Praise for *Accelerating Performance*

"Some business books excel at data-based analytical rigor, others at strategy, leadership, or soft skills. *Accelerating Performance* integrates all these vital components and teaches leaders how to drive fast with vision."

—**Tom Glocer,** founder of Angelic Ventures LP, director of Merck & Co. and Morgan Stanley, and member of the supervisory board for Publicis Groupe

"An ambitious, breakthrough book! Who wouldn't want their company to be in Colin and Sharon's group of super-performers? Drawing on original research, illuminating cases, and practical advice, they show us a surprising— even unfashionable—route for companies to get there: not by reinventing themselves but by becoming significantly better versions of who they already are! Smart, funny, with a very high 'PIPSI' (provocative ideas per square inch)."

—**Robert Kegan,** Meehan Professor of Adult Learning and Professional Development, Harvard University, and coauthor of *An Everyone Culture: Becoming a Deliberately Developmental Organization*

"Delivering sustainable, standout performance is the holy grail for business leaders. Colin and Sharon present a compelling agenda to help leaders increase the metabolic rate in their business, thereby creating the conditions for long-term success. Boards and CEOs should take note—and take action."

—**David Roberts,** chairman, Nationwide Building Society

Accelerating Performance

Accelerating Performance

How Organizations Can Mobilize,
Execute, and Transform with Agility

COLIN PRICE
SHARON TOYE

WILEY

For Cameron and Jodie and the love of knowledge

Contents

Foreword

One of the great pleasures of writing this book is that we had the opportunity to spend time with the CEO or other senior executives at so many of the 23 companies around the world that our research identified as the most successful in recent years. These 23 "superaccelerators" have cracked the code. They have managed to be both big and agile, pulling away from the pack through the sort of disciplined approach to acceleration that we lay out in this book.

The stories these executives told us give life to many of the concepts in the pages to follow. For example:

HDFC Bank can provide customers with a "10-second loan." Paresh Sukthankar, the bank's deputy managing director, told us that a profile can be developed in the background based on the information a customer provides online, and the subsequent loan can be processed and granted for a modest sum within seconds. We talk in the book about the need for "digital dexterity," and the Indian financial services company provides a shining example.

While we talk about the need to "speak truth to power," MasterCard has a pithy saying that addresses that need: "Good news takes the stairs, and bad news takes the elevator." President and CEO Ajay Banga told us that he gets tired of all the self-congratulatory e-mails that are common in business: "So I've told everybody I don't need good news." Instead, he asks to hear first about the problems that need to be resolved.

Cigna, the huge health insurer, provides examples of two key points. First is the need to generate a strong sense of purpose, because it can make sure that everyone is pointed in the same direction and can get employees to provide their "discretionary effort"—the effort that they don't have to provide to get by but one that turbocharges performance when employees can be motivated to provide it. Cigna president and CEO David Cordani said he stresses that employees aren't just processing insurance policies. Instead, he says: "We exist to improve the health, well-being, and sense of security of the individuals we serve."

Second, Cordani provided a vivid description of the benefit that comes from having a real dialogue with employees, viewing change as something you do *with* people, not *to* them (the traditional approach). Cordani said that his frequent meetings with employees allow him to connect face-to-face: "For example, are [employees] thinking and acting like owners—or renters? Are they looking forward and setting the bar higher, or looking backward and trying to justify what happened in the past? Seldom do you come away with a singular 'aha' moment. But you can get a lot of pearls, and when you string them together, you have a lot of value."

Starbucks provided a great illustration of the value of reducing priorities to a handful, to avoid the kind of complexity that strangles so many businesses. Scott Pitasky, executive vice president and chief partner resources officer, notes that Starbucks' focus "is on our partners [what the company calls its employees], on our coffee, and on the experience that we create in the store for our customers."

Explaining the power of working outside the hierarchy (while not ditching it entirely) and of the need to create space for innovation, Matt Brittin, president of EMEA business and operations at Google, described how the company lets innovation bubble up from the bottom. Engineers can start to work on projects or ideas and try to rally support. If others join the effort, demonstrating potential, then Google starts to provide a little structure, partly by arranging for groups with similar ideas to work together. Brittin says Google has become big enough that it can no longer really go on letting "a thousand flowers bloom." Instead, the company aspires to more "coherent bouquets" of innovation efforts.

For its part, BlackRock, the global investment firm, exemplifies a dedication to good old-fashioned execution—a quality that our research found to be a competitive differentiator in organizations more broadly. Speaking of the connection between talent management and success, Jeffrey Smith, BlackRock's global head of human resources, told us: "I don't think the magic for us is tied up in seeking out the most innovative, new talent thing that somebody can think of. Instead, the key is executing. We would rather support, drive, reinforce, and actually *do* the things that companies all know they're supposed to do but frequently overlook."

BlackRock's pragmatism also extends to how it supports collaboration. "We spend a lot of time talking about what it means to 'be a good peer,'" noted Smith. "That really matters around here."

Jeff Sprecher, founder and CEO of Intercontinental Exchange, told us that he encourages collaboration outside hierarchy, even to the point of designing his headquarters to make chance meetings likely. Among other things, he puts only certain soda flavors on each floor, so someone wanting a certain type might have to go to a different floor—and bump into someone interesting along the way.

He also provided great examples both of how crucial it is for leaders to be aware of how they're thinking and acting and of the importance of leaders' role-modeling behaviors (including humility) for the rest of the organization. Sprecher told us: "I'm a terrible manager. I am just a terrible manager. And so you say, 'Okay, how does a terrible manager manage an organization?' The only thing I could come up with is to lead by example, to run my own behavior the way I would want my employees to run their behavior, and do it in a way that is quite obvious and transparent and hope that people will try to emulate the leader."

We talked with our interviewees about the need to see the world through customers' eyes—we believe, like Peter Drucker, that solving a customer problem should be the core aim of any business. Connie Ma, vice president of human resources at TSMC, takes this attitude to heart when she maintains: "[Customers'] success is our success, and we value their ability to compete as we value our own."

Natarajan Chandrasekaran, CEO of Tata Consultancy Services, epito-mizes this customer-focused outlook: "Whether you are in the front office, the back office, or the CEO of the company, every employee should know how what they do affects the customer." Thyagi Thyagarajan, an indepen-dent director at TCS, echoed this view, telling us that employees there "have no fear of being fired by the company" but that they do fear "being fired or rejected by the *customer*. If the customer is unhappy, that's what employees fear."

There's more, actually much more, but those quotes should give you a taste of what is to come. We hope you appreciate the insights from these leaders as much as we do.

Acknowledgments

A book is a team effort. The players on this team were a delight to work with. Ruben Hillar, our chief researcher, applied boundless curiosity matched only by his inexhaustible energy. Becky Hogan mined the data with a ferocious intensity. David Turnbull was the bass player of our little band; his cool logic and unflappable calm kept us on track. Toomas Truumees and Camelia Ram led the charge on Chapter 6. Krishnan Rajagopalan, Jeff Sanders, and Samantha Smith brought decades of executive search experience to Chapter 12. Carolyn Vavrek and Bonnie Gwin took the lead role on Chapter 13 and brought us invaluable insights. Susan Moore was tireless and painstaking in her editorial efforts, and Heloisa Nogueira, with the assistance of Thomas Fleming, Rachel Swift, and Melissa Haniff, managed the publishing process with aplomb. Paul Carroll took our words and made them readable.

Thank you.

About the Authors

Colin Price is an executive vice president and the global managing partner of the Leadership Consulting Practice at Heidrick & Struggles. He has advised many of the world's largest corporations, several national governments, and a number of charitable institutions. His books include *Mergers* (with David Fubini of McKinsey & Company and Maurizio Zollo of INSEAD), *Vertical Take-Off* (with Sir Richard Evans, former chair of British Aerospace), and *Beyond Performance* (with Scott Keller of McKinsey & Company). He holds degrees in economics, industrial relations and psychology, and organizational behavior. He has presented at many prestigious conferences, including the World Economic Forum and the Harvard Roundtable series. He is an associate fellow of Saïd Business School at Oxford University and a visiting professor at Imperial College London.

Sharon Toye is a partner in Heidrick & Struggles' London office and a member of its Leadership Consulting Practice, where she heads up the global service line for accelerating team performance. An organization development expert, qualified psychotherapist, and highly skilled consultant, she has more than 20 years of experience as an executive and top-team coach. She has served as a leadership advisor to many top global companies in a range of industries, including investment and wealth management banking, engineering, and telecommunications, as well as to the top teams of PE-backed market leaders. She holds an MBA from the London Business School, an MSc in organizational psychology from Birkbeck College at the University of London, and an MSc in integrative psychotherapy. She has been published in *Business Strategy Review* and *strategy+business* as well as in *Managerial Forensics*.

INTRODUCTION

Why We Wrote This Book
The Data Sets You Free

When companies talk about "big data," they're talking about how to better understand the great, big world out there, beyond their corporate walls. What happens inside those walls has historically been seen as too fuzzy, too qualitative, to lend itself to rigorous research and management of big data. The internal workings, especially where people are involved, have been seen as "the soft stuff" and shielded from hard science. Certainly, there have been employee morale surveys and the tracking of retention rates, but organizations haven't done the kind of work that would allow them to understand what really works and what's folklore when it comes to managing organizations in ways that will win in the marketplace. People bring a lot of intellect and common sense to management, but common sense isn't always enough—witness what behavioral economists are teaching us about the quirks of customer behavior versus the old approach to economics that assumed that all actors were perfectly rational.

It's time to recognize that "the soft stuff" is really the hard stuff and to bring hard science to management.

Moving organizational behavior into the realm of science is the core mission of this book. We prefer facts over fiction. We think HR, for instance, needs less PowerPoint and more Excel. We're not saying all the facts are easy. Markets and businesses are ecosystems, not machines, so interactions can be hard to discern. But we have to get beyond generalities and form "rebuttable presumptions," clear hypotheses that can be tested and potentially disproved. To quote Lord Kelvin, the physicist known for determining the value of absolute zero: "When you can measure what you are speaking about and express it in numbers, you know something about it, but when you cannot measure it, when you cannot express it in numbers, your knowledge is of a meager and unsatisfactory kind." It's time that our understanding of organizational behavior moves beyond the "meager and unsatisfactory."

We do that by building on the work that led up to Colin's 2011 book with Scott Keller, *Beyond Performance: How Great Organizations Build Ultimate Competitive Advantage*. That book also took a strong research focus, drawing on 600,000 survey responses, including from 6,800 CEOs and other senior executives, at more than 500 organizations. The book largely focused on how to improve organizational health. For this book, we have broadened the scope of the analysis to look at all organizational behavior issues that drive performance at all relevant levels—strategy, teams, and leaders, in addition to the organization level. We have done so through many thousands of additional surveys and interviews, including in-depth interviews at many of the 23 companies that we identified (based on methodology described in detail in Chapter 4) as the world's most successful over the past seven years.

As Alan Mulally said when he took over at Ford as CEO in 2006 and began an epic turnaround of the company, "The data sets you free."[1]

The research for this book pulls together numerous strands of work, notably those represented by our decades as consultants and advisers. Colin comes at the problem from a background in economics—he taught at Oxford—and in management consulting. He was the fourth consultant hired at Price Waterhouse, right before *In Search of Excellence* was published in 1982 and sent interest in management consulting through the roof. As the practice grew at Price Waterhouse, he ran the organization in England, then in Europe, and then worldwide. He then spent 15 years at McKinsey, where he became a director (senior partner) and led the Organization Practice globally; he drove the development and use of McKinsey's Organizational Health Index, the tool that was used as the empirical basis of *Beyond Performance*.

Sharon began in organization development at National Power and further developed her experience in organizational transformation at Accenture. During this time, she collected an MBA from the London Business School, an MSc in organizational psychology from Birkbeck College at the University of London, and an MSc in integrative psychotherapy. She is also a licensed psychotherapist and a master certified coach (ICF MCC). She founded Co Company to apply her expertise in organizational change and leadership development to performance enhancement in companies. When Colin left McKinsey in 2014, he joined Co Company, which Heidrick & Struggles acquired in 2015. Colin is now the managing partner of the Leadership Consulting Practice for Heidrick & Struggles; Sharon is a partner in the Leadership Consulting Practice in the London office, where as the developer and author of the team accelerator methodology she leads the firm's work in this area. She has published on the topic in a number of books and journals, including *Managerial Forensics, Business Strategy Review,* and *strategy+business*.

We think of our work as a living combination of the hard stuff and the soft stuff—economics, management consulting, psychology, and therapy.

We have, of course, also greatly benefited from the decades of experience of our colleagues at Heidrick & Struggles, who have seen what works and what doesn't at the senior-most levels of corporations.

In many ways, the argument we make should be easier for people to accept now than it would have been in the "pre-Lehman" era. Lehman Brothers was the fourth-largest investment bank in the United States before going under in 2008, essentially signaling that the dam had burst and that the U.S. federal government was no longer going to stand in the way of a financial collapse that wiped out $14.5 trillion of the value of companies on the world's stock markets, or a third of the total. Lehman Brothers employees were earning gobs of money by engaging in incredibly risky behaviors, but, in the pre-collapse days, warning signs weren't spotted because those overpaid employees were as happy as could be.

The hard stuff hadn't yet come to the soft stuff, so it was hard to see the effects that a toxic culture would have on Lehman Brothers and then the whole global financial system. In the "post-Lehman" era, by contrast, the need to go well beyond traditional measures of financial performance should be evident.

The answers won't all be in this book. That's not what science does. Besides, there's so much uncertainty in the environment these days that a certain amount of good fortune will always be required.

But we believe the saying that "luck is the residue of design," and we intend to equip you so well on the design piece that you will be in a great position to capitalize on opportunities for luck.

We, and many others, will continue to build on what's here by constantly testing what's working and what isn't and quantifying how to proceed.

Let the science begin!

Note

1. Bryce G. Hoffman, *American Icon: Alan Mulally and the Fight to Save Ford Motor Company*, New York: Crown, 2012.

Move Fast or Die Faster

As promised in the Introduction, this section follows the data and fleshes out the core argument of this book: that organizations can generate enormous benefit by taking an empirical approach to management.

In Chapter 1, we set the stage by showing why the current approach to managing institutions isn't working—and can't work. At fabled institution after fabled institution—BP, the British Army, Parliament, HSBC, and on and on—major failures have occurred because of dysfunctional cultures. But current approaches to management don't adequately address the issues that would have prevented those disasters. We're doomed to repeat them unless we greatly update our thinking, recognizing that the soft stuff really is the hard stuff and taking the series of actions that the data shows will help today's institutions achieve breakthrough success.

Chapter 2 covers the basics of our META approach, which stands for Mobilize, Execute, and Transform with Agility. We start by showing how two of the mantras among executives today—the need to go faster and the need to look for disruptive business models—can take organizations into blind alleys. Businesses can land in an "acceleration trap," where they aren't discriminating enough about their search for speed and actually go more slowly. Our research also found that there is more opportunity for improvement by being more effective in the markets where you already operate rather than by taking the more disruptive approach and moving into different industries or new geographies. That's a key point that many businesses miss. They may spend so much time looking for the next big thing that they miss the even bigger opportunities that are right in front of them.

Chapter 3 shows in living color how important META can be, by detailing how Bain Capital Private Equity has become a catalyst for acceleration. We walk through three case studies of companies in the Bain Capital portfolio to see how principles from META have unlocked enormous potential. For instance, Nets Holding, a payments processor in Scandinavia, has gone from declining revenue to organic growth of 6 percent in recent quarters. It has seen profit margins increase by 14 percentage points since Bain Capital, Advent International, and ATP bought the company from a consortium of

180 banks in 2014. Nets has explicitly followed many of the META principles we lay out in this book. It developed a detailed plan anchored in a thorough understanding of its markets, customers, competitors, and profitability. It quickly got alignment among its top team, partly by hiring new talent and capabilities for the 60 percent to 70 percent of roles where moving fast was especially important. Nets Holding also generated quick wins that produced momentum and freed up cash and identified 10 operational issues that had to be fixed immediately.

In Chapter 4, we describe the research journey that took us to META. We dove into the details of the management at half of the FT 500 companies, interviewed senior executives at many of the top-performing companies we identified in our research, surveyed 20,000 global leaders, conducted in-depth interviews with 150 of them, analyzed data from 3,000 teams, drew from our library of more than 10,000 executive assessments using our latest tool and from our experience of placing more than 4,000 executives a year—and more. Research rarely makes for great reading, but we felt the need to demonstrate the extraordinary amount of work that went into META, as long as we're arguing for a data-driven approach to management—and we certainly hope that you find our journey interesting.

Chapter 5 provides a baseline for you as you approach the rest of this book. It gives you two quick ways to see where you fall on our acceleration scale, one based simply on the compound annual growth rate of your organization and your industry, and the other based on answers to 16 questions. Armed with the answers, you can start to see how much work, and what sort of work, you have ahead of you.

CHAPTER 1

The Soft Stuff Really
Is the Hard Stuff

It's a pleasant evening in central London, and we just finished our last meeting—a wide-ranging discussion at Chatham House about some of the changes that could occur in the global political climate. We decide to walk to our dinner appointment.

Walking around St. James's Square takes us past BP's global headquarters, and a bad memory surfaces. BP, founded more than a century ago, has been a revered institution in the United Kingdom and has positioned itself for the future with aggressive moves into renewable energy. But there's that memory of April 20, 2010, when the Macondo oil well erupted below BP's Deepwater Horizon rig, killing 11 workers and injuring 16 others. The explosion caused the massive rig to become engulfed in a fireball and sink into the Gulf of Mexico. A sea-floor oil gusher flowed for 87 days, and more than 200 million gallons of oil and 225,000 tons of methane gas spilled into the ocean and along more than 1,000 miles of coastline of all the Gulf states—the catastrophe is described as the largest accidental marine oil spill in the world and the largest environmental disaster in U.S. history. The toll on local businesses is still being calculated, but it appears that in claims, cleanup efforts, fines, and victim compensation, BP will pay out more than $65 billion.[1]

How could this happen to such a great company? The investigation into what went wrong blamed "a culture of complacency." William Reilly, co-chair of the commission that investigated the disaster, said there was "emphatically not a culture of safety on that rig."[2]

As we continue our walk to dinner, we carry on to Trafalgar Square and then head down Whitehall, sticking to the streets rather than walking through St. James's Park, as we're looking for a cash machine. We pass the Old War Office building on our left and the Household Cavalry Museum on our right. We're reminded that all isn't right with the military, either.

It seems the U.K. Army had become a bloated bureaucracy, especially at the top levels. As reported in *The Times* [of London], the new head of the army, General Sir Nicholas Carter, decided to reduce the number of colonels, brigadiers, and generals to "stop the rise of 'yes men.'" He also wanted to curb the widespread tendency among officers to "put the interests of their 'tribe' before those of the wider force." The article places the blame on "flawed leadership" and "an institutional malaise in which commanders are rarely held to account. . . . [B]ureaucracy takes precedence over common sense and people are not encouraged to take risks."[3]

Hurrying down Whitehall, still not having found a cash machine, we pass a throng of demonstrators—taxi drivers with signs protesting that Uber is unfairly putting them out of business. In reality, their industry is yet another great London institution that didn't keep up with the times. London's black cabs are famous, and its drivers are arguably the best informed in the world. They have to pass "The Knowledge," a test about routes and landmarks first administered in the mid-1800s; it is so exhaustive that drivers need an average of 34 months to succeed. Today The Knowledge has to compete with its lowercase equivalent—the knowledge drawn from satellite navigation systems and embedded in every smartphone—and with the new business model represented by Uber, Lyft, and others. And the taxi industry didn't adequately prepare.

Pushing our way through the protestors, we pass on our left Richmond House, the headquarters of the Department of Health, responsible for one of the treasures of the modern British state, the National Health Service (NHS).

Ahhh, the healers. Arrggh, the healers.

In March 2009, problems were exposed at Stafford Hospital, run by the Mid Staffordshire NHS Foundation Trust. Based on investigations, press reports suggested that between 400 and 1,200 more patients died between 2005 and 2009 than would have if the proper actions had been taken by hospital staff. The public inquiry cast grave doubt on those numbers, saying they were the product of flawed statistical methods and finding against the hospital in only four deaths, two of which occurred in the years at issue. Still, the inquiry uncovered "an insidious negative culture involving a tolerance of poor standards and a disengagement from managerial and leadership responsibilities. . . . There was an atmosphere of fear of adverse repercussions; a high priority was placed on the achievement of targets."[4]

Eventually, we get to Parliament Square, where the BBC is taking advantage of the pleasant weather to interview politicians on the green outside the Houses of Parliament. The BBC is such a symbol of integrity, except that . . .

In January 2014, *The Guardian* reported that "[s]enior BBC figures are facing calls to reform the corporation's 'culture of secrecy,' as an internal inquiry is expected to reveal Jimmy Savile sexually abused up to 1,000 children while working for the corporation."[5] Savile, who died October 29, 2011, at the age of 84, was a media personality best known for hosting a BBC show called *Jim'll Fix It*, which featured letters from children making wishes that the show then granted. The show ran for almost 20 years. In October 2012, 18 years after the show ended (and after Savile's death), allegations of child abuse were made against him, including claims that he devised some episodes to gain access to potential victims. The BBC had previously been warned about problems and spent six weeks investigating but, in December 2011, dropped the probe and, instead, aired programs over the Christmas and New Year's holidays that year that paid tribute to Savile. However, the police opened an investigation ("Operation Yewtree") and, in January 2013, confirmed that there were 450 alleged victims of sex abuse by Savile.[6] An inquiry into the BBC's dropped investigation of Savile found that "crucial information . . . was not shared" inside the BBC and that "no-one seemed to grasp what should be done with the information. . . . Efforts were hampered in part by an apparent adherence to rigid management chains and a reluctance to bypass them."[7]

Turning away from the interviews, our eye falls on the somewhat dilapidated Palace of Westminster, home to Parliament. Still more problems there . . .

In May 2009, *The Daily Telegraph* published the first in a series of articles that exposed a scandal involving the abuse by many British Members of Parliament (MPs) in claiming their business expenses. It was front-page news for more than a year, and the upshot was that more than half of all 646 MPs (at the time) had been claiming outrageous expenses—so much so that this particular group of MPs were dubbed the "rotten Parliament."[8]

Worrying about MPs' expenses reminds us again that we need to find a cash machine, so we hurry into the Tesco Metro Express next to Westminster Station. Tesco, we now recall, was itself the subject of an accountancy scandal, when it was discovered that it had overstated its profits by hundreds of millions of pounds.[9]

Now in search of light relief, we look among the Sunday papers for the *News of the World* to laugh at the celebrity gossip, before remembering that it folded a few years ago.

In the summer of 2005, complaints arose about probable voice mail hacking, implicating the British tabloid publication *News of the World* (NoW). Over the next 10 years, more and more information was released, with the end result involving more than 1,000 victims—ranging from Prince William to 9/11 victims and including a missing teenager, whose phone messages were allegedly deleted to free up space, causing her parents to believe she was still alive (the teen was later found to have been murdered). The investigation also revealed the hacking of phones belonging to J. K. Rowling (author of the Harry Potter books), actor Hugh Grant, Sarah Ferguson (the Duchess of York), an MP, the U.K.'s former deputy prime minister, and many others. Former *News of the World* journalists claimed that phone hacking was "a common practice at NoW."[10] Though Andy Coulson, editor of NoW, claimed to have no knowledge of the hacking, he resigned from his position in 2007. *News of the World* folded in July 2011, ending 168 years of publication. Several high-level executives of its parent company, Rupert Murdoch's News International, resigned, including the CEO, the head of the Dow Jones division of News Corp and publisher of *The Wall Street Journal*, and James Murdoch (son of Rupert), who was chair of U.K. satellite broadcaster BSkyB. Coulson, amid the fallout of the scandal, also resigned from his subsequent position as British Prime Minister David Cameron's spokesman and spent five months in prison. Millions of pounds in fines were paid to the victims, and several people were arrested and convicted, with jail time, of conspiracy to intercept phone messages. A formal inquiry found "a failure of systems of management and compliance. None of the witnesses were able to identify who was responsible for ensuring compliance with an ethical approach to journalism."[11]

We finally find a cash machine at Barclays Bank, in business for 325 years and the very image of security. But Barclays summons its own bad memory. In 2012, Barclays was fined £290 million (almost $500 million) by U.S. and U.K. regulators for attempted manipulation of the Libor and Euribor rates (i.e., the average interest rates at which banks borrow funds from one another).[12] The bank's stock price declined more than 15 percent, which wiped out about £3.5 billion from the bank's market capitalization, and both the chair and CEO of Barclays resigned their positions. The investigation into the scandal found that "the business practices for which Barclays has rightly been criticised were shaped predominantly by its cultures" (plural, because there were multiple subcultures). The report added: "[A]cross the whole bank, there were no clearly articulated and understood shared values—so there could hardly be much consensus among employees as to . . . what should guide everyday behaviours."[13]

A broader study, by New City Agenda and London's Cass Business School, indicted the whole industry for its "near-death experience" and noted: "The banks have paid out £38.5 billion [over $60 billion] in fines and customer redress relating to their retail operations since 2000. Banks have also received 20.8 million complaints between 2008 and the first half of 2014." The volume of complaints about banks lodged to the Financial Ombudsman Service more than quintupled between 2008–2009 and 2013–2014, going from 75,000 to more than 400,000. The report found that one of the most important causes of this extreme situation was the aggressive sales culture of many banks, which rewarded employees for selling financial products that customers didn't necessarily want or need.[14]

All right then. Moving on.

We can't use our card at Barclays because the machine is out of cash, so we head down the street to HSBC, the U.K.'s largest bank. HSBC does business in 80 countries and employs 240,000 people (44,000 of them in Britain). But, oh yes, in 2012 HSBC was fined $1.9 billion for helping drug cartels to launder money;[15] the ensuing investigation revealed—surprise, surprise—that the root of the problem was the organization's culture.

Given how many institutions have been fined throughout the banking industry, it's clear that these settlements actually settle little, and the details of the poor cultures that lead to them are being swept under an already lumpy carpet.

That reminds us that poor organizational health is a problem of not only individual banks but the U.K. banking system overall. The Bank of England (which functions in much the same way as the U.S. Federal Reserve) was revealed as woefully unprepared for the financial crisis that occurred in 2007: "Bank directors did not properly challenge executives, while managers often failed to give members of its court—or board—a full account of the breakdown in the U.K.'s regulatory regime, particularly the dysfunctional relationship between the Bank and the Financial Services Authority, then the City watchdog."[16]

And who knows what will happen after Brexit? Will the Bank of England and other institutions handle the departure from the European Union any better than they have past convulsions in the market?

Oh, enough already. We decide to stop this walk. It's depressing. Let's find a pub so we can stop in before dinner and have a stiff drink or three.

■ ■ ■

We aren't intentionally picking on the United Kingdom here. Every country has its list of institutional scandals these days. Germany's Volkswagen has acknowledged a broad cheating campaign designed so that its diesel cars could pass emissions tests. Japanese carmakers have also been caught cheating on mileage tests. In the United States, financial institutions—including blue-chip firms such as Goldman Sachs and JPMorgan Chase—have paid more than $110 billion to settle charges related to their role in selling mortgages to people who couldn't afford them and feeding the Great Recession. Boeing's chief financial officer illegally offered a job to a U.S. Air Force official while the official was negotiating with potential suppliers for a $23 billion contract for aerial refueling tankers; he was sentenced to four months in prison in 2005.[17] The Air Force official pleaded guilty to favoring Boeing on four contracts and was sentenced to nine months in prison.[18]

We're making a broad point, about institutions in every country, and felt it was worth taking that rather long walk to do so. We have deliberately offered an almost obsessive repetition to make our point that, no matter where you look, the same dynamic is revealed. The *culture* of these organizations is driving their behavior. The soft stuff drives the hard stuff—as in, the numbers in the financial results that tend to draw our focus.

Why do so many institutions fall down? We believe it is because the actors become more important than the audience. In other words, the people in the institution place greater value on their own well-being than on the people whom the institution is serving. BP's managers were more concerned with profitability than with the safety of the drill operators. Executives in several banks looked after themselves rather than their customers. Members of Parliament were also looking after themselves, rather than their constituents, when they fiddled their expenses. *News of the World* was more interested in publishing gossipy stories that would appeal to readers than it was with protecting the privacy of the people whose phones it hacked to get those stories. The Mid Staffordshire NHS Foundation Trust was more concerned with keeping costs down than with taking care of its patients. There is a psychological term called the *iron law of oligarchy*, which says that, as soon as you give an institution power, it will begin to obsess about itself rather than the people it is supposed to serve. People see the world as divided between the have-nots and the have-yachts—and decide they'd like to join the latter.

These cultural failings fit in a larger context because they aren't generally seen as being as important as some of the other dynamics driving business these days. The emphasis everywhere is on disruption, not on the fundamentals of managing a business as effectively as possible, taking what could be drag factors and turning them into factors that drive the business forward. Disruption wasn't the issue with these failings. BP didn't have a well blow up because its market was being disrupted by, say, fracking. HSBC didn't launder money and Barclays didn't fix interest rates because of pressure from start-ups such as Lending Tree. People didn't die at Stafford Hospital because of new molecular therapies. These institutions—and so many like them—had problems because they didn't pay attention to the soft stuff that drives the hard stuff.

There is no doubt that any leader has to have one eye on disruption. Look at digital photography, the move to online retailing, the reinvention of the music industry, and all the other changes we read about. But to read the news these days you'd think that the whole game is to find a new business model or at least new markets. In fact, as we'll prove in this book, moving into a new industry or geography generally isn't the best answer. You should be ready for any disruption but will miss an awful lot of opportunities in the meantime if that is your primary focus.

The fear of disruption leads to an indiscriminate emphasis on speed. Every part of the organization has to go faster, faster, faster, all the time. In fact, while we all feel that we're going faster, based on the deluge of information that fills our in-boxes every day and that we have at our fingertips through our smartphones, much of that feeling is an illusion. The rate of consumer product launches has changed little for years. The same is true for the rate of production in factories—in fact, productivity in general has improved so little, despite all the technology being deployed, that economists are puzzled. A U.S. think tank, the Conference Board, actually projected a decline in productivity for 2016, the first drop in three decades.[19] The period over which a company could achieve sustainable competitive advantage, as measured by return on capital in the S&P 500, hasn't changed since 2000.[20]

Some change is even slowing down. The median tenure of a CEO increased to 5 years in 2014, from 3 years in 2007, and the average S&P 500 CEO retiring in 2014 had held the position for 10 years, the highest number since 2002.[21] A survey of 2,000 project managers at more than 60 companies around the world found that, in 2015, it took an average of 63 days to hire an employee, up from 42 in 2010, and the time to complete an IT project rose from 9 months to 10, on average. The process by which one company sells something to another takes 22 percent more time because five or more people now have to approve a deal, up from one or two.[22] Yes, the world is speeding up in many ways, but it's important to separate reality from the feeling of speed.

The right answer—the one that will deliver the most return, most reliably—is to increase the metabolic rate of your organization through a process that lets you increase speed, but only in certain places, in certain ways, at certain times, designed for maximum effect. We call this process META for two reasons. First, META is an acronym for Mobilize, Execute, and Transform with Agility. Second, as economist Paul Romer observes, "Perhaps the most important ideas of all are meta-ideas—ideas about how to support the production and transmission of other ideas."[23]

This metaphoric process isn't about finding a single breakthrough of the sort that would lead to the next Airbnb. It's more about taking a series of threads, each not especially strong, and weaving them into a fabric that is very strong. Let's use one more analogy: In thinking about how to solve problems, people often talk about getting rid of the bad apples. We think that the issue isn't just the apples; it's also the barrel makers. We will help you build better barrels so you have better apples.

We will spend the rest of this book showing how we arrived at META and then explaining in detail how to implement it. We do so based on our personal work with clients over decades and on definitive research done specifically for this book. We seek to be rigorous, empirical, and evidence based. Too many organizations are managed by "anecdata," a sprinkling of data used to justify personal opinions. The recommendations that you will find here are based on thorough analysis.

If you can increase your corporate metabolic rate, you will accelerate your business, and you will win. Even if the world isn't all disruption and unmitigated speed, there are still enormous opportunities to make your business more profitable.

You know the opportunities are there. You can see them and feel them. We'll help you find them, explore them, and exploit them.

In the spirit of that optimism, let's briefly remind ourselves of the progress that the world's organizations have enabled in the past century-plus, rather than risk leaving you with a depressive hangover after the walk that opened this chapter. Observe the following:

- Mortality among children under the age of five in the world has dropped by half just since 1990, to 46 per 1,000 live births, thanks to the collaboration of research institutions, pharmaceutical companies, and health systems. In 2015 the Bill & Melinda Gates Foundation predicted that the rate can be cut by half again by 2030.[24]
- The adult literacy rate has nearly quadrupled, from 21 percent of the world's population in 1900 to 83 percent in 2010, thanks to the spread of education.[25]
- At the time of this writing, we had either just passed or were about to reach the point (methodologies vary) where more than half of the world's population has access to the Internet and, thus, essentially all the world's knowledge and each other. That figure was less than 1 percent in 1995.[26] The change will drive a new era of transparency and accountability.
- The number of people living in extreme poverty (with an income of $1.90 or less a day) fell below 10 percent for the first time, in 2015.[27] The figure was 44 percent in 1981.[28] The decline means that some 1.2 billion people climbed out of extreme poverty in those three and a half decades, and the World Bank pledges to end extreme poverty by 2030. Some 700 million people are still living in extreme poverty, and we as a global community should surely set our sights higher than an income of $1.90 a day, but the progress is enormous.

Organizations made the progress happen, despite their many flaws. Although there is no doubt a dark side to failing organizations, the drive that organizations can provide for our species and our planet holds the promise of more progress in the next 100 years than we can possibly imagine.

Notes

1. National Commission on the BP Deepwater Horizon Oil Spill and Offshore Drilling, *Deep Water: The Gulf Oil Disaster and the Future of Offshore Drilling*, Report to the President, January 2011.

2. Suzanne Goldenberg, "US oil spill inquiry chief slams BP's 'culture of complacency,'" *Guardian*, November 9, 2010, theguardian.com.
3. Deborah Haynes, "Army chief takes axe to 'bloated' top brass," *Times* [of London], January 24, 2015, thetimes.co.uk.
4. Robert Francis, Chair, *Report of the Mid Staffordshire NHS Foundation Trust Public Inquiry*, Executive Summary, February 2013, gov.uk.
5. Jason Deans, "Culture of secrecy blamed for BBC's failure to stop Jimmy Savile's crimes," *Guardian,* January 19, 2014, theguardian.com.
6. David Gray and Peter Watt, *Giving Victims a Voice: Joint Report into Sexual Allegations Made Against Jimmy Savile*, a joint Metropolitan Police Service (MPS) and National Society for the Prevention of Cruelty to Children (NSPCC) report, January 2013, nspcc.org.uk.
7. Nick Pollard, *The Pollard Review: Report*, ReedSmith, December 18, 2012, bbc.co.uk.
8. Robert Winnett, "More than half of MPs guilty of over-claiming expenses," *Telegraph*, February 5, 2010, telegraph.co.uk.
9. Caroline Binham and Scheherazade Daneshkhu, "Serious Fraud Office launches Tesco accounts probe," *Financial Times*, October 29, 2014, ft.com.
10. "UK phone hacking scandal fast facts," CNN Library, updated April 24, 2016, cnn.com.
11. Lord Justice Leveson, *The Leveson Inquiry: An Inquiry into the Culture, Practices, and Ethics of the Press*, Executive Summary, November 2012, gov.uk.
12. Harry Wilson, "Barclays hit with £290m fine over Libor fixing," *Telegraph*, June 27, 2012, telegraph.co.uk.
13. Anthony Salz, *Salz Review: An Independent Review of Barclays' Business Practices*, April 2013, euromoney.com/downloads/2013/Barclays -Salz-review.pdf.
14. New City Agenda and Cass Business School, *A Report on the Culture of British Retail Banking*, Executive Summary, November 2014, newcityagenda.co.uk.
15. Jill Treanor and Dominic Rushe, "HSBC pays record $1.9bn fine to settle US money-laundering accusations," *Guardian*, December 11, 2012, theguardian.com.
16. Harry Wilson and Philip Aldrick, "Minutes reveal Bank in chaos as financial crisis hit," *Times* [of London], January 7, 2015, thetimes.co.uk.
17. Peter Pae, "Ex-Boeing CFO gets jail for tanker scandal," *Chicago Tribune*, February 18, 2005, chicagotribune.com.
18. Renae Merle and Jerry Markon, "Ex-Air Force official gets prison time," *Washington Post*, October 2, 2004, washingtonpost.com.
19. Sam Fleming and Chris Giles, "US productivity slips for first time in three decades," *Financial Times*, May 25, 2016, ft.com.

20. "The creed of speed," *Economist*, December 5, 2015, economist.com.
21. "The creed of speed," *Economist*, December 5, 2015, economist.com.
22. Tom Monahan, "The hard evidence: Business is slowing down," *Fortune*, January 28, 2016, fortune.com.
23. Paul M. Romer, "Economic growth," in *The Concise Encyclopedia of Economics*, Second Edition, ed. David R. Henderson, Library of Economics and Liberty, 2007, econlib.org.
24. Bill & Melinda Gates Foundation, *2015 Gates Annual Letter: Our Big Bet for the Future*, 2015, gatesnotes.com.
25. Max Roser, "Literacy," *Our World in Data*, 2016, ourworldindata.org.
26. "Internet users," *Internet Live Stats*, internetlivestats.com.
27. "World Bank forecasts global poverty to fall below 10% for the first time; major hurdles remain in goal to end poverty by 2030," press release, World Bank, October 4, 2015, worldbank.org.
28. Poverty overview, World Bank, April 13, 2016, worldbank.org.

CHAPTER 2

How to Increase Your METAbolic Rate

L ots of management advice taken as authoritative is actually anecdotal. Some of it is explicitly so, such as in the currently popular books by Richard Branson and Mark Cuban on the lessons that they draw from their successful careers (and that may or may not be applicable to yours). Some is so breezily anecdotal that readers can peruse the material for pleasure but know not to take it seriously, such as in books on the wisdom to be drawn from Winnie the Pooh, the crew of the Starship *Enterprise*, or Genghis Khan. But a great deal of management advice is in the dangerous middle ground: based on a certain amount of experience with reality, but not so much so that the lessons drawn can be broadly applied.

This treatment of anecdote as data—what we call "anecdata"—is pervasive and pernicious enough that it has prompted the beginnings of a backlash. In *Leadership BS: Fixing Workplaces and Careers One Truth at a Time*, for instance, Stanford professor Jeffrey Pfeffer notes that the leadership industry has no barriers to entry and argues, buttressed by research studies, that some concepts such as "authentic leadership" should be taken with a grain of salt. For example, if the CEO is in a lousy mood, he should probably hide it rather than be authentic. He's expected to play a specific role and provide energy to those around him, so he has to act his part, even if he isn't feeling it. In fact, Pfeffer says that currently one of the most popular classes at the Stanford business school is called "Acting with Power"; drawing from the world of theater, it teaches students how to play a role.[1]

We need to look to hard data for how to address the core question for businesses today: How can we thrive in a fast-paced, digital world where profound long-term and short-term forces collide in unpredictable ways?

Our extensive research (described in Chapter 4) points to a single answer: acceleration. By that we mean the ability to reduce time to value by building and changing momentum more quickly than your competitors. The research also shows that the way to accelerate is through a process we call

META: Mobilize, Execute, and Transform with Agility. Following META will allow your company to improve its metabolic rate, making it much fitter and better able to succeed in today's accelerating, taxing business environment.

Research has found that cows addressed by name produce more milk—one of many, many studies that show correlation, not causality. The cows produce more milk not because they have names but because they receive better care.[2] In our own research, we've been careful to identify causality, not just correlation. In other words, we won't tell you to name your cows.

We'll describe META later in this chapter, but first we need to put into perspective two other issues that dominate much of the conversation about management these days. First is the need for speed. Second is the need to prepare for disruption.

The Need for Speed

Speed is certainly important. As Figure 2.1 shows, the world is moving so much faster than in the past that adoption rates for new technologies have become almost vertical.

FIGURE 2.1 Technological change is accelerating

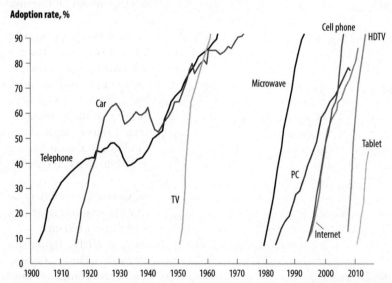

Source: Horace Dediu, "Seeing what's next," Asymco.com, 2013. Reprinted with permission.

While the telephone and other older technologies took decades to get to near total adoption, more recent technologies such as the smartphone and the tablet have compressed the time from decades to years.

Some organizations move at a geologically slow pace, but the rest of the world is moving at a frenetic clip. The speed of walking has picked up 10 percent since the 1990s. We check our phones more than eight billion times a day. The average shot in a movie has gone from 10 seconds in the 1940s to 4 seconds today. Even chickens are speedier: They grow four times faster than they did 50 years ago. ADHD is the quintessential modern disease.[3]

The internationalization of business is happening so much faster these days. While it took Walmart 32 years to establish its first presence outside the United States, it took Amazon only 3 years. Hilton Hotels needed 24 years; Airbnb, 1 year. Visa took 16 years; PayPal needed just 2.[4]

With the world moving so much faster these days, it's widely accepted that businesses have to greatly increase their rpms just to stay in place against the competition and go even faster if they're to keep up with customer expectations. But those statements gloss over some important distinctions. For one, not all industries are changing at the same speed or at the same time—while music was upended 15 years ago, for instance, insurance is just now seeing glimmers of innovation because the forces at work there play out over the longer term. For another, change isn't always that fast—look at the low number of new consumer products and the generally steady speed of production. It's not enough just to mandate speed all the time, in every part of an organization and at every level.

Yes, everything having to do with the customer needs to be done at the speed that the customer requires—which is almost always faster than it's being done now. That need for speed is even greater than it used to be because customers now have so many more ways to complain publicly. When United Airlines' baggage handlers badly damaged a $3,500 guitar owned by musician Dave Carroll, he couldn't get the airline to compensate him or even apologize. So he wrote a song about United's mishandling of the situation. He posted the song on YouTube and got 9 million hits within a year. *The Times* [of London] estimated that the public debacle cost United $180 million in revenue.[5]

Still, there needs to be considerable understanding and subtlety about where to speed up and where not to and how to marshal the right kind of change inside an organization and accelerate overall performance.

Paresh Sukthankar, deputy managing director at HDFC Bank, one of our 23 superaccelerators, told us, "Business is about balance. Of course, satisfying shareholders is important in a publicly listed company. But that shouldn't be pursued to the extent of taking on a risk profile that is not prudent and that damages customers' trust in us. Without our people, we are just another portfolio of assets. It's the active balancing of the shareholder, the customer, our people, and the community that has enabled our growth."

He played the role of what people at the bank called "Doctor No" during a stretch when Indian banks were rushing to make loans to finance infrastructure—loans they now very much regret. He described perfectly how to negotiate the acceleration trap in a newspaper interview: "What's the function of a brake?" he asked. "It gives you the confidence to drive fast."[6]

Leaders need to take an approach that rhymes with the one in Daniel Kahneman's brilliant book, *Thinking, Fast and Slow*, to apply the right type of discipline to each sort of issue. Putting too much emphasis simply on speed can lead companies into what we call the "acceleration trap" (in other words, adopting a frantic pace in all of their activities without ever taking the time to stop and reflect on what is going on). Even in Silicon Valley, known for speed at all costs, Eric Ries, the author of the popular recent book on innovation, *The Lean Startup*, says he advises companies to "slow down and learn."[7]

In aeronautics, there is a concept called max Q. Based on air density and speed, it is the maximum aerodynamic stress that a vehicle can withstand. With the space shuttle, max Q occurred at about 35,000 feet; engines were throttled back by about two-thirds as shuttles approached that altitude to avoid catastrophe. Similarly, in business, it is sometimes necessary to throttle back to avoid falling into a trap that can devastate performance, productivity, and retention. A constant, frenetic pace saps employee motivation and makes employees less willing to accompany the management team in its quest for better performance. Stress-related health problems start to arise, absenteeism and medical leaves increase, and, ultimately, with no end in sight, people start to leave to go to companies with more sustainable rhythms.

The impact on employees is also transferred to those in closest contact with them, customers and suppliers, who feel neglected. In a frantic organization, employees cannot dedicate time to listening to their customers' concerns because that slows them down. Employees also do not have time to attend to the needs and requirements of their suppliers, which also operate at a frantic rhythm and require attention. Pretty soon, customers and suppliers start defecting to competitors.

Too much focus on speed can not only leave bodies in your path—be they disgruntled or disengaged employees, customers, or suppliers—but also cause communities to feel betrayed and ignored or damage ecosystems. Companies need to be able to focus on the long term for the places where they operate and, indeed, for the whole planet.

If you're in quicksand, the worst thing you can do is thrash about, but that's just what many companies do.

Speed is important. It just isn't the be-all and end-all.

Disruption

Neither is disruption the be-all and end-all. Clayton Christensen, who popularized the idea through his important book *The Innovator's Dilemma: The Revolutionary Book That Will Change the Way You Do Business*, has even seen how it's possible to be led astray by focusing too much on the idea of a world in upheaval. Christensen very publicly advocated that Harvard Business School (HBS), where he is on the faculty, reinvent its curriculum to allow for the effect of massive open online courses (MOOCs), which he saw disrupting all of education.[8] A MOOC allows anyone to take a class over the Internet, and enrollment in some early MOOCs reached the six figures. A few years ago, many thought that MOOCs would overwhelm traditional higher education, and Christensen argued for radical change at HBS. But MOOCs fizzled. Enrollment might still be in the tens of thousands for some classes now, but completion rates are in the low single-digit percentages. There's still interest in how the Internet can supplement traditional education, but MOOCs turned out to be a fad, and HBS is surely glad that it didn't do anything rash.

In Silicon Valley, people like to caution: "Never mistake a clear view with a short distance." And the assumption that every business needs to constantly be ready to move to a new business model or into new markets can lead to that sort of confusion about timing. Constantly assuming disruption is right around the corner can also distract management from the day-to-day work that can deliver real benefit. It can lead an organization to bounce from one unrealized idea to another—companies can wind up with corporate ADD, always chasing the next idea *du jour*.

Disruption is certainly powerful, when it happens. Ask Kodak, Blockbuster, newspapers, and a host of others. But not every change is swift or total. Travel agents were supposed to be wiped out by the Internet, but about 40 percent of those operating during the industry's peak are still in business,[9] and the number of bank tellers has actually increased since the advent of the ATM.[10] So not every business needs to become "the Uber of" or "the Airbnb of" something.

In any case, while breakthroughs in strategy are still important, they don't provide the sort of long-term competitive advantage that they once did. Strategies are easier to copy in these fast-moving times, when innovation no longer requires enormous resources.

Disruption, like speed, is important and should be watched for but has to be kept in context.

META

All of this leads us to acceleration and META.

When we began our research into the sources of success, we considered the possibility that they relied on being in the right industry or geographic market. However, as Figures 2.2a and 2.2b illustrate, we found that, while industry and geographic location do matter, what matters more is a company's performance within its chosen industry or geographic market.

The difference between being average in the most and least profitable industries is 19 percentage points of margin. Similarly, the difference between being average in the most and least profitable geographies is 16 points. But the differences within industries and within geographies are far greater. The average variation between the best-performing and worst-performing companies within an industry is 34 points, and the average variation between the best-performing and worst-performing companies within a country or region is 38 points.

FIGURE 2.2a Execution trumps strategy: Industry view

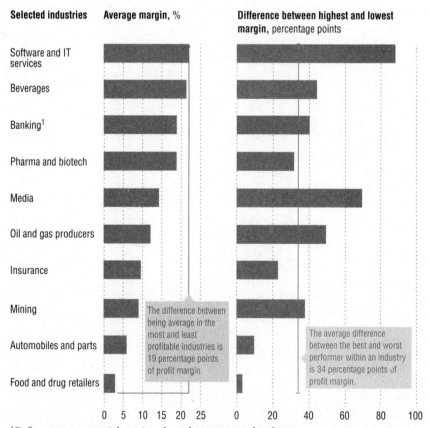

[1] Refers to commercial, regional, and investment banking.

Source: Heidrick & Struggles analysis of FT 500 data; Investopedia

FIGURE 2.2b Execution trumps strategy: Geographic view

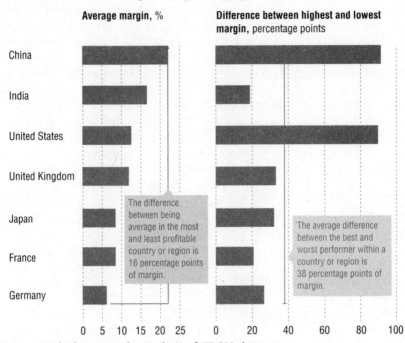

Source: Heidrick & Struggles analysis of FT 500 data

In other words, instead of having success depend on the sort of radical change that an emphasis on speed or disruption would dictate, our research found that the majority of competitive differentiation now occurs based on companies' ability to exploit new sources of growth while sustaining the source of today's competitive advantage—they are able to make sense of changes in their current environment, not a radically new one, and act in a timely manner.

Do this same analysis for companies 20 years ago, and you will find that industry and geography mattered more then than they do now. Go back 40 years, and you'll find that industry and geography mattered even more. Why? Essentially, the reason is the "creative destruction" effect of the globalization of capital. There used to be wide variations in the attractiveness of industries, but as capital has become ever more global, liquid, and informed (largely driven by the twin forces of deregulation and privatization and by the rise of powerful, activist investors), the less-productive industries have been "Uber-ized." If an industry or subindustry doesn't earn its cost of capital plus a healthy margin over a business cycle, death approaches. Think buggy whips. Picking the right industry and geography matters a lot. But the importance of the right-hand side of Figures 2.2a and 2.2b is climbing.

A company's growth rate and its potential for improvement in profitability both correlate much more strongly with performance on certain management metrics than they do with moving into a different industry or geography. Our research has found, for instance, that accelerating teams move faster and deliver 22.8 percent more economic impact than derailing teams. Individual leaders who are adept at accelerating performance are as much as four times more productive than their peers.[11] Although managers invariably point to external events to explain poor results, the fact is that every business faces storms. What matters most, we found, is the resources you place on the boat to prepare for changing circumstances as well as how you handle the boat and crew and navigate the waters while you're in the storms.

Our data shows that sustaining acceleration in companies requires having a portfolio of initiatives composed of long-term commitments as well as small bets, balancing speed and quality, and providing access to the right information. Focus on increasing the number and speed of only the right activities. Do not raise performance goals across the board; follow your acceleration pathway. Shorten innovation cycles in the areas that most need it—it may be product development, but it can also be internal management innovation or continuous improvement plans.

To be as precise and helpful as possible, we have identified a series of what we call drag and drive factors, at each of the four levels—strategy, the organization, teams, and individuals. When companies get these factors right, our research shows, they accelerate. Done wrong, and the companies create drag.

While we'll go into the drag and drive factors for each of the four levels in the chapters on how to accelerate at those levels, we'll give you a preview here of the 13 factors at the organization level, to show how strong the correlation is between these factors and performance. As Figure 2.3 shows, within each quintile of corporate performance, the companies that scored better on our diagnostic based on these 13 key factors had better financial results.

We found that derailing companies are shrinking revenue by more than 8 percent a year, while accelerating companies are growing revenues by more than 8 percent a year, with the remaining categories falling between these poles.

To make the drag and drive factors at each level easier to act on, we have organized them into META, whose acceleration formula is shown in Figure 2.4.

You need to have some level of excellence in all four of the META areas, but acceleration can still be present even if one of the areas is little developed. For instance, in a mature industry with well-established processes, such as steel or pulp and paper, the ability to transform may matter less than the other areas in driving acceleration.

Let's look at each of the META areas one by one.

FIGURE 2.3 Why drive factors matter

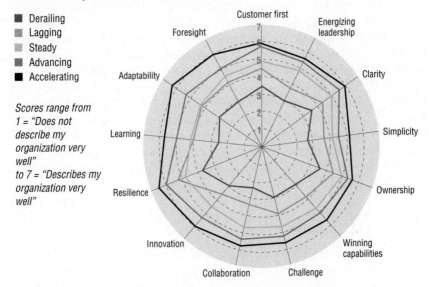

■ Derailing
▨ Lagging
▨ Steady
▨ Advancing
■ Accelerating

Scores range from 1 = "Does not describe my organization very well" to 7 = "Describes my organization very well"

FIGURE 2.4 META

M + E + T + A = Acceleration	
Mobilize	Inspire aligned action based on a compelling purpose and a simple set of strategic priorities.
Execute	Fully harness and streamline resources to consistently deliver excellence in the core business.
Transform	Experiment and innovate to create new growth engines and to reinvent existing businesses ahead of the market.
Agility	Spot opportunities and threats; adapt and pivot at a faster pace than competitors to create competitive advantage.

Mobilize

Mobilizing requires the ability to inspire aligned action based on a compelling ambition and purpose and a simple set of strategic priorities. This is Napoleon's army as it marched out of Paris, not as it straggled back from the gates of Moscow. This is a school of fish sensing a predator and immediately taking on a very precise shape to avoid that particular attacker.

An organization that is dragging here will feel overtaken by market disruptions and experience chronic service failures and high customer attrition. The company will witness performance indicators in the red and see key projects delayed or never finished. It will have no clear purpose and a message so complicated that it deters people from even trying to get it.

To turn this drag into drive, you need to put the customer at the center of all decision making and be able to read changes in the external ecosystem through the lens of your customers. You need to operate with leadership that can energize and gather the organization behind a purpose so powerful that everyone will feel that they own it and want to make it happen. Mobilizing is also about having clarity, challenging long-held assumptions, minimizing priorities, emphasizing flexibility over optimization, aligning cultural and brand values, developing a high-engagement environment, and creating an organizational story that is easy to understand, is told at every opportunity, and can accelerate decision making to drive aligned and purposeful action.

Execute

Execution is about fully harnessing and streamlining resources to consistently deliver excellence in the core business. It is based on a shared understanding of the critical few strategic capabilities required, the extent to which those capabilities exist in the organization today, and the feasibility of closing the gaps. Key trade-offs and risks are explicitly considered.

This is General Electric under Jack Welch, who, Peter Drucker said, would come up with a list of priorities, and then narrow it down to one priority and focus on that one priority for five years. After five years, he wouldn't go to the second priority on his list. He'd start over with a new list and settle on a new most-important priority. He backed up his priorities with extensive resources to develop talent and match it to the opportunities.

When your people and resources are stuck in complex, hierarchical structures, waiting for sign-offs; when there is little or no diversity of thought among decision makers; and when there is poor talent mapping and management, you are experiencing execution drag. You can tackle that drag and turn it into drive by reducing bureaucracy and creating a culture of meritocracy where leaders demonstrate accountability for how they perform and how they manage others. This will allow you to attract the best talent and release new energy to accelerate performance.

Transform

This is where companies experiment and innovate to create growth engines and to reinvent existing businesses ahead of the market; sometimes, transformation results from a dramatic breakthrough, while other times it comes from a steady, long-term effort through a process such as Six Sigma.

More than the other areas of META, transformation implies a change in the way people in the organization think and in the way resources are allocated. It implies breaking with tradition and internal fiefdoms, rethinking the ways things are done, embracing change and innovation, and not tolerating mediocrity, even at the expense of personal relationships.

The willingness to experiment is the ethos that has developed in Silicon Valley, and, while not every practice in the valley could or should be emulated by other companies, this ethos should be. Initiatives that are implemented achieve a balance between commitment and flexibility, informed by well-defined performance metrics. You will have a clear mechanism for managing those with a stake in the initiatives on a continuing basis. You and your people will be freed to experiment, learn to trust each other, stretch each other, and work as one joined-up organization driving forward.

Agility

The key element of acceleration, agility implies being able to spot opportunities and threats and to adapt and pivot faster than peer organizations to create a competitive advantage. It also means being able to prepare for, withstand, and recover from setbacks quickly.

If the organization is slow to adapt to market changes, suffers from analysis paralysis, keeps applying old solutions to new problems unsuccessfully, and has leaders who are slow to adopt new ideas, it is dragging. To turn this around, focus on nimbleness, decode signals indicating that change is coming, and act in a timely manner. Embrace change as an opportunity for continuous improvement, and look for leaders who are open-minded and can adjust to new internal or external conditions.

Agility is what Walmart is trying to develop to keep from being "Amazoned," as so many companies have been before it. Walmart has been phenomenally successful by developing great supply chain capabilities, among other things, but now must learn to cope in the fluid online environment. Although known for developing capabilities internally, Walmart bought online retailer Jet.com for $3.3 billion in 2016 to accelerate its efforts. Agility is what the president of Toyota, Akio Toyoda, thinks the company needs to emphasize. Even as he reported strong annual earnings for the year ended March 31, 2016, he said in the same remarks that the company had "become too big to respond speedily to severe changes in the business environment." He said that, to become agile, the company needed to make major changes, including reaching out to partners instead of "being obsessed with doing everything ourselves."[12] Agility is what enabled a major media company to use digital signals to detect with 75 percent to 90 percent certainty that a subscriber was about to cancel. It could then try to entice the customer to stay, and with every percentage point reduction in churn, the company stood to gain millions of dollars in profit.[13]

A survey of 322 senior executives found that 95 percent felt that their organizations need to be more agile to survive in the long term. Twelve percent felt their organizations (especially those with at least 500 employees) have actually become less agile in recent years.[14]

■ ■ ■

META and the drag and drive factors it represents must be addressed at the four levels. They must be part of the strategy-setting process, which must become a continual exercise—no more five-year plans, at least as the guiding document for an organization. The factors must be addressed in terms of general management of the organization, guiding many away from traditional "command and control" approaches and even breaking down barriers between companies and their partners, suppliers, and customers. The factors must guide the management of teams, which can be far more effective than they currently are. And these drag and drive factors must be considered in terms of individual leaders, who, after all, determine much of the success or failure of an organization.

Although most companies pursue many of the goals in META, they miss key aspects. In particular, companies often don't do enough to be agile, which can act as an amplifier of the work in the other three areas.

We began our work thinking that elite organizations used a different approach to management than did lesser performers, but what we found was that companies across the spectrum emphasized the same things. All wanted to put the customer first. All wanted clarity within the management structure. All wanted to innovate. What we discovered, though, was that elite companies were far more effective in attacking the same set of issues.

META provides the guide that will help you join that elite group. But keep two things in mind. First, META is a contact sport. It requires that you fight against the tendency of managers to go along to get along and requires that hard choices be made, often, to keep the organization as fit as possible. Second, you haven't accomplished acceleration unless it costs you money and you make money; in other words, it doesn't come for free, but it has a big payoff.

In the next chapter, we will walk you through some examples of companies in the Bain Capital portfolio that demonstrate just how powerful META can be.

Notes

1. Bill George, former CEO of Medtronic and author of *Authentic Leadership,* says Pfeffer and other critics misstate the concept. See Bill George, "The truth about authentic leaders," *Harvard Business School Working Knowledge,* July 6, 2016, hbswk.hbs.edu.

2. Caroline Gammell, "Cows with names produce more milk, scientists say," *Telegraph*, January 28, 2009, telegraph.co.uk.
3. For more on our accelerating modern world, see Robert Colvile, *The Great Acceleration: How the World Is Getting Faster, Faster*, London: Bloomsbury, 2016.
4. Chris Outram, *Digital Stractics: How Strategy Met Tactics and Killed the Strategic Plan*, London: Palgrave Macmillan, 2016.
5. John M. Bernard, *Business at the Speed of Now: Fire Up Your People, Thrill Your Customers, and Crush Your Competitors*, Hoboken, NJ: John Wiley & Sons, 2012.
6. MC Govardhana Rangan, "Paresh Sukthankar succeeding Aditya Puri as HDFC Bank CEO will give shareholders a reason to cheer," *Economic Times*, January 8, 2014, economictimes.indiatimes.com.
7. Paul Michelman, "Why Eric Ries likes management," *strategy+business*, November 12, 2013, strategy-business.com.
8. Jerry Useem, "Business school, disrupted," *New York Times*, May 31, 2014, nytimes.com.
9. Rebecca L. Weber, "The travel agent is dying, but it's not yet dead," CNN, October 10, 2013, cnn.com.
10. W.W., "Are ATMs stealing jobs?" *Economist*, June 15, 2011, economist .com.
11. Similarly, research conducted at MIT suggests that firms that excel at agility grow revenue 37 percent faster and generate 30 percent higher profits than firms that lack the capability. See Peter Weill, "IT portfolio management and IT savvy—rethinking IT investments as a portfolio," Center for Information Systems Research, MIT Sloan School of Management, June 14, 2007.
12. Kana Inagaki, "Robotics hire signals Toyota fightback against tech groups," *Financial Times*, June 20, 2016, ft.com.
13. Martin Reeves and Mike Deimler, "Adaptability: The new competitive advantage," *Harvard Business Review*, July–August 2011, hbr.org.
14. Chandler Macleod Group, *Organisational Agility: Navigating the Maze*, October 9, 2014, chandlermacleod.com.

CHAPTER 3

A Learning Laboratory

Private equity firms can function as learning labs for all of us because they work on whole portfolios of companies, not just one at a time. They test and learn, and test and learn, and test and learn. They have huge incentives not only to deliver returns but also to do so quickly. So in a world where acceleration is key, they offer even more valuable insights than they have historically.

We've had the pleasure of working with Bain Capital Private Equity in Europe, in particular with one of its global investment leaders, Dwight Poler, and with Stuart Gent, who heads the firm's portfolio operations, so we're going to describe in some detail in this chapter how three of its companies have accelerated. Bain Capital has been focused on transforming companies for more than 32 years and has developed a clear approach to do this. The principals at Bain Capital are careful to note that the success of their companies is led and driven by their management teams. They look to find companies at an inflection point and partner with great CEOs and management teams who then drive change and deliver the results. They also work with other private equity firms as coinvestors and see those firms as key, active partners.

Poler says Bain Capital's global investing strategy focuses on "driving a transformation in results—how we can achieve a discontinuous improvement in performance. We will look at areas like how to accelerate growth, drive margin expansion, expand into new markets, and improve capital efficiency. Our goal is far more than pulling a simple lever, like cutting costs; we aim to systematically build a great company, as we know that company will be highly valued when we decide to sell."

Although private equity is often viewed as based on a particular capital structure, Bain Capital views itself more as a different governance model, with capital, that can be more effective when companies are trying to drive major change. "Over our history," Gent says, "we have continuously looked to improve our tool kit for accelerating change. Over time we have built on our commitment to the strategy and project management side of change by investing further in organizational health and agility. The ability for an organization to identify, align, resource, and implement real change on its own over time is the key to long-term value creation."

Once Bain Capital is involved, Gent says it invests time, money, and human resources to "make sure the company has a clear strategy, anchored in the facts of its industry, customers, competitors, and economics. We build the plan *with* the top team, a process that builds alignment and that helps us look to add capability to the team, where needed." He adds that Bain Capital focuses on building alignment throughout the company, starting with perhaps the top 20 people, then moving to the top 100, and so on. He says that getting alignment up front is crucial because it allows for better interactions and much quicker decisions down the road.

"We invest real resources in driving change where it matters most," he says. "We measure progress by the real impact achieved, not by measuring activity or process, and we consistently follow up. Once change is under way, we focus on what we need to put in place to make it sustainable."

He acknowledges that "a lot of what we do may sound obvious, but companies rarely seem to drive change in such a focused and disciplined way."

Gent says that Bain Capital "tries to accelerate the results of a company quickly" through short-term levers such as pricing, procurement, cost reductions, simplification, and so on "to financially get ahead of our investment case, because then you have more time to think about the profound change you want to drive and you have more cash to invest in making it happen."

He offers a wry observation about the need to put real talent behind the changes: "When we look to build teams to lead key initiatives, I always question the first set of names discussed. Real change needs the best people in the company, and by definition they are the busiest and so are rarely offered up for key projects. Their managers know how good they are— which is exactly why we want them."

Following the recent financial crisis, Bain Capital applied its tool kit to itself. "The macro environment was very tough," Poler says. "And we needed to both navigate the challenges in our portfolio as well as decide how and where to invest in the post-crisis world. During that period, we spent time and resources refining and recommitting to our strategy. We took the full team away from the office to dedicate the time needed to align with and commit to the plan, and we worked extensively on our effectiveness as a partnership team, making some key changes. We also refined our core behaviors and culture, building on the strengths of our heritage."

A closer study of the experiences of Gent, Poler, and their colleagues at Bain Capital's portfolio companies offers lessons for other organizations interested in honing their ability to accelerate performance, as you'll see as we look at Atento, Nets Holding, and NXP.

Atento

Atento began life in 2000 as a carve-out of the call center assets of Telefónica, the main telecommunications company in Spain and a major player in Latin America. The plan was not only to provide services to Telefónica but also to be able to provide outsourced CRM services to others throughout Spain and Latin America. Atento became the third-largest provider of CRM and BPO services in the world, with more than 150,000 employees in 14 countries. Bain Capital bought Atento in 2012 for $1.3 billion.

Following the acquisition, Bain Capital confirmed as CEO Alejandro Reynal, who had been appointed to the position about a year earlier. Reynal then spearheaded the nine-month-long development of a strategic plan to strengthen Atento's position as one of the global leaders of its sector while evolving the company into a provider of value-added customer experience solutions. He says some of the opportunities were apparent but just had not been possible to realize as a subsidiary of Telefónica. For instance, Atento could now quickly grow its client base by offering its services and expertise to telco companies other than Telefónica. It could also leverage its size to gain economies of scale on procurement and drive improvements in operations productivity. The company could, in addition, undergo technological changes to increase efficiency and bring its value proposition up to speed with the digital age. Equally important, the team was now empowered to shape Atento's own future and unveil its full potential as an independent company.

To start, Reynal made some changes to his top team to position the company for this transformation. "That didn't mean replacing 100 percent," he says. "We had people who are very good at execution." Nevertheless, he did want new people in the "more horizontal," or functional, roles to support the new direction and hired, among others, a new CFO, chief operating officer, and, over time, chief commercial officer.

Reynal took the new top team of 10 on a seven-day journey to break down their assumptions about how the company should operate and to build alignment. He had the team meet in Madrid and then took them away without telling them where they were going. He said people tried to figure out their destination on their mobile devices—one guessed the Czech Republic—and were surprised to see Moroccan flags when they landed. Then the team was taken on a very challenging journey moving between different cities every day, spending nights in the desert, completing long cross-country walks, and sleeping in lodgings with just cold water in the showers. The agenda for each day never unfolded before breakfast that same day.

"It was a once-in-a-lifetime experience for all of us. These are senior executives who want to be in control, who want to know what will happen next," Reynal says. "But we needed to build a team eager to deal with just the opposite. After a while, they surrendered. You knock down some barriers. Then you start building trust."

As the week went on, the team moved from the general experience into specific, guided discussions about the plan for transforming and growing the company and ended the week feeling that they knew each other far better and were united in their purpose.

The time then arrived to roll out, across the entire organization, the plan to transform and grow Atento. A companywide engagement and mobilizing campaign was launched under the theme "Lead the Transformation." It kicked off with a three-day summit in Brazil for the top 100 leaders of the company. From there on, the new strategic plan and transformation agenda permeated the whole organization through a series of strategic workshops and engagement activities held in each country. The process is repeated every year, with the necessary adjustments, to reignite the transformation process and continue executing the strategic plan.

The result has been significant achievements at the growth, efficiency, and people levels. For instance, Atento has taken out $150 million of annual costs through economies of scale and process improvements. In a significant change from how things were done three years ago, the company is now managed from three command centers, with more than 100 call centers across three continents serving more than 400 clients and monitoring interactions with 500 million consumers. Reynal says the company is also positioned to take out additional millions of dollars in efficiencies, partly because of its latest digital initiatives.

Reynal also figures that the company has about 10 percent less absenteeism and attrition because of efforts to transform Atento into a high-performance organization. This commitment calls for innovations in the hiring process, continual training and development of employees, and strong communication—all key levers for a company that sees the talent of its employees as a fundamental component of the value proposition.

With momentum generated by the early successes on the efficiency and people sides, Atento has expanded into adjacent, but still new, markets, including the United States, where it routes calls to its centers in Latin America. Atento has also expanded into value-added services. For instance, rather than having an operator handle a marketing call for, say, a credit card company and then pass an interested customer on to that company to complete the transaction, Atento can manage the process end to end. Removing the handoff greatly shortens processing times for clients while reducing errors. Value-added solutions have gone from approximately 10 percent of revenue to 24 percent in four years, Reynal says. The company retains more than 99 percent of its clients each year.

He acknowledges that he needs to stay alert because the external environment changes quickly. Social media, artificial intelligence, and other technological developments are transforming how interactions with customers are handled, so he has a formal process for evaluating emerging technologies to be sure he stays ahead of the game. Reynal also monitors social and economic conditions, which can be volatile in his markets. For instance, during Brazil's recent downturn, inflation rose 11 percent in 2015, leading to significant wage increases for his employees—a huge percentage of his total costs. To offset the impact of such a situation, the company has to pass a percentage of this increase in cost to its clients and become even more efficient.

In 2012, when Bain Capital bought Atento, research firm Gartner listed the company in the "challengers" quadrant of its Magic Quadrant[1] for the business process outsourcing sector. Compared with its peers, Atento was rated above average for its ability to execute but was seen as lacking vision. In 2015, Atento was firmly in Gartner's "leaders" quadrant; it was rated the company with the highest execution ability and well above average on completeness of vision. For the third consecutive year, Great Places to Work Institute put Atento on its list of the 25 best multinationals to work for, the only company from its sector listed among Google, Microsoft, Coca-Cola, and other household names.

Nets Holding

Nets Holding traces its history back 50 years to when some 180 Danish and Norwegian banks set up a joint back office to handle payments. Nets, which is based in Denmark, consolidated into an operating business in 2010 and bought the largest processor in Finland in 2012. The parent companies decided in 2013 that, while Nets was the biggest processor in the four Nordic countries, it needed considerable capital to stay viable. The parents chose to sell rather than invest, and Bain Capital, Advent International, and ATP bought Nets for $3.1 billion in 2014. Bo Nilsson, whom the banks brought in as CFO to organize the sale, was kept on as CEO.

As happened with Atento, Nilsson looked for quick wins that would fund the investments needed for the transformation and found some.

"I don't know if you can imagine 180 banks owning a business," Nilsson says. "They showed great foresight by setting up Nets and did as much with it as they could, but the ownership structure was inherently complicated. Board members couldn't even discuss many issues, because they were competing with each other."

He quickly changed 60 percent to 70 percent of the top team. "Sometimes you want to take things step-by-step, but it was important not to have people around who were never going to come around," Nilsson says.

"Those are tough decisions. You are losing people who have quite a lot of knowledge about customers and the product. But you have to have only people with the energy and capabilities to make it long term."

He changed the compensation structure to pay-for-performance, "which is very challenging in my neck of the woods because that concept isn't that well known" in Scandinavia. He decided that 10 operational issues, such as improving onboarding of customers, were crucial priorities for 2014, and "we were going to focus just on those few things rather than try to change the world."

Recognizing that driving costs down was paramount, he did a performance-based analysis of procurement that led him to essentially re-place the entire team with outsiders. Nilsson also invested heavily in digital capabilities, including through a series of acquisitions that brought key technologies in-house. Among the acquisitions were the top e-commerce platform in Finland and a company with mobile capabilities.

Nilsson initially focused hard on building alignment among his top 25 executives and then expanded to his top 85 people, whom he took out of the office together for a week to build a strong leadership team, break down silos, and ensure that all 85 understood the plan and their role in making it happen. He's now expanding the alignment effort to include the top 250 at Nets.

Using our analytical tools, including the one diagnosing team effectiveness (the TAQ), he generated what he considers to be important insights. "Our strategic alignment is very strong," he says. "That's the good news. But it was also clear that we need to work on our meeting discipline, in order to ensure stronger and more aligned decision making." Based on practical suggestions, Nilsson says, "I immediately changed the way we set up meetings, who runs them, how we provide feedback. If you look at what we've done without really having top-performing teams, imagine if we could get teams performing at the top level."

To spur change quickly, he set up teams that worked outside the normal hierarchy, which is made up of seven business units. For instance, he didn't think each of the seven units would be able to develop an effective, Nets-wide plan for mobile payments, so he set up a team that crossed all seven businesses. Nilsson chaired the group and established quick approval processes. He did something similar for data analytics and set up fast-moving steering committees for areas where he saw the need for major change. Once the efforts were far enough along, he folded the teams and turned the responsibilities over to the businesses.

He took the same sort of approach with employees. After focusing on achieving alignment with his top 250, he turned his attention to the company's more than 2,000 other employees, who had been in full-on transformation mode for years, without necessarily fully understanding why. To relieve some of the pressure, Nilsson moved toward a business-as-usual approach, focusing on the people side, on deliveries to customers, and on managing stakeholders. He also turned his attention more to changing the culture and values.

The result of all the work has been a 14 percentage point improvement in margins and an uptick in organic growth, to 6 percent in the final quarters of 2015. At the time of this writing (September 2016), Nets Holding unveiled plans to launch an IPO and is projected to receive a valuation of $3.9 billion to $4.8 billion—a gain of at least $800 million in just two short years. In a *Financial Times* interview, Nilsson described the IPO as "the next step in the development of the Nets group following a period of rapid growth and considerable investment, during which the business has been transformed."[2]

NXP

NXP's history goes all the way back to 1953, when Dutch giant Philips N.V. set up an electronics business. A group of private equity firms, including Bain Capital, bought 80 percent of Philips Semiconductors in 2006 at a price that valued the entire company at $9.4 billion. Today, renamed NXP, it is the fifth-largest semiconductor maker in the world, outside of the memory-chip market—it is known especially for chips for cybersecurity, cars, and digital networks; the company carries a market valuation of $29.7 billion.

During the four-year stretch that Bain Capital was involved with NXP, before it went public in 2010, Bain Capital partners worked closely with Ruediger Stroh, who ran a major division. He, too, began with a six-month effort to deeply understand the business and develop a growth strategy. He set a truly ambitious goal. He wanted to have at least 1.5 times the market share of his nearest competitor in his various lines of business, even though the business had roughly 0.8 the market share of the largest competitor when he took over.

Stroh decided that his division was just cherry-picking opportunities. It was looking for high-end markets, but they tended to be small. So he decided to push in several areas to identify mass markets, including contactless smartcards that, among other things, can be scanned by readers and used as fast, secure, convenient tickets on buses and trains. He also saw, back in 2009, how important cybersecurity would be and has won big with the sorts of chips that are used in bank cards, including in China's massive market. (He acknowledges that focusing on cybersecurity gave him more of a tailwind than he could have expected.)

With the plan in place, he, too, organized a journey, taking his top 50 team members on a four-day trip to Spain that forced people out of their routines, disoriented them to break down barriers, and saw the group return as a tight-knit team.

"Our CEO said, 'Are you nuts? We're almost bankrupt, and you want to do what?'" Stroh recalls. "I said, 'Do you think you could win a Super Bowl with people who haven't met each other? Well, how can I turn the business around with a team that doesn't know each other?'"

When the group returned, it focused intensely on role-modeling crisp decision-making behavior. "We don't just make decisions," Stroh insists. "We make fierce commitments." He said his team's philosophy is like that of Yoda, who told Luke Skywalker in *The Empire Strikes Back*: "Do. Or do not. There is no try." Stroh says, "Once we commit, we go for it." He says that he insists on delegating responsibility to get decisions made at the right level.

His team has developed standards for how to conduct productive meetings and gives itself a score in each one. "When we have meetings that suck, we address the issue," Stroh says. He puts three empty chairs in each meeting, to stand for other team members, for shareholders, and for customers. He sometimes has someone sit in one of those chairs and advocate for whomever it represents. His mantra is "Focus. Speed. Customers."

His division has gone from the bottom quartile in Gallup's employee engagement surveys to the top quartile. Stroh says employees bought into his vision that radical growth was possible.

Of course, getting the team dynamics right is just part of the equation. There are a lot of effective teams in Silicon Valley, where Stroh has lived for 20 years, that don't accelerate, because they don't navigate the fast-changing technology market well enough.

Stroh's division worked closely with customers and prospects to anticipate their needs because lead times on new products can be exceptionally long. The team shifted from an internal to an external focus and from selling just products to providing real, value-added solutions. The work with customers has gone so well that Stroh says that NXP's Net Promoter Score has risen from 5 percent to 42 percent.

In the process, Stroh achieved his targets—and then some. He went from 0.8 of his biggest competitor's market share to 3 times the share in some lines and to 8 times in others. Revenue rose from $300 million a year when he took over to $1.3 billion four years later, in 2013. It has since continued the surge and become a multibillion-dollar business, mostly through organic growth. (He has also been given some additional lines of business.)

As Stroh says, "Impossible is really just an opinion."

■ ■ ■

While Bain Capital Private Equity is just in the background in these stories, we've worked with the company enough to know that it does any number of things exceptionally well and has worked to constantly refine and improve its approach to transformation over time. To generate sustained impact and build great companies, it puts a real premium on speed and on accelerating the cycle rate of change. Bain Capital keeps learning from its ever-evolving portfolio of companies and works to share that learning with all of them. It measures real impact, not just the activities and processes that are *supposed* to produce impact. The partners at Bain Capital also select and invest in a global team of very talented people to drive performance.

As you'll see, many of the drivers of success for these companies will show up as major themes in the rest of this book—the need to quickly assemble the right top team and get it aligned behind your strategy, the power of building momentum through early successes, the importance of getting team dynamics right and of role-modeling behavior, and much more. We'll start to really explore these topics in the next chapter, where we explain the research journey that brought us to acceleration and META.

Notes

1. For an explanation of this type of analysis, see Gartner, "Research methodologies: Gartner Magic Quadrant," gartner.com.
2. Martin Arnold, "Danish payments processor Nets Holding plans IPO," *Financial Times*, September 1, 2016, ft.com.

CHAPTER 4

Our Journey to META

In 1962, renowned economist Milton Friedman said, "There is one and only one social responsibility of business— . . . to increase its profits."[1] We all know where that line of thinking got us.

Jack Welch was seen as the paragon of generating shareholder value. He produced a steady march of profit increases that led to a $484 billion market valuation for General Electric when he stepped down as CEO in 2001, after a 20-year stretch in the top job for the company, which had a $14 billion market valuation when he began. But even Welch said, in 2009, that "shareholder value is the dumbest idea in the world. Shareholder value is a result, not a strategy. . . . Managers and investors should not set share price increases as their overarching goal."[2]

The focus on shareholder value has led to distortions, such as a huge increase in CEO pay relative to that of lower-level employees; CEOs reaped the reward from options that were designed to give them incentives to increase the stock price but that often made them rich regardless of how the company fared or how much credit they could claim—boards typically didn't want to disappoint their CEO once the prospect of huge stock gains had been put on the table. The emphasis on shareholder value also contributed to scandals such as those at Enron and WorldCom, where senior executives tried to feed the beast that is the stock market long after the underlying businesses failed to justify a lofty valuation.

The emphasis on shareholder value didn't even accomplish its main goal: increasing profits. The return on assets and on invested capital fell by three-quarters for U.S. companies between 1965 and 2009.[3]

By contrast, we side squarely with Peter Drucker, who wrote in 1954, "There is only one valid definition of a business purpose: to create a customer."[4] Yes, businesses are designed to generate profits, but, at their core, they are to fill a need for customers. Once senior executives start overfocusing on some other constituency—whether themselves, their employees, their shareholders, or any other group—they risk losing their way and walking into the sorts of problems that we address throughout this book.

Trying to solve a problem for a customer gives a company a mission, and it's better to have companies run by missionaries than by mercenaries.

Our belief that customers, not profits, should be the focus for companies drove our decision on what metric to make central in our research. (We understand that a description of research methodology isn't the most scintillating of topics, but we promised to stay close to the data, so we need to explain the research.)

We debated extensively and looked at all available financial metrics: total shareholder return (TSR), revenue, margin, and earnings before interest, taxes, depreciation, and amortization (EBITDA). We chose revenue growth. More specifically, we decided to use compound annual growth rate (CAGR) to determine a constant growth rate over a specified period because it dampened the volatility that big up or down periods can cause in other measures, because it allowed for easier comparisons, and because it is hard to tamper with.

Because revenue is nothing more than the amount of goods or services sold multiplied by the price that customers pay for them,[5] growing revenues are a good indication that a company is meeting customer demands. When revenues go up, it is because volume goes up, prices go up, or both. Increases in volume or price indicate that the consumer is willing to buy more of the product or service offered or to pay a higher price for it. Revenue growth that stays high over time suggests that the connection between the company and the customer is strong and will remain so for at least the near future.

Revenue growth, which drives shareholder value in the long term, is achieved by pursuing growing market segments, by finding new customers, and by improving the retention of existing customers, all of which are at the core of accelerating performance.

Research shows that, for top-quartile companies, revenue growth is the most important contributor to TSR over the long term. But revenue growth is hard to achieve. Analysis by Bain & Company finds that the leaders of Global 2000 companies are projecting to outgrow their markets, on average, by two times in terms of revenue. But 90 percent of these companies fail to achieve their growth ambitions over 10 years. Among the reasons why companies struggle: internal organizational issues such as complexity, missing capabilities, and an inability to focus.[6]

Having decided that revenue CAGR was the right metric, we began our research with the FT 500 list of the world's largest publicly traded companies and searched it for companies that are elite—not just good or even great, but elite. We wanted companies that had demonstrated real success for an extended period, even in these fast-changing times.

The first pass at the data produced a standard bell curve (Figure 4.1). In other words, some companies grow fast, some are stable, and some shrink. No surprises there. The paradox of growth is alive and well: All companies want growth, but growth brings scale, and scale brings complexity, which in turn chokes growth. This is not a new insight.

FIGURE 4.1 The paradox of growth

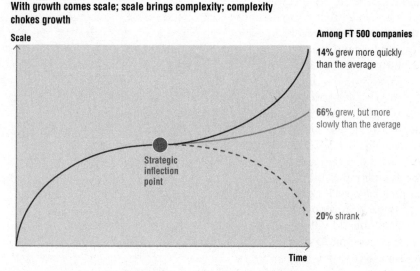

With growth comes scale; scale brings complexity; complexity chokes growth

Scale

Among FT 500 companies

14% grew more quickly than the average

66% grew, but more slowly than the average

Strategic inflection point

20% shrank

Time

Source: Heidrick & Struggles analysis of FT 500 data

However, when we applied additional screens, we found a surprising reality. We looked for companies on the FT 500 list that were in the top 20 percent for revenue growth in both the last three and the last seven years, to ensure that success was sustained. We screened for companies that generated no more than 20 percent of their growth inorganically, to avoid any that were primarily expanding through acquisitions. We identified companies that received no more than 20 percent of their revenue from their home government. We also looked for companies that had not seen their profit margin reduced by more than 20 percent as a percentage of revenue as they grew—growth can destroy value if companies pursue revenues so aggressively that they take a hit to their profit margins, and we wanted to avoid any that had done so. Those four "rules of 20," as we came to call them, produced a startlingly small number of companies. Out of our original list of the 500 companies with the largest market valuations—the most successful companies on the planet—only 23 met these tests. We call them the "superaccelerators."

To make sure we were onto something by studying these superaccelerators and what made them tick, we looked at how they performed in the stock market. As we've said, we made the deliberate choice not to use stock market performance to identify the superaccelerators—in keeping with John Kay's idea of obliquity, we believe that stock market success is something that happens as an outcome of doing the right thing, rather than the target to be pursued at all costs. But, as a double check, we calculated what would have happened had you invested $100

FIGURE 4.2 Superaccelerators' stocks outperform

■ Superaccelerators ■ Remaining FT 500 companies

Total return on $100 investment, $

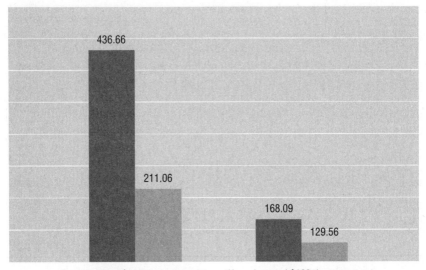

If you invested $100 seven years ago   If you invested $100 three years ago

Source: Heidrick & Struggles analysis of FT 500 data

in the 23 superaccelerators and in the rest of FT 500, both three years and seven years ago. To accurately calculate this scenario, we carefully corrected share price movement for things such as share buybacks and stock splits, and we assumed that you reinvested dividends back into the original stock. Figure 4.2 shows the results.

The good news is that you would have made money in all four scenarios. But if you'd invested $100 in our 23 superaccelerators seven years ago, you would now have a portfolio worth some $437, an increase of $337. If, instead, you'd invested in the rest of the FT 500, your portfolio would be worth $211, an increase of only $111. In other words, the increase in wealth from investing in the superaccelerators compared with the rest of the FT 500 over the last seven years is more than three times greater.

In a sense, this may not be surprising. Companies that grew revenue profitably would be expected to outgrow the stock market. If you had put money on the winning horse, you would be taking home more money than if you had bet on the horse that came in second. But that is not the point we are making. Based on our research, including into the superaccelerators, we are making two different, more subtle arguments about the importance of accelerating performance.

First, we are arguing that the most profitable growth was driven by the ability to accelerate performance: Because its presence *predicts* future outperformance, developing the ability to accelerate performance will help your organization to outperform.

Our second argument is that predicted growth is an important part of how investors determine a company's value. Research shows that around 40 percent of a company's valuation derives from estimates of future growth.[7] A company that can accelerate performance can achieve that growth more quickly. In a business-as-usual scenario for a publicly listed company, that increased speed will show up in a higher valuation in the stock market. For a company owned by a private equity (PE) investor, it will reduce the length of time the PE company needs to own the portfolio company. And for a company undergoing a transformation, the increased speed can help minimize the length of time taken up by disruptive changes.

We're not intending to give investment advice; that's not our topic. What we are saying is that our recommendations will help companies grow more profitably than they would have otherwise. As well as being a good thing in its own right, that will also make those companies worth more.

The 23 Superaccelerators

Although no company is guaranteed continued success—as "lookbacks" at the list of companies in *In Search of Excellence, Good to Great,* and other business books have shown—the 23 superaccelerators (listed in Figure 4.3, by total revenue) have demonstrated great enough success for

FIGURE 4.3 The superaccelerators

1 Apple
2 Ping An Insurance (Group) Company of China
3 Alphabet
4 Comcast
5 SoftBank Group
6 Cigna
7 Gilead Sciences
8 Taiwan Semiconductor Manufacturing Company
9 Danaher
10 Starbucks
11 Tencent Holdings

12 Tata Consultancy Services
13 Visa
14 Cognizant Technology Solutions
15 BlackRock
16 Biogen
17 MasterCard
18 The Priceline Group
19 Shire
20 HDFC Bank
21 Cerner
22 Intercontinental Exchange
23 Illumina

Average compound annual growth rate (CAGR) of revenue for superaccelerating companies over the past 3 years is 24%—almost 9 times the average CAGR for the whole group of FT 500 companies over the same period.

Average CAGR for 7 years is 20%, which is 4 times the average of the FT 500 companies over the same period.

a long enough stretch that they can yield important lessons. Seven years of great success is a long time in this day and age.

Note that, while the list includes Apple and Alphabet, the companies come from a wide range of industries, not just high tech. Nor are the companies all from the United States or any other specific region; they span the globe. (Descriptions of the 23 companies are in the Research Appendix.) Any company can become elite, or at least make major strides in that direction.

The list is absent some iconic companies—for example, Amazon, Southwest Airlines, and Qualcomm. They fail our test on maintaining or growing profitability (or seeing margin decline less than 20 percent) in the seven-year period. For sure, some companies not on our list are growing strongly. But the margin test was put in place to avoid rewarding companies that grow at the expense of remaining profitable consistently. This does not mean that in the future they can't become elite companies by our definition. But right now, they are not part of the elite group.

The Journey

We were more than intrigued to find out what drove the outstanding success of the superaccelerators. What capabilities and characteristics do these companies possess that can be applied to others? This question took us on quite a journey.

We conducted in-depth interviews with senior executives at many of the 23 superaccelerators, and we were privileged to be able to study nearly 250 of the FT 500 companies and to dive into the minutiae of their management practices. We combined that research with what we have learned from years of research into how hundreds of companies have achieved acceleration at the four levels: strategy, the organization, teams, and individuals.

For the *strategy level*, we drew on our consulting work, on a study conducted by Wharton faculty affiliated with DSI (now a Heidrick & Struggles company), and on surveys of more than 20,000 global leaders.

The question driving the research was the following: What aspects of strategy enable an organization to thrive under changing conditions? Our underlying hypothesis was that, in today's constantly evolving world, the organizations that accelerate are capable of sensing and acting in a timely manner.

A study conducted by faculty at Wharton Executive Education, which surveyed 1,200 leaders from a variety of industries, found that 60 percent of senior executives admitted that their organization had been blindsided by three or more high-impact events within a five-year period, and this impeded their ability to accelerate performance. Of those executives, 97 percent said that their organization lacked an adequate early warning system, leading to unforeseen impacts on the core business or product lines.

This information, combined with our consulting work and research in strategy and decision making, formed the basis for developing a conceptual adaptation of what it takes to accelerate strategy. This conceptual model was also informed by draft surveys with more than 20,000 global leaders in companies representing diverse geographies and functions.

This helped us to define and measure the aspects of strategy that drive organizations to see sooner, scan wider, and learn faster, enabling them to outperform their competitors.

For the *organization level*, we asked the following question: What is it about great organizations that enables them to beat the competition consistently?

Based on years of consulting with companies about growth and acceleration, we developed a set of hypotheses about what practices allow companies to accelerate. We crafted a survey that received almost 250 responses from major organizations, and we conducted interviews with clients around the world. We asked executives to self-rate their level of META and then correlated the ratings with actual financial performance and found that the self-ratings on our acceleration factors matched well with corporate revenue growth, as shown in Table 4.1.

Not surprisingly, CEOs and members of their boards painted a more positive picture, while those at lower levels, such as department heads and general managers, depicted a more negative one. (The findings suggest that the further someone in an organization is from the customer, the more likely that person is to have a distorted view of the company's position.) To smooth out such variations in responses, we introduced variables such as the stage of business growth.

There was a strong positive correlation ($p < 0.01$) between our measure of acceleration (i.e., META) and the stage at which an organization was in its business cycle, irrespective of a respondent's position within the organization. In other words, if companies were accelerating, they were more likely to be in the early growth to mature phases, while those derailing were more

TABLE 4.1 Acceleration and performance

	CAGR of revenue over 7 years	META survey classification
Derailing	−1.17%	−1.40%
Steady	5.36%	6.31%
Accelerating	17.34%	14.87%

likely to be in the mature to decline phases. Linking the stage in the business cycle with our objective measure (revenue CAGR at seven years), we found a strong positive correlation ($p < 0.01$) between the two measures: Those companies that are accelerating are more likely to have a higher revenue CAGR at seven years; those companies that score low on META have more trouble leveraging the drive factors to accelerate performance and may, in fact, be turning some of them into drag factors (see Figure 4.4).

FIGURE 4.4 Scores on organizational drive factors

Scores range from 1 = "Does not describe my organization very well" to 7 = "Describes my organization very well"

n = 1,118

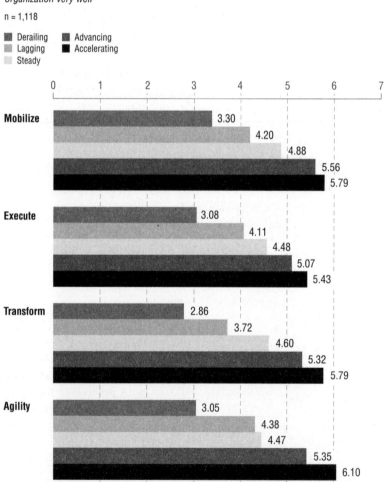

Companies in developed economies find acceleration easier to achieve. In addition, the smaller the organization, in terms of revenue and number of employees, the more accelerated it was likely to be—consistent with the paradox of growth.

For the *team level*, we started from the premise that organizations are a collection of teams and asked the next logical question: What makes teams more effective?

We analyzed data from 3,000 teams across a wide number of organizations, functions, and geographies, in industries as diverse as banking, private equity, insurance, engineering, telecommunications, health care, and charitable institutions. We measured team acceleration through the application of a tried and tested questionnaire, the Team Accelerator Questionnaire (TAQ), which has robust reliability and validity. We have used this instrument to take the temperature of teams from within the team as well as through the perceptions of key stakeholders outside the team. Crucially, we have also correlated team acceleration with financial performance data from organizations.

Team acceleration was calculated based on the number of respondent groups rating above 3.8 on a 5-point scale across the 16 tests of teams. The respondent groups included all four of the interested and affected parties of teams—the members, the leader, the line manager of the leader, and the team's stakeholders. Teams have been categorized as *accelerating* when all four respondent groups scored above 3.8; *advancing* when three respondent groups scored above 3.8; *steady* when two respondent groups scored above 3.8; *lagging* when only one respondent group scored above 3.8; and *derailing* if none of the respondent groups scored above 3.8.

Figure 4.5 shows the distribution of teams within these five classifications.

As you can see, using 3.8 as the standard produces a normal distribution curve. We also found that, true to our prediction that acceleration is not a naturally occurring phenomenon for most teams, only 13 percent of the teams we studied could be defined as accelerating, whereas roughly 27 percent were lagging or outright derailing.

Here is the critical question: Do accelerating teams deliver superior performance? Organizations use various measures to assess performance of their people, teams, functions, and the enterprise as a whole. In our research, we looked at bonuses as a proxy for economic performance. We applied a multiple regression analysis and found that being an accelerating team, as opposed to a derailing team, explains 13 percent of the variance in performance. As Figure 4.6 shows, across all the teams we studied, accelerating teams, on average, had an economic impact 22.8 percent higher than that of derailing teams.

Accelerating teams reduced costs more quickly, got to market more effectively, and launched products more smoothly. Additional research

FIGURE 4.5 Team performance

n = 1,118
% of teams

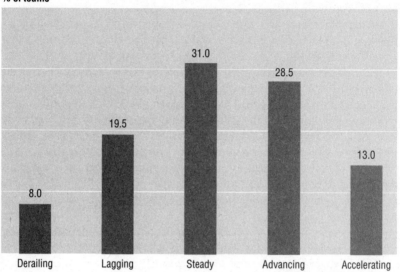

FIGURE 4.6 The clear benefits

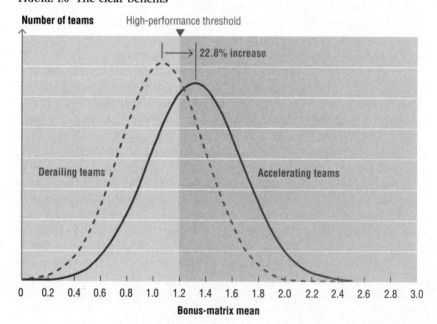

FIGURE 4.7 Teams at the top struggle

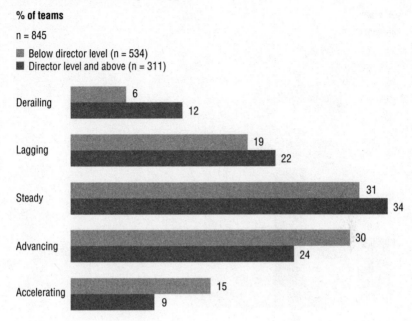

% of teams

n = 845

░ Below director level (n = 534)
■ Director level and above (n = 311)

Derailing — 6 / 12

Lagging — 19 / 22

Steady — 31 / 34

Advancing — 30 / 24

Accelerating — 15 / 9

Note: Numbers do not sum to 100%, because of rounding.

found that senior teams do worse than the rest of the teams in the organization (Figure 4.7) and that the closer a team is to the customer, the more likely it is to be accelerating its performance (Figure 4.8).

For the *individual level,* we drew on our experience from placing 4,000 senior executives a year; on research done for *The CEO Report*, published in 2015 and developed through a partnership with Saïd Business School at the University of Oxford; and on our proprietary leadership profiling tool, Leadership Signature®. Given that individuals make up teams, here was the final question for our research: What characteristics do the leaders who best drive acceleration have that others lack?

Years of experience placing CEOs and other senior executives across different industries have given us a comprehensive understanding of what makes an effective senior leader. In 1999, we developed our proprietary leadership competency framework called LEEED (Learn, Envision, Execute, Engage, Deduce), which provided a library of 19 competencies with a 7-point anchored scale that has been used in more than 10,000 executive assessments over the years. A similar number of assessments has been performed with other leadership frameworks tailored to the unique context of the client.

FIGURE 4.8 Teams close to customers do better

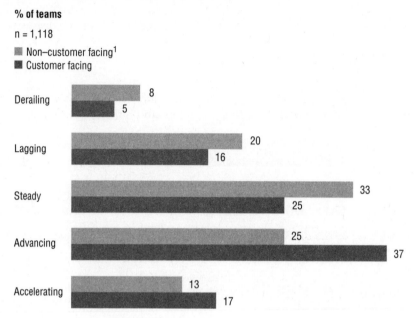

% of teams

n = 1,118

▨ Non–customer facing[1]
■ Customer facing

- Derailing: 8 / 5
- Lagging: 20 / 16
- Steady: 33 / 25
- Advancing: 25 / 37
- Accelerating: 13 / 17

[1]Numbers do not sum to 100%, because of rounding.

In 2014, we decided to develop a new approach to thinking about leadership competencies that would incorporate the rich empirical evidence collected through our years of doing assessments, the emerging knowledge from the accelerating performance thinking in a VUCA (volatile, uncertain, complex, and ambiguous) world, our in-depth interviews with more than 150 leading CEOs in partnership with the Saïd Business School at the University of Oxford, and our close collaboration with clients.

In addition to this research, we developed Leadership Signature, an executive assessment tool that considers the following question: How will this person lead? The online tool consists of 36 questions and provides insight into a senior leader's style in leading the organization and his or her team. Leadership Signature assesses eight behavioral patterns that individuals draw on when in leadership positions.

The result of all this research was a framework aligned to the critical areas that can accelerate performance through META. In 2015, we ran a customized survey to try to understand what the practices of accelerating organizations, teams, and leaders are. The results showed that individual leaders who are accelerating tend to do much better at META and the drive factors than those who are not.

Putting all of this information and experience together became the foundation of our Leadership Accelerator Questionnaire (LAQ), which can help diagnose the level of acceleration that individual leaders are capable of driving in their organization.

■ ■ ■

Based on all this research into the superaccelerators and a host of other companies at the strategy, organization, team, and individual levels, we are confident that we have identified the key issues.

We have identified how companies win—by outperforming in their current space rather than moving into a new industry or new geography.

We have learned how companies accelerate—through META. We will describe META further in Section II, showing how it plays out at the strategy, organization, team, and individual levels.

We have uncovered how companies know what to do, and in Section III, we will explain how to find the right recipe of actions to accelerate performance, how to drive change, how to handle people, and how to find the right role for the board.

We have also identified the four capabilities that are the differentiators—ripple intelligence, resource fluidity, dissolving paradox, and liquid leadership, which we further describe in Section IV. There are, of course, other important skills (e.g., reading a balance sheet, making presentations, etc.), but these four capabilities separate those that can from those that can't.

However, before we move on, we will first explain how you can diagnose where your organization fits on our scale of derailing to accelerating, so you can identify your starting point as you begin this crucial journey to acceleration.

Notes

1. Milton Friedman, *Capitalism and Freedom*, Chicago: University of Chicago Press, 1962.
2. Steve Denning, "The origin of 'the world's dumbest idea': Milton Friedman," *Forbes*, June 26, 2013, forbes.com.
3. Steve Denning, "The origin of 'the world's dumbest idea': Milton Friedman," *Forbes*, June 26, 2013, forbes.com.
4. Peter F. Drucker, *The Practice of Management*, New York: Harper & Row, 1954.
5. There are, of course, industries, such as financial services, where the calculation of revenue gets more complicated because income comes in different forms—interest rates, fees, commissions, etc.

6. See James Allen and Chris Zook, "The strategic principles of repeat-ability," Bain & Company, May 4, 2012, bain.com; and James Allen, "The five pillars of sustainable growth," Bain & Company, February 12, 2014, bain.com.
7. Economist Intelligence Unit, *Creating Growth in a Flat World: How to Identify, Quantify, and Capture New Growth Opportunities,* 2016, eiu .com.

CHAPTER 5

What's Your Current Pace?
A Diagnostic

To be able to start the journey toward accelerating performance, you need to get a good understanding of the current status of your organization—what the metabolic rate of your organization is today. One good place to start, mirroring the analysis that we have done, is to look at your financial performance over the past three and seven years.

You will need two key ingredients to be able to do this analysis: your company's financial data for the last seven years and your competitors' (revenue and operating margin is all you need). If there is an industry index that measures revenue compound annual growth rate (CAGR) and operating margin, you can use that, as well.

First, calculate the revenue CAGR for your organization for the past three years, and compare it with that in the industry. Next, do the same for the past seven years. If your company is in the top quintile for both periods, and you meet our other "rules of 20"—no more than 20 percent of your revenue growth was due to acquisitions; your home government didn't drive more than 20 percent of your revenues; and you didn't lose more than 20 percent of your margin over the past seven years—then congratulations. You are a superaccelerator!

More than likely, though, you are not, because only a few achieve that status. Do not be disappointed by this. Many highly regarded companies simply aren't accelerating as much as the elite ones are.

To see where you do fit, try to determine where your CAGR places you against your peers, either by using the direct data that you have about your competitors or by comparing yourself against the industry breakdowns we provide in Figures 5.1 and 5.2.

Depending on which quintile you're in, you occupy one of the five categories of acceleration we've identified (Figure 5.3).

Superaccelerating companies are a subset of accelerating companies; they are the ones that successfully meet all four rules of 20. If your organization is

FIGURE 5.1 Revenue CAGR 2013–2015, industry averages

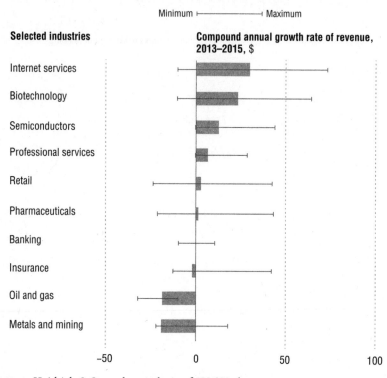

Source: Heidrick & Struggles analysis of FT 500 data

in the lowest (fifth) quintile for your peer group, then you are derailing. If you are in the fourth quintile, you are lagging, and so on. Please remember that this is only the financial analysis aspect of the diagnostic. However, as our research shows, this is a pretty accurate indication of where your company would fall in the continuum after all diagnoses are completed.

A derailing organization is one mired in drag factors. Nothing seems to be working correctly. Customers are defecting to competitors, suppliers are abandoning ship as well, and employees are becoming disenfranchised. High levels of bureaucracy and a silo mentality prevent the free flow of resources and information to attend to the most promising opportunities. The organization fails to see the future and anticipate changes. The company's vision is either unclear or poorly communicated. Twenty percent of the FT 500 companies fit this classification.

At the other extreme, accelerating organizations are firing on all cylinders. The customer is king, suppliers are satisfied, and employees are happy and become the biggest advocates for the organization in competitive talent markets.

FIGURE 5.2 Revenue CAGR 2009–2015, industry averages

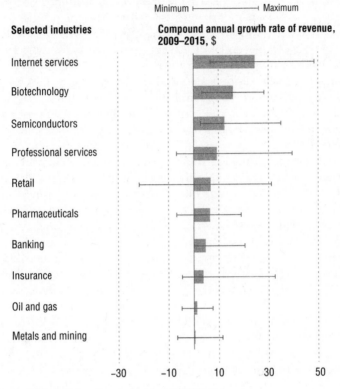

Source: Heidrick & Struggles analysis of FT 500 data

FIGURE 5.3 The five categories of acceleration

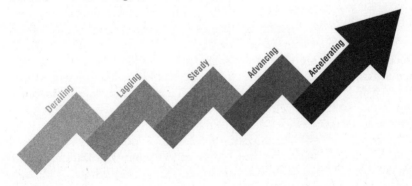

There is a high level of simplicity across business and management processes, across organization structures, and in the approach to measuring performance. Uncertainty is a normal part of doing business, and the company knows how to handle setbacks in a way that quickly transforms them into valuable learning opportunities. Sixteen percent of FT 500 companies fall in this category.

The remaining 64 percent of companies fall in between these two extremes, almost equally divided among the lagging, steady, and advancing categories. To understand the difference between these three categories, let us describe what the middle category—steady—looks like. Organizations in this category are neither excelling nor failing. They are, for the moment, clinging to their customers, employees, and suppliers. They are weathering attacks from competitors and disruptors, and they seem to be content with maintaining the status quo. Companies in this position are walking a delicate balance that can tip the scale in one direction or the other very quickly. If your organization is in the steady category, you need to make sure you are taking measures to quickly move in the advancing direction. Too long in a "steady state" position may be untenable as the drag factors start increasing their weight and pull the organization toward the derailing end of the spectrum.

Being in the lagging category can mean you are in the process of becoming a derailing company, or perhaps that you are recovering from a derailing situation. To be able to determine more accurately which situation your company faces, you need to understand where you are coming from. If you are heading in the direction of a derailing company, things are not totally dire yet, but you are getting awfully close. By contrast, if your company is recovering from a derailing situation, the fact that you are lagging may indicate that some drive factors are starting to have a positive impact on your organization's performance but that the drag factors are still too strong.

If you are advancing, meanwhile, it may indicate that things are improving—or worsening. You are not excelling like an accelerating company, but you are getting close. The drag is not so strong as to prevent the effectiveness of the drive factors. Companies in this category are probably implementing many of the tools that accelerating companies use to stay ahead of the competition, although some drag elements still prevent them from achieving their full effectiveness. The big worry here is the risk of complacency, which allows drag to build up and undermines the positive effects of the drive factors.

To gain an understanding of the overall level of acceleration in your organization, we have developed a self-assessment tool (also available online at www.accelerationassessment.com) that provides a quick glance at where in the continuum your organization falls. Take a look at the statements in Table 5.1, and evaluate how much they reflect your organization. Pick the statement that best reflects your organization, and make note of the score (1 through 5) for each one.

TABLE 5.1 Self-assessment tool

STRATEGY

1	2	3	4	5
We can't agree on our purpose and our direction for the organization.		We're clear about our purpose but confused about our direction.		We're clear about both our purpose and our direction.
We don't know what strategic capabilities are required to execute successfully.		We understand the strategic capabilities required to execute, but can't develop them quickly enough.		We have (or can quickly develop) the strategic capabilities we need to execute successfully.
We're unable to prioritize initiatives, leading to confusion and disunity.		We have prioritized some great initiatives but don't know how to manage them.		We have prioritized great initiatives, and we're able to move them forward successfully.
We're just not geared to adapt to change—we're followers, not leaders.		We're aware of threats and opportunities but slow to adapt.		We quickly spot threats and seize opportunities ahead of the competition.

ORGANIZATION

1	2	3	4	5
We don't have a vision that inspires us to action.		We are able to move forward but would benefit from a more inspiring vision.		We have a clear and compelling vision that drives us forward.
Unit managers do not share resources.		We're experimenting with resource-sharing on an ad hoc basis.		Resources are shared across organizational units, are streamlined, and consistently deliver excellence.

(Continued)

TABLE 5.1 (*Continued*)

ORGANIZATION (*continued*)

1	2	3	4	5
We're comfortable with what's familiar and spooked by new ideas.		We innovate occasionally, but it's not the norm.		We beat our competitors by reinventing our businesses constantly.
We don't know how to recover from setbacks.		We recover from setbacks, but take too long to regroup.		We're quick to learn from setbacks and develop corrective processes.

TOP TEAM (CEO AND DIRECT REPORTS)

1	2	3	4	5
Our top team is confused about our purpose and out of touch with customers and stakeholders.		Our leaders know our purpose and our market but don't know how to turn that knowledge into business value.		Our top team has a clear vision based on putting the customer at the center of everything we do.
Our top team can't organize resources to deliver on our mission.		Our top team has the skills to deliver but takes too long.		Our top team is able to deliver quickly and effectively.
Our top team lives in the past, is incapable of reinvention, and can't build beneficial relationships either internally or externally.		Our top team innovates sporadically and finds it hard to build beneficial business partnerships.		Our top team uses trusted relationships to reinvent our business ahead of the competition.
Our top team fails to anticipate and adapt to change.		Our top team is defensive and can't see change until directly confronted with it.		Our top team is brilliant at responding rapidly to change

(*Continued*)

TABLE 5.1 (*Continued*)

INDIVIDUAL LEADERS

1	2	3	4	5
Our leaders can't connect the dots or see the way ahead very clearly.		Our leaders see only what's blindingly obvious to everyone else.		Our leaders connect the dots of disparate events and take action before our rivals catch on.
Our leaders can't anticipate change quickly enough to match resources to opportunities.		Our leaders know how to allocate resources but are hampered by not having proper processes.		Our leaders constantly optimize the matching of resources to opportunities.
Our leaders can't think beyond the present.		Our leaders know only how to play win or lose.		Our leaders are comfortable with ambiguity, and adept at win-win solutions.
Our leaders are authoritative and hierarchical.		Our leaders use their informal networks but prefer to lead through hierarchy.		Our leaders network well and lead in a fluid, consultative manner.

Add up your scores for each of the statements to get a total score. If your results are 16 or below (you could score below 16 if you did not answer some of the questions), you are derailing. You should focus urgently on corrective actions.

If your score is between 17 and 32, you are lagging. Remember that lagging can mean that you're on the path to derailing or that you are beginning to recover from that state. You need to understand where you are coming from and then determine what is dragging the organization down, focus on addressing those factors, and put yourself on a path toward acceleration.

If your score falls between 33 and 48, you are steady. This is neither good nor bad news. It means that there is a lot of potential to go in either direction. Some drive factors are in place, but also some are exerting an important drag. In this situation, you need to make a conscious decision about how to eliminate or reduce the impact of the drag factors so that you can leverage what you are doing well in the drive factors.

If you scored between 49 and 64, you are advancing. This is good news. It means that your drive factors outweigh your drag factors and you are on the right path. Efforts here should focus on eliminating drag factors altogether so that you can join the elite companies in the accelerating category.

Scores between 65 and 80 indicate acceleration. Does this mean that you have nothing to do? No. Even when you are accelerating, you need an agenda in place to ensure that acceleration can be maintained. Drag factors have a tendency to creep back in (complexity, in particular), so it is imperative that you embed acceleration in your culture and that it becomes business as usual. You can't become complacent. You must remain alert to the troubling signs of drag, however small or incipient they may be.

We are very confident that these results will match the results you obtained with the financial analysis. Sometimes, however, as is the case with very successful organizations such as Southwest Airlines and Amazon, there is a contrast between the soft (measured in the tool above) and the hard (financial) measures of performance. This can be due to market characteristics (e.g., a rise in the price of oil that affects airline travel costs) or a longer-term strategy that is not reflecting well in the current financial performance (e.g., the desire to be the main outlet for everything on the Internet).

In the following chapters, we will show how you can move your company to the accelerating end of the spectrum at all four levels: strategy, the organization, teams, and individual leaders. You may have noted in your assessment that one of those four levels in particular has notably lower scores than the others, which suggests that the chapter on that particular level may merit closer attention. As you will see, there are many things you can do to improve your ability to accelerate. However, it is unnecessary to do everything. Your journey has to be built around the elements that make the most sense for your aspirations.

The Acceleration Imperative

Now that you have seen the basic outline for META, this section takes a deep dive into the specifics, at each of the four levels where META applies: strategy, the organization, teams, and leaders.

Chapter 6, on how to accelerate strategy, observes that many companies do a curious thing: They may focus 100 percent of their effort on things they can control, even though analysis shows that 45 percent or more of a company's profitability depends on events in the environment, outside its control. This chapter explains how to sense better what's going on in the environment and then respond faster, to turn that 45 percent-plus from uncertainty into opportunity. The chapter goes through 13 factors that can either create drag or drive performance. For instance, it explains how to fail fast—most companies hold on to failing strategies for too long. The chapter explains how to check for "execution feasibility"—many companies set strategy without fully understanding whether they can make it work, rather than trying to develop a strategy with the fewest execution hurdles in front of it. The chapter also describes how to respond rapidly, based on less-than-perfect information, and how to get to the goal ahead of the competition.

In Chapter 7, on how to accelerate organizations, we note that it has been a very long time since there has been fundamental innovation in organizational structure. As a result, developments in technology and other factors that change the pace and nature of work are creating real pressures that need to be resolved. Given the complexity of these nuanced issues, the only way to act with accuracy is through the data. So, based on our research, we lay out the 13 factors that our analysis has shown determine drag and drive at the organization level, and then we delve into the 3 actions that are most important to take for each of the 13 factors—so, 39 action steps in all. We describe how to co-innovate with customers and how to use a higher purpose as fuel that can excite employees and align them behind the company's goals. We also explore how to get employees to speak truth to power, how to act as one firm, how to learn from mistakes, how to either improve or atomize the corporate center, how to develop what we call digital dexterity—and much more.

Chapter 8, on how to accelerate teams, provides a telling statistic: Our research found that, on average, a high-performing team (called accelerating, on our scale) delivered 22.8 percent more economic value than a low-performing team (derailing, on our scale). We also found that teams that dealt directly with customers generally performed far better than those with an internal focus—suggesting that ways need to be found to put all teams, especially top teams, directly in contact with customers. Creating "psychological safety" is also crucial, to allow for open and productive conversations—a study by Google found that that was the most important factor in determining the success of its teams. In all, we identified 16 drag and drive factors for teams, with two key actions that will generate the best performance for each factor. The chapter includes an extended look at Nationwide Building Society, where the chief operating officer has been working on these accelerating principles with his top team since 2012. While he would acknowledge that he still has work to do, he has made such progress that, in the first quarter of 2016, Nationwide was ranked number one for customer service satisfaction among its peers and has assets larger than the remaining 44 British building societies combined.

In Chapter 9, on how to accelerate leaders, we observe that, in a world where capital costs essentially nothing, all value comes from leaders who harness and implement ideas better than their competitors do. Yet most companies say their leaders only reliably get 50 percent of the full potential of their people. As we sought to understand this crucial issue of leadership, our research identified 11 drag and drive factors that must be addressed. How leaders manage energy turned out to be a key issue. For instance, the best leaders adopt tactics such as looking at the 80-20 rule and deciding that, if 80 percent of the outcomes come from 20 percent of the activities, they will identify the 20 percent and ignore the rest. Our research also turned up a plethora of other practical advice—for example, that leaders need to embrace the power of doubt and that, no matter how hard it may be to act otherwise, it's not okay to be grumpy.

A note on examples: We use lots, to illustrate our points, and name names wherever we can. We typically use a company as an example only once, in the interests of readability, but we make an exception for the super-accelerators. The material from our interviews with them was so rich, and their success so significant, that we include their observations and stories wherever they are relevant, even though that means repeating names at times.

CHAPTER 6

Accelerating Strategy
Less Plan, More Planning

Imagine it is the late 15th century; you are an explorer, preparing to sail into the fog. No one has ever come back from the fog, so you do not know what is on the other side. As the captain, how do you pack for the journey? What will help you deal with rapidly changing and uncertain conditions on the other side of the fog?

This is the challenge that many business leaders face today in the midst of the rapid and confusing change we're all experiencing. Leaders confront a foggy future without a reliable guide—no one has been to the future and returned. Yet they need to make critical decisions that will set their organization up for success many years into the future.

With limited and imperfect information, business leaders must pack and plan so well that they not only survive but also thrive no matter what future environment they find themselves in.

This requires a series of steps within our META framework to achieve acceleration at the strategy level. The steps allow you to make crisp decisions in the face of uncertainty and then adapt as circumstances change and, ultimately, get to the destination much faster than you would have otherwise—and then start moving to the next destination.

But most leaders don't see themselves as explorers of the unknown. They dislike uncertainty. So they tend to focus on what they can control. To the extent that they think about the unknown, they talk about "future-proofing" their organizations. This is a fool's errand.

"I've been doing business plans in banks for 30 years, and they've all been wrong," says Juerg Zeltner, the CEO of UBS Wealth Management. The world is just too ambiguous. A major study found that, on average, approximately 45 percent of a company's profitability depends on how beneficial or detrimental external and industry events are for its performance—in other words, on what happens in the fog (Figure 6.1). That study was completed before some of the most significant black swan events of the modern era,

FIGURE 6.1 Half the business is left to fate

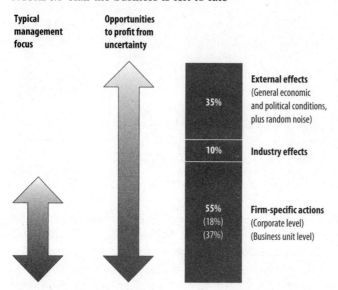

Note: The percentages refer to how much of the variance in return on assets is due, on average, to various influences. The data reflect over 100 U.S. manufacturing firms consisting of at least two strategic business units covering 160 industries. *Source:* Jaime A. Roquebert, Robert L. Phillips, and Peter A. Westfall, "Markets vs. management: What 'drives' profitability?" *Strategic Management Journal,* October 1996.

such as the 9/11 attacks and the 2008–2009 financial crisis, and volatility and uncertainty have only increased in recent years.

On average, oil and gas businesses have about 90 percent of profitability driven by the external environment (the price of oil). Over the past 10 years, in working sessions with hundreds of leadership teams within the financial services and health care industries, we found that the C-suite perceived profits to be approximately 70 percent dependent on external and industry events (regulatory change, economic shocks, changing customer preferences, disruptive new entrants, etc.) and rising. Before the financial crisis, the banking industry generally created 25 percent return on capital. Now the new normal is about 10 percent, and banks are struggling to adapt.

Yet organizations typically spend 100 percent of their time and resources on managing the manageable 55 percent (or less) and fall into traps that prevent them from creating an accelerating strategy.

Organizations that wish to develop or maintain an accelerated strategy must spend more time and resources on understanding the 45 percent (or more) that is unmanageable and learning how to "read the tea leaves" better. Instead of passively accepting the environment around them, accelerating organizations seek to make it work for them—or even influence it when possible by shaping regulations, customer preferences, and other drivers of change. These organizations find a balance between flexibility and optimization, have an inquisitive attitude that leads to experimentation, and are committed to continuous learning. They understand that the benefits of seizing opportunities exceed the cost of making mistakes—which is central to the ability to reduce time to value.

Most companies aspire to these "learning" behaviors, but, when market conditions become even slightly challenging, they fall back into the traps.

To drive the right behaviors, think in terms of the four areas of META:

- **Mobilize:** There must be a shared understanding and broad ownership of why the organization exists, where it wants to go, and what it is great at. The company must also agree on the high-impact trends and uncertainties that will shape its industry.
- **Execute:** The company must zero in on the critical few capabilities that the strategy requires while understanding the extent to which those capabilities exist in the organization today and the feasibility of closing gaps. The company must also be able to objectively identify and discontinue underperforming initiatives.
- **Transform:** The organization must be able to pursue strategic ambitions while sustaining performance in the short term.
- **Agility:** Companies need the ability to prepare for and recover from setbacks quickly, in a manner that balances performance and learning, while pursuing emerging opportunities before they become obvious to the rest of the industry.

We break these META areas down into the 13 drive factors that, based on our extensive research, will allow you to accelerate your strategy and win (Figure 6.2).

Mobilize: Embrace Uncertainty

Decision making slows when uncertainty exists. An accelerated strategy needs to acknowledge that uncertainty but still achieve absolute clarity and alignment among the leadership team on the most important forces shaping the future. That way, critical decisions can be made at pace—and adapted as circumstances turn out to be not quite what was expected.

FIGURE 6.2 The SAQ model

Uncertainty is not the enemy; it is where some of the most profit-able opportunities exist. As Nathan Rothschild, a prominent member of the second generation of the illustrious banking family, is reputed to have said, "Great fortunes are made when the cannonballs are falling in the harbor, not when the violins are playing in the ballroom."

As we've noted, our research found that fully 60 percent of the respondents in a major survey said that their organization had been repeatedly blindsided by high-impact events, and 97 percent said their organization lacked an adequate early warning system. Yet organizations still focus on managing the more predictable events, using traditional tools such as extrapolative forecasting, net present value analysis, and decision trees. Organizations don't focus enough on the more ambiguous and unpredictable possibilities in the environment. To do so, they need to adopt tools such as influence diagrams, real-options analysis, and system dynamics modeling (Figure 6.3).

Embracing uncertainty means focusing on solving the problems of the future rather than just addressing the operational pressures in front of the organization. This requires dedicated time—which means allocating much more time than many executives do now—to clear space on the calendar.

FIGURE 6.3 A shift toward greater ambiguity

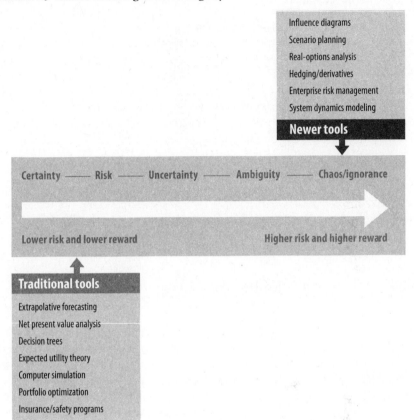

That time must be used to explore very specific cases to see where new markets might lie and to play with assumptions to see when they might become large, new opportunities.[1] Lots of ideas should be generated because, conventional wisdom to the contrary, there is no trade-off between the quantity of ideas and the quality. A large quantity of ideas leads to quality.[2] Embracing uncertainty means building a deep understanding of the highest-impact forces that are shaping the future of an industry and preparing for a range of alternative futures.

For example, a global pharmaceutical company recognized that it was struggling with its annual strategic planning process. Once-routine decisions on how to manage its multibillion-dollar portfolio had grown increasingly cumbersome. The decisions had also become inconsistent and did not align with the biggest drivers of change for the industry. Company leaders asked the 10 core business units to submit operational plans for the next three years that were "more strategic" rather than entirely oriented toward finance, and they worked with business unit leaders to agree on a definitive perspective on how health care in the United States could evolve over the next five years.

This definitive perspective allowed for a better balance between long-term and short-term decisions and for faster decisions. Strategic choices that routinely took weeks to debate and approve now typically require only a few hours.

In an interview with the *Financial Times*, Masayoshi Son—the CEO of SoftBank, a superaccelerator—describes his approach to long-term planning, using the ancient game Go as an analogy: "The experts do not put the stones right next to the earlier stones. They put them in a completely different part of the board. That is what I do. I try to look in the future and think backwards."[3]

Mobilize: Pressure-Tested Decision Making

Often, context needs to be broadened so that new options can surface. What seems to be a harsh, either/or choice can become a much easier decision. Continually reframing business challenges must become a best practice, to enable pressure-tested decision making.

Current approaches to decision making can produce behavioral and organizational blinders that impair our ability to make tough decisions and set an accelerating strategy. People are not naturally wired to be good strategic decision makers. It is human nature to have mental filters—they help us to efficiently manage information overload and to make many routine decisions without hesitation—but these shortcuts come with a cost. These filters often lead people to see what they expect to see rather than what is actually there. Overconfidence can also cloud judgment, as people are far too certain that the current view they hold is correct. As Christopher Cerf and Victor Navasky explain in their book *The Experts Speak*, even people at the top of their field are often dead wrong. Confirmation bias means people have a penchant for evidence that confirms their view and filters out information that contradicts it.

As imperfect decision-making beings, we need to constantly recognize and work to overcome our biases. One approach is to employ an outside-in, pressure-tested decision-making process that takes inventory of the biggest decisions for the near term and long term as they relate to external change. This technique is used to determine which decisions the organization is prepared to make and which will require more information to fill gaps. Consider the 40–70 rule of Colin Powell, the former U.S. secretary of state and chair of the Joint Chiefs of Staff. The rule says you need between 40 percent and 70 percent of the information available to make a good decision. Anything less is too little, and anything more will lead to analysis paralysis.

Companies often struggle with making decisions under uncertainty, particularly when there is significant investment at stake. It is critical to make swift decisions with discipline while battling against the cognitive biases that can hinder decision making.

A global supplier for the food, beverage, and other industries shows how this is possible. It was positioned to be first to market with a sugar substitute and needed to decide whether to spend $60 million to expand production capacity. It was uncertain about the regulatory environment and customer demand, and time was of the essence. FDA approval for new sugar substitutes was pending, and a much larger competitor was preparing to enter the market as a fast follower. Looking at both the short term and the longer term through pressure-tested decision making, the organization recognized that the decision was not a $60 million one but a $180 million one because of the additional investment that would be required to support the first decision on the expansion in capacity.

This realization prompted leadership to think more strategically about the consequences of all its options, including how the new sugar substitute would fit with the other products in its global portfolio. This analysis led leadership to realize that it could sell the new capacity for $40 million if the profit pool for the new product was not as attractive as once thought. This realization greatly reduced the risk and accelerated the action to expand capacity.

Mobilize: Shared Vision

A strong, shared vision enables leadership to remain committed to a strategic direction in times of crisis or great opportunity. If an organization can embed this type of guide to action at all levels, it can make decisions faster and more confidently to find new profit pools, ultimately improving performance.

Extensive research shows that companies that specifically state where they are going, and why, do remarkably better than those that do not. For instance, in *Corporate Culture and Performance*, Harvard Business School professors John Kotter and James Heskett reported on a four-year study of 10 firms in each of 20 industries. They found that firms with a strong corporate culture and vision grew revenue more than 4 times faster; their stock price grew 12 times faster; and their profit performance was 750 percent higher.[4]

It is often difficult to align on a vision in times of certainty, let alone set a bolder vision to guide the organization during times of uncertainty and disruption. Most visions are incremental and stifle an accelerated strategy, promoting the status quo and limiting change to minor investments in new capabilities that support the core business. But a bold vision is often a bridge too far, creating a state of paralysis by presenting the prospect of radical changes to the business model. Most accelerated strategies find a hybrid vision in the elusive sweet spot between incremental and bold, balancing the familiar with a distinct north star for the future.

Ajay Banga, president and CEO of MasterCard, one of our superaccelerators, has rallied the company around a clear and compelling vision: "a world beyond cash."

"Eighty-five percent of the world's retail payments are still made using cash, but the tailwinds of urbanization and globalization are driving the gradual conversion of cash to electronic forms of payment," he told us. "Even if we change that 85 percent to 84 percent and we just maintain our market share, we will grow revenue by 7 percent. That's remarkable, and very few companies are benefiting from that sort of change. The real challenge, and hence opportunity, is to actually grow market share and grow faster—that's the kind of runway our business has. My predecessor's strategy was to close the profitability gap between us and our competitors, which addressed the need at the time. When we are in a situation, as we are now, where smart reinvestment in the business has the potential to yield very high returns in growth and revenue, we should pursue that path. Moreover, foregoing reinvestment in favor of achieving very high operating margins in the short term has the potential to attract new competitors and regulatory oversight."

The reframing of the vision led Banga to focus on growth, not margin, and to think not just about competing for share against Visa and other traditional rivals but also against cash and checks. "The answer is simplicity of mission and vision of what the industry is," he said. "Cash is still king. Let's put our energy against that. How do we do it in a smart way, both with existing products and with digital innovation, and take advantage of the trends in the market and build? How do we build the culture that cares about winning all the time, as compared to being okay with just growing at the 7 percent? We couldn't have grown the business without a big change in the culture. And I couldn't have changed the culture without laying out a vision of what the market is all about and directing the resources to where the opportunities were, rather than trying to satisfy everybody while also growing profitability."

To achieve the growth strategy meant not only a cultural transformation but also some key changes in the people and technology underpinning it. According to Banga, "We began to recruit more technology-oriented staff and more people who were focused on building external partnerships. We also made a number of strategic acquisitions whereby we gained cutting-edge technology and the people around it. This growth was global rather than U.S.-focused because, while the United States remains the world's largest consumer market and our largest market, the opportunity to displace cash is worldwide."

Similarly, John Murabito, executive vice president of human resources and services at Cigna, one of the superaccelerators, told us: "Our overall enterprise strategy ends up being the fuel for all of the substrategies, whether that be at the business unit level or at the functional level. So there's a really strong tie-in to support the strategy from deeper in the organization and at all the key levels—business, function, and otherwise. All employees have a good sense of how they can personally contribute to the strategy. The alignment in the organization is as strong as any I've seen."

Execute: Future Core Competencies

Today's winning capabilities are tomorrow's table stakes. Organizations must identify what capabilities world-class competitors will possess in the future and begin to invest now. These competencies are the foundation on which the organization's shared vision is built and executed.

These competencies must provide advantage over competitors; be hard to replicate, imitate, or transfer; not be available to be bought or sold; provide value to customers; apply across markets or product lines; exist broadly across groups of employees; and be sustainable.

Focusing on future core competencies will, first of all, make the organization skilled at methods and processes that matter most. Each competency will reinforce and improve the others more rapidly than competitors are able to. Second, as the same competencies are applied across more products and services, the organization gets more value out of them. The organization can afford to hire specialists, because the cost of building capabilities is amortized across the entire portfolio. Third, money will be spent where it is needed most, and less will go to table stakes, the necessary competencies and skills that every competitor brings to the market. Fourth, there will be greater alignment, as people in different product lines and geographies are attuned to the same capabilities system. They are more likely to understand one another and make independent decisions that are more or less in sync. They can combine forces and share resources more easily. They will be able to execute faster and with more force because they are all pulling in the same direction.

With rapid changes occurring in the energy industry, executives at one of the world's largest electric and gas utilities were concerned that their business strategy would not sustain their performance and began thinking about future competencies. It was not evident what they needed to change, so they looked at how customers' needs might evolve. They uncovered several organizational shortcomings and developed initiatives to bridge these competency gaps. In addition to reducing risk by sizing up new initiatives long before any actual investment and by recognizing early warning signs, the utility can better manage expectations of stakeholders, including regulators and suppliers.

Execute: Execution Feasibility

Many attractive strategies exist. However, not all are possible for every organization. Investing in strategies with low feasibility is a losing path. Leadership needs to recognize that how they will win may be different than the path for their competitors. Selecting strategies that have the least number of execution hurdles and the highest probability of closing capability gaps is vital.

A high percentage of strategic initiatives fail because not enough people understand the strategy and because incentives and budgets aren't linked to the initiatives. A global survey of senior executives by PwC found not only that more than half of those surveyed did not believe their organization had a winning strategy but also that two-thirds believed their company lacked the needed capabilities to realize its strategy.[5]

Before making any moves, therefore, organizations should inventory the principal strategic decisions for the near term and long term and then evaluate their readiness to execute. By honestly evaluating the probability of success for alternative strategies, leaders can eliminate those that appear attractive but lack a high likelihood of realizing their expected value.

In a major U.S. market, a host of problems with obstetric care created a great opportunity for several hospitals to transform the practice in the region. However, here was the question: Could the hospitals seize the opportunity? Three institutions were working to create a truly differentiated experience for mothers and infants by merging practices into one program. But success required complex cooperation by all three entities on this $500 million-plus project, including on culture and expansion of infrastructure construction.

The leadership team did an exceptional job defining the business case and had a strong understanding of all the execution elements for the multiyear project. To help anticipate problems, the team used extreme scenario analysis and conducted a Monte Carlo simulation (an analysis used to model ranges of possible outcomes and their probabilities). A critical hurdle to feasibility was spotted—a team had been identified, but the assignment of roles, responsibilities, and accountabilities was not as well defined as necessary. An early symptom of this problem manifested in a lack of urgency, given the long-term nature of the project and given other demands on people's time. To close the feasibility gap, the team set up milestones to build momentum and alignment across the three organizations and to move resources quickly to the critical path items that were behind schedule and threatened to derail the overall effort.

Execute: Adaptive Playbook

Relentless testing of alternative strategies is imperative to an accelerated strategy. Organizations need more than one strategy at the ready, as market conditions often change and new threats and opportunities emerge.

Most organizations plan as if the world were predictable, developing point forecasts, budgets, and initiatives that will succeed as long as the external environment cooperates. But the business landscape is changing in many industries, and the rules of engagement are also changing. Unfortunately, most leaders realize this only after a significant value-destroying event.

Organizations must become intimately familiar with their competitors' inner workings and pain points to better understand how competitors will possibly react to specific tactics. To build this competitor-centric approach, leadership teams should regularly employ an internal role-playing exercise to simulate the competition's strategic intents. This behavior will help an organization anticipate the actions of current and future competitors.

A playbook of strategic choices can better prepare organizations to act quickly when the environment changes. The ability to master the principles of game theory is core to building a truly adaptive playbook. Leadership must be prepared to swiftly shift resources to new priorities when the primary strategy and portfolio of initiatives are no longer creating their intended value.

One of our clients, a pharmaceutical company, saw the value of an adaptive playbook as it prepared to launch a potential blockbuster in the diabetes space. The class of drugs had one well-established player and one that was widely assumed to be next to market. Given the sequencing of FDA approvals, industry consensus was that our client's drug would be the third to enter the class. The leadership team rehearsed their strategy in a competitive war game and surfaced several what-ifs, including the possibility of a change in market-entry position. At first, the team felt that preparation for this unlikely event was not the best use of their precious prelaunch time. However, leadership decided to test several core market assumptions and created an alternative playbook. Fast-forward six months, and the FDA surprisingly placed considerable new data demands on the product that was expected to be second to market, delaying that company for years. Our client was ready and captured the upside of being second into the market because of that alternative playbook.

Transform: Balanced Portfolio

A portfolio approach to investing for the future is essential for any accelerated strategy. It creates a structure to enable short-term resource fluidity while simultaneously providing the discipline required to meet long-term growth aspirations.

Strategic transformation requires the seeds of growth and innovation to be planted while maintaining the core business, enabling rapid scaling when those seeds start to bear fruit. A well-constructed portfolio balances investments with knowable return on investment (ROI) in the short term along with investments that have long-term potential and can't be evaluated with such traditional financial metrics. Traditional metrics assume that the source of competitive advantage will stay the same or at least be predictable many quarters and years into the future—but that's not how the world works these days. Portfolios need to incorporate varying levels of risk and multiple time horizons to address the growth problems that plague many organizations.

For example, a leading global chemicals manufacturer recognized that it was losing its edge, particularly when it came to long-term innovation, because near-term initiatives with a clear ROI were siphoning resources from research and development (R&D) and the next generation of products. So the company devised a disciplined portfolio management approach that allocated its investments into three distinct categories: core, new, and experimental. Each category comes with a specific time horizon and risk level: Core is short term/low risk. New is medium term/medium risk. Experimental is long term/high risk. Budgets are allocated for each category, with strict structures in place to prevent longer-term budget dollars from getting pulled into short-term, core investments. Only investments within the same category can compete for budget dollars. This helps ensure that short-term focus never crowds out long-term investment, minimizing the potential for a growth gap later on.

Transform: Fail Fast

Every organization has limited resources. An organization with accelerated performance can objectively assess which strategies are working and which are not, allowing it to pull the plug on those that are failing, double down on those that are working, and invest in new ideas. An organization burdened with too many stagnant strategic initiatives quickly faces a drag on overall performance.

Most organizations cling too long to failing strategies. That is partly because of a lack of discipline, especially if a leader feels some attachment to the strategy—but letting go of a failing strategy sooner instead of falling prey to the sunk-cost fallacy is important to minimizing losses. Organizations also must learn how to reward failure and celebrate related learnings rather than penalizing failure.

George Day from the Wharton School brings much-needed discipline to failing fast through his "real, win, worth it" framework. Management teams need to repeatedly ask themselves, "Is the opportunity still real?" "Can we still win?" and "Is it worth doing in terms of the expected return?" This type of framework pushes leaders to constantly challenge thinking and track performance. Early on, managers must establish critically important triggers that enable them to pull the plug on a failing effort faster than they would have otherwise.

A company used this sort of approach when it had to decide whether to aggressively increase production capacity to meet demand in the Chinese tire market, by asking the following questions: Will the market continue to grow as assumed? Was the opportunity still real and worth it? Investing heavily would exploit current opportunities but leave the company with significant overcapacity in the longer term once the Chinese market slowed. Choosing to limit investment would eliminate the long-term problem but result in a significant loss of market share and profits in the short term.

The company engaged in a stress test of capital investments and the business model in relation to the possibilities of global overcapacity and change in the Chinese market. Leadership uncovered significant risks in the medium and longer term. As a result, the company pivoted its resources elsewhere, accepting a small loss but avoiding a much more significant market collapse.

Transform: Rapid Response

Rapid response requires the ability to sense threats and opportunities in the market. Sensing is not enough, though—organizations must relentlessly pursue improvement in how they respond when signals emerge. These skills are critical to maximizing the upside and minimizing the downside as part of an accelerated strategy.

Responding to a threat or opportunity more quickly than competitors, based on less-than-perfect information, can be the difference between just being average or being accelerated. Most organizations struggle to act swiftly and commit resources because the near-term risks of being wrong far outweigh the long-term reward of being right.

It's important for organizations to understand how well they sense threats and opportunities. In a *Harvard Business Review* article, George Day and Paul Schoemaker introduce a simple but powerful idea, as exemplified by Table 6.1: An organization can sort through threats and opportunities, both seen and unseen, by categorizing them. (Most organizations find it

TABLE 6.1 Threats and opportunities matrix

	Seen	Unseen
Threats	Mitigated risk	Blindsiding loss
Opportunities	Captured upside	Unrealized potential

Source: George S. Day and Paul J. H. Schoemaker, "Scanning the periphery," *Harvard Business Review*, November 2005, hbr.org

easier to see threats than opportunities, so they will need to work harder to spot the opportunities.)

No company is perfect, of course, but every company must strive for a healthier balance between the opportunities and threats that are seen versus those that are unseen.

It's also crucial to remember what we've written about the acceleration trap. You can't just go fast all the time. You have to pick your spots, and sometimes you have to go slow first before you go fast. A study of 343 companies found that those that focused on "strategic speed"—reducing the time it takes to deliver value rather than just operating at a greater pace—had 40 percent higher revenue and 52 percent higher profit over a three-year period.[6]

A global pharmaceutical company had to strike this balance as it was preparing to launch an oncology drug that had been granted breakthrough therapy (BT) designation by the FDA. Its main competitor was preparing to launch a combination treatment in the same time frame, with both companies seeking to gain much more lucrative indications (that is, approval for additional uses) in the 12 to 18 months following the launch. The pharma company needed to understand how and when to engage its key stakeholders to build interest among those making and influencing treatment decisions. The brand leadership team worked to understand how to differentiate their treatment from that of their competitor and win over key influencers. The team then developed a road map for how and when to engage each stakeholder group for the initial indication as well as the targeted second and third indications. The strategy garnered support from key influencers, positioning the company well for substantial market share once its treatment achieved a second indication 15 months later.

Agility: Foresight

Most organizations are skilled at sensitivity analyses of one issue in isolation, but few can conduct deeper-level examinations of how issues interact in a complex system.

The current volatile, uncertain, complex, and ambiguous (VUCA) environment demands that organizations reevaluate their strategies and strengths, lest they become one of the many casualties of industry disruption. Yet research shows that leaders are lacking in their ability to anticipate. In our assessment of nearly 25,000 executives in more than 175 countries on the "six key elements of strategic thinking," we found that predicting competitors' potential moves and likely reactions to new products or initiatives ranks as the least-developed skill among the most important strategic behaviors. This is alarming. Leaders must encourage investigation of a broader range of potential outcomes to avoid overconfidence traps related to forecasting.

A global pharmaceutical giant, for one, sought to determine what factors could have the most impact on the evolution of global oncology pricing, which is seeing a sharp change away from traditional assumptions—drug companies can no longer count on high margins and low price sensitivity. We helped the company create a "signaling" system to regularly monitor the events that would have the greatest impact. This mechanism informed the timing and nature of initiatives to improve pricing and contracting arrangements.

Agility: Learning

You must continuously test assumptions about yourself, your market, your customers, and your competitors. It's important to understand which assumptions might be vulnerable and to "unlearn" associated behaviors. By walking in the shoes of your competitors, you can experiment with different actions and learn about your market.

In a world of certainty, operational excellence routinely wins. In a world of greater uncertainty and risk, organizations that learn faster win more often. Operational excellence is increasingly becoming a table stake in many industries, with true differentiation stemming from a learning culture that is externally focused, experimental and innovative, collaborative, and comfortable with risk.

In a typical organization, most resources are focused on its central task. That limits the ability to pick up the barrage of weak signals from the periphery. Our survey of more than 200 senior executives found that their expected need for peripheral vision outstripped their current capacity, creating a "vigilance gap."

Organizations with accelerated strategy seek to close the vigilance gap and develop the ability to scan the periphery and capture the relevant signals.

This is the sort of approach taken at Aurizon, Australia's largest rail freight company, which has established a permanent unit that monitors shifts in key markets for coal and other commodities. The executive team reviews the dashboard to see when it needs to change emphasis among a predetermined set of strategic plans.[7]

Similarly, in 2012, a longtime champion of the electronic payment processing sector began to realize that its position at the top was not immune to competition. Its primary revenue source was waning, and its solutions began to seem less and less relevant in the lives of customers. Competitive threats from the four horsemen (Google, Apple, Facebook, and Amazon) led the company to seek partnerships to fortify its position and set up opportunities for additional revenue.

The organization recognized the value of war gaming to understand how competitors might react to any partnerships. This was accomplished through a structured, two-day, multiround simulation with members and heads of various divisions, including market research and strategic planning. Divided into six teams, each put on the hat of one competitor and participated in the simulation through an external lens. Armed with this additional insight, the organization surfaced potential partnership opportunities and a likely future layout of the competitive landscape and industry ecosystem as well as potential game-changing threats to its position.

Particularly valuable was the organization's self-reflection on its own attractiveness as a strategic partner. As a leader in the space, the organization assumed it could take its pick of potential partners. This exercise in outside-in thinking, however, led the team to realize that the capabilities that had made the company an industry leader were not the same as what today's technology goliaths would find valuable as they entered the online payments space.

Agility: Adaptability

Even the most successful companies must adapt to ensure that they stay on top. As one scholar famously put it, writing on *The Origin of Species*, "It is not the most intellectual of the species that survives; it is not the strongest that survives; but the species that survives is the one that is able best to adapt and adjust to the changing environment in which it finds itself."[8] Leaders must recognize that existing strategies and processes, even if successful in the past, might need to be changed dramatically to ensure continued performance in the future.

Once-great companies fail due to a lack of adaptability. Long-lived organizations, meanwhile, are characterized by several traits, as outlined by Arie de Geus in *The Living Company*. First, the organizations are financially responsible, maintaining a healthy balance sheet and avoiding excessive leverage. Second, they have deeply embedded and shared values that guide action. Third, they are skilled at seeing around the corner and sensing change in their environment. And last, they are adept at experimenting on the edges of their market and evolving their business accordingly.

Organizations that accelerate strategy can adjust to changing circumstances by applying existing resources to new purposes and modifying actions and behaviors accordingly. This allows the organization to take advantage of new opportunities in good times and bad.

An industry-leading asset manager shows how to adapt. It had weathered the financial crisis fairly well, but its executives recognized that their business needed to evolve in a rapidly changing environment. Looking at how others had struggled, the company sought to adapt its offerings and processes to boost performance. It invested heavily in passive trading, despite its heritage business of active trading. Executives also studied their investment managers and identified several problems, such as groupthink, excessive risk aversion, disengagement, and disproportionate conviction in a model or process.

The senior leadership team leveraged behavioral economics research to understand the suboptimal behaviors along with the signals of each behavior, the conditions that foster the behaviors, and the most effective ways to intervene. Leaders then developed customized tools for both their investment managers and their risk managers to encourage more efficient behaviors. For teams with the greatest need, the organization provided intensive real-time coaching, delivering investment process recommendations to mitigate bias and optimize decision making.

This effort created a win-win situation for investment managers, the company, and its clients through targeted interventions.

Agility: Resilience

Many organizations have too narrow a view of the plausible range of outcomes, and often a disruptive event turns into something that is crippling rather than a small setback or even an opportunity. Any accelerated strategy must minimize the possibility of being blindsided or disrupted and maximize the odds of capturing new opportunities. Although we cannot predict future outcomes, we can pressure-test our ability to withstand rapid shifts around us.

Organizations that accelerate strategy ensure that a robust, continuous-improvement infrastructure is in place. Mechanisms exist to self-regulate so disruptions do not cascade to cause a catastrophe. It is critical to surface and examine mental models—the key assumptions underlying a business's strategy. By considering which assumptions might be vulnerable and looking at a broader range of outcomes, leaders can combat overconfidence and prepare for challenging operating environments.

A large offshore drilling contractor showed the value of this approach, in the face of an exceptionally challenging environment: Offshore drilling rates from 2001 to 2011 showed periods of high demand, short rig supply, and high day rates (e.g., 2005 to 2007), followed by periods of low demand, excess rig supply, and low day rates (e.g., 2009). Honing the ability to adjust to changing circumstances was crucial. In particular, the company wanted to minimize damaging surprises. For instance, salaries had doubled between 2005 and 2010 due to a lack of labor availability in roles requiring high skill and experience—and personnel costs accounted for about 60 percent of operating expenses. Retirement of the baby boomer generation, increased competition for talent, and rapid technological developments relating to frontier projects further highlighted the need to manage risk.

We worked with a range of internal stakeholders to frame the future of HR in the context of industry changes such as the oil sands boom in North America and political instability in the Middle East. Analysis revealed a shortfall of as much as 20 percent for some roles—bigger in prospective markets. The critical gaps were in nonsupervisory positions, contrary to conventional belief inside the company.

This analysis highlighted the need to increase resilience by better understanding reasons for attrition at more junior levels, leveraging the global workforce locally to improve flexibility of key talent, and recruiting and developing nationals in prospective markets such as Mozambique and Tanzania.

■   ■   ■

In today's world, many of the tried-and-true, financial-based strategic planning tools are much less effective, leaving organizations ill-positioned for sustainability—let alone success—in a dynamically changing marketplace.

A well-known Scandinavian proverb says, "There is no such thing as bad weather, only inappropriate clothing"—and many companies need a different approach to their strategy for dealing with a harsh environment. A central theme in strategy is not to frame any future as "good" or "bad." Your job is to figure out what that future holds and prepare for it, no matter what it is.

An accelerated strategy gives a company a much better chance of winning. It enables sustained, high-level performance by providing organizations a superior ability to anticipate and respond to the competition, an unquestioned clarity of strategic intent, and an adaptive plan built to thrive in complex, uncertain environments.

Notes

1. Duncan Simester, "The lost art of thinking in large organizations," *MIT Sloan Management Review*, June 3, 2016, sloanreview.mit.edu.

2. Adam Grant, *Originals: How Non-Conformists Move the World,* New York: Viking, 2016.
3. Kana Inagaki, Leo Lewis, and Arash Massoudi, "Masayoshi Son: The unrepentant visionary," *Financial Times,* July 22, 2016, ft.com.
4. John P. Kotter and James L. Heskett, *Corporate Culture and Performance,* New York: The Free Press, 1992.
5. Paul Leinwand, Cesare Mainardi, and Art Kleiner, "5 ways to close the strategy-to-execution gap," *Harvard Business Review,* December 22, 2015, hbr.org.
6. Jocelyn R. Davis and Tom Atkinson, "Need speed? Slow down," *Harvard Business Review,* May 2010, hbr.org.
7. Martin Toner, Nikhil Ojha, Piet de Paepe, and Miguel Simões de Melo, "A strategy for thriving in uncertainty," Bain & Company, August 12, 2015, bain.com.
8. Leon C. Megginson, "Lessons from Europe for American business," *Southwestern Social Science Quarterly,* June 1963.

CHAPTER 7

Accelerating Organizations
Turning Drag into Drive

The history of innovation has many heroes. Go back to the ancient Greeks, and you find pioneers in philosophy, theater, and geometry. From the ensuing centuries, we celebrate scientific heroes who identified fundamental properties of our universe, such as Sir Isaac Newton and Albert Einstein, or those who discovered some of its building blocks—such as Niels Bohr, who laid out subatomic structures, or Joseph Priestley, who discovered oxygen. More recently, our awe about scientific discoveries has extended to those whose products have changed our lives, so we venerate Steve Jobs and Sir Jonathan Ive for designing the iPhone and put on a pedestal founder-CEOs such as Mark Zuckerberg of Facebook. We have, in some cases, even moved beyond products to focus on developers of new business models, with the success of Uber, Airbnb, and other "asset-light" businesses.

But what about developments in organizational structure and in managing at the organization level? There is a general consensus that the future of business competition will depend much more on talent and on agile organizations, and this doesn't just mean finding better people as part of a war for talent. The shift in emphasis also requires better thinking about how we organize and deploy that talent.[1] All sorts of developments in technology have radically changed how we interact with each other in businesses. And yet, in the years since Alfred P. Sloan created the modern structure of a corporation at General Motors, from the 1920s to the 1950s, has anyone emerged as an innovator in organizational structures? Is there even anyone who comes to mind?

We need to rethink our organizational structures from front to back—starting with the customer and then working back to everything else. We also need to rethink how we manage people within those structures. Now is the time.

Too many organizations have become herbivores. Not enough are velociraptors—lightning-fast and ready to pounce on any weakness. So we

FIGURE 7.1 The OAQ model

have pored through our research and identified 13 key factors that can either drive an organization forward or that can create the kind of drag that comes from a diet of eucalyptus leaves (which has koalas sleeping for most of the day). As with the other three levels we address—strategy, teams, and individual leaders—these 13 factors fit neatly within the META structure, and we have organized them that way (Figure 7.1).

If you focus on these factors, and on the actions we describe in this chapter that can turn drag into drive, you will at the very least begin to operate much more efficiently. You may also be able to identify some truly innovative approaches, whether in managing teams or in breaking down corporate boundaries and collaborating with external resources as effectively as you now do with your own.

The 13 Drag and Drive Factors

Figures 7.2 and 7.3 summarize the 13 drag and drive factors, organized into the META framework.

FIGURE 7.2 Drag factors for organizations

Mobilize

Internal focus	Fatigue	Confusion
Chronic service failures	KPIs in the red	Unclear purpose and strategy
High customer attrition	Key projects delayed	Lack of focus
Overtaken by market disruptions	Disengagement	Too many conflicting priorities

Execute

Complexity	Unclear accountability	Skills gaps
Too many layers	Overlapping accountabilities	Weak talent pipeline
Unjustified process variation	Rewarding effort, not impact	Losing the best people
Complicated metrics	Victim mentality	Avoiding tough people decisions

Transform

Fear	Complacency	Competition
Missed value opportunities	Acceptance of mediocrity	Silos and politics
Stagnation	Taking too long to remove poor performers	Distrust
Outdated products and services	Avoiding straight talk	Information hoarding

Agility

Hindsight	Immunity	Inflexibility	Frailty
Always looking at the past for answers to current problems	Inability to learn from mistakes	Slow to adapt to changing circumstances	Unable to recover from setbacks
	Avoiding failure at all costs		Weakened by setbacks

Let's break each of these drag and drive factors down by category:

- **Mobilize**: Mobilizing requires the ability to read changes in the external ecosystem through the lens of your customers and to energize the organization with a crystal clear message.

Drag factor	Drive factor
Internal focus	Customer first
Fatigue	Energizing leadership
Confusion	Clarity

FIGURE 7.3 Drive factors for organizations

Mobilize

Customer first
Always responsive to changing customer demands
Low customer attrition
Consistent service excellence

Energizing leadership
High-energy buzz
Empowerment at every level
Strong role models who inspire others to bring their best performance

Clarity
Everyone aligned and committed to purpose, ambition, and clear priorities

Execute

Simplicity
No bureaucracy
Lean processes
Streamlined structure

Ownership
Meritocracy
Delivery culture
Integrity-driven processes

Winning capabilities
Talent magnet
Great talent-development processes
Best talent in key roles

Transform

Innovation
Culture of disruptive thinking, idea generation, and experimentation
Fast adoption

Challenge
Supportive, frank feedback and debate
Highest performance expectations

Collaboration
Work as one organization
High level of trust
Joined-up processes and communication

Agility

Foresight
Think ahead to anticipate and plan for changing circumstances

Learning
Learn quickly to avoid repeating past mistakes
Improve continuously

Adaptability
Quick to adapt to changing circumstances

Resilience
Recover quickly and emerge stronger from setbacks

- **Execute:** Execution at the organization level requires the ability to fully harness and streamline resources in order to consistently deliver excellence in the core business. It also requires a simple organizational structure, centralized ownership of resources, and the right capabilities.

Drag factor	Drive factor
Complexity	Simplicity
Unclear accountability	Ownership
Skills gaps	Winning capabilities

■ **Transform**: This is where companies experiment and innovate to create growth engines and to reinvent existing businesses ahead of the market. This often requires a different, more aggressive approach to innovation. It also means being willing to face challenges and to collaborate when tackling them.

Drag factor	Drive factor
Fear	Innovation
Complacency	Challenge
Competition	Collaboration

■ **Agility**: The key element of acceleration, agility implies the ability to spot opportunities and threats and to adapt and pivot faster than competitors to create a competitive advantage. It also means the ability to prepare for, withstand, and recover from setbacks quickly.

Drag factor	Drive factor
Hindsight	Foresight
Immunity	Learning
Inflexibility	Adaptability
Frailty	Resilience

Of course, here is the big question: If both high- and low-growth companies attempt to be great on these 13 drive factors, what are the winners doing that differentiates them?

The 39 Differentiating Actions

We dug deep into the management practices of the superaccelerators and identified 3 actions for each of the 13 drive factors. We think of these 39 actions as similar to the elements on the periodic table. They can be combined in a vast range of important ways. No one company we observed implemented all of these actions; instead, the superaccelerators adroitly combined the most critical ones into a winning recipe, given their context.

Thirty-nine actions is a lot, and not all will require new thinking at every organization. But, in our experience, many will serve as a sort of mirror; when an organization holds that mirror up to itself, it will find that it doesn't look quite like it hoped it did or thinks it should. So we suggest running through the list of actions to see which ones resonate and then digging deeper into those. In later chapters, we'll explain how to develop the capabilities necessary to make changes and to turn your list of needed actions into a recipe for success.

Following are the 3 actions you should consider for each of the 13 drag and drive factors.

Mobilize: Customer First

1. **Immerse yourself in the customer experience.**

Every organization in the world aims to be customer-driven. Most are not. How much of the time of your top 100 leaders is actually spent with customers? Do you have a seat in the office or a seat in your car, as you go visit your customers? How much of your energy is spent "feeding the beast" rather than being in direct service to your customers? You must free your teams and organization to focus on the customer. Spend time in your customers' shoes. Visit them, investigate their experience, understand their world, and connect personally. You also must invest in data, insights, and intuition to understand which customer segments are most attractive. Share your personal customer insights with your teams to scale your customer impact.

According to legend, Henry Ford said that if he had just asked customers what they wanted, they'd have asked him to design faster horses, but he knew more about their needs than they did. Really understanding the customer is even more important than it used to be because of the end of information asymmetry. Companies used to have a huge information advantage over customers. Companies could pretend to be great, shiny brands even when they were not. No longer. Customers know better now.

Adobe recognized that it was not, in fact, putting customers first, despite intending to do so. It discovered that its customers found the company not always easy to do business with, and it was not consistently delivering the level of service its customers expected. So Adobe set up a Customer Immersion Program to allow senior leaders to play the role of a customer and experience Adobe for themselves. One way senior leaders put themselves in the shoes of customers was to interact with customer service by calling in with a problem or need. Leaders learned, among other things, about how to reduce complexity in pricing and offerings that had been frustrating customers.[2]

Brian Cornell, who became CEO of Target in August 2014, is personally immersing himself in the customer experience as he tries to return the retailer to the days when it was known both as chic and as a discounter. Although known as a huge consumer of data, he pops into stores unannounced—previously, visits by the CEO were scripted scrupulously— and talks anonymously with customers to gain insights that he then probes with his team. Cornell moved out of the newly redone corner suite occupied by his predecessor and took a smaller office so he could be just steps away from Target's global data nerve center, where 10 staff members monitor social media and television to track, moment by moment, how customers react to product announcements, news events, or online posts. He receives briefings from the team twice a day.[3]

2. **Co-innovate with customers.**

You must break down barriers to your customers. Embed yourself in the value chain and innovation process for your B2B customers. Be a partner, not a vendor. Help to shape and create the future needs of your customers by challenging assumptions about what delights them and anticipating competitors' responses rather than merely reacting to them. While protecting your critical intellectual property, invite your customers to take the journey with you. Always make decisions as if your customers were in your meeting.

Zara became an international phenomenon by, essentially, coinventing with customers at great speed as part of what is known as "fast fashion." Zara designs clothing and stocks the items in its stores, but that is just the start of the process. Zara's sales associates watch to see which items customers consider buying but then put back. Associates ask for feedback from customers and communicate it instantaneously to the design team, which modifies items and quickly fills stores with products that reflect customer preferences. Zara makes clothes only in small batches and locks in just 50 to 60 percent of its line at the start of the season versus the industry average of 80 percent. As a result, Zara has unusual flexibility to adapt as certain items become hot sellers. This approach required that Zara shorten its supply chain by setting up manufacturing facilities close to its big markets in the United States and Europe, which means slightly higher costs. But the co-innovation with customers means that Zara marks down only 15 to 20 percent of its merchandise, while the industry average is 50 percent, and Zara's profit margins are consistently double the industry average.[4]

Restaurant chain Red Robin introduced a test burger in a small number of restaurants and had servers communicate feedback from customers instantly to the test kitchen. This allowed Red Robin to quickly make changes to the burger based on customer preferences, and it was able to roll the burger out nationally in four weeks rather than the 18 months the process normally took.[5]

3. **Gear your measurement systems to start with customers and follow with finance.**

All revenue shortfalls, margin deficits, and cost overruns originate in the lack of customers, the lack of the right customers, or the lack of a proper response to customers' needs. Look at your measurement array, and if it gives you greater insight into finance than into your customers, you've got it wrong. Don't weaken your financial rigor, but match it with customer insight.

Zappos CEO Tony Hsieh built the online shoe company on a radical approach to service that very much started with the customer and worked backward. He let customers return for free any shoes they didn't want, even though he knew customers would order lots of pairs and perhaps keep just one or two. He put such emphasis on customer service that a friend of his, who had spent a night barhopping and was disappointed to find when she returned to her hotel that room service had shut down for the night, called Zappos customer service to find out where she could order a pepperoni pizza in Santa Monica, California, at three in the morning—and was given five phone numbers for places that would deliver. Hsieh made sure the economics worked at Zappos, but only after taking care of the customer first.[6]

James H. Gilmore, coauthor of *Authenticity: What Customers Really Want*, marvels that so many companies claim to focus on customer service yet don't deliver it: "They focus exclusively on ROI (return on investment) and instead get RODNN (return on doing nothing new, pronounced 'rotten')."[7]

Mobilize: Energizing Leadership

4. Role-model urgency.

The CEO and the top team are the rate-limiting valve of any organization. Set shorter meetings, with excellent process management. Discuss issues once, thoroughly, and then move on to implementation. Follow up relentlessly. Be a visible symbol for what you expect of others—your decisions, how you prioritize your time, and the way you engage. Keep yourself healthy, and watch out for burnout. Your physical, mental, and emotional state affects your ability to win the race and sets the example for others. Be in tune with your mood, and manage your energy and its impact on others. Light up the room when you enter, not when you leave!

UBS showed great urgency after the collapse of Lehman Brothers in 2008. UBS and Credit Suisse had very similar valuations at the time, and the two executive teams could almost hear each other from their respective head offices on either side of Bahnhofstrasse in Zurich, but it was only UBS's new CEO, Sergio Ermotti, who moved with haste. He downsized and refocused the investment bank, returned to the core franchise of wealth management, and led a top-to-toe cultural change program. Credit Suisse is doing all those things but almost a decade later; at the time of this writing, UBS has twice the market capitalization of Credit Suisse. Speed wins the day.

5. **Stop "sucking up" accountability.**
   The natural tendency in top and senior teams to take hold of more and more accountability creates drag. You must not let senior leaders "suck up" all the authority; they must push it through the organization to those at the customer interface. Be relentless in holding leaders to account for using empowerment to create capability. Develop a team culture that encourages functional/business units to compromise to do the right thing for the organization as a whole. Ensure that every single team member, without exception, points in the same direction (though, of course, without stifling useful discussion).
   Home Depot thrived by not letting managers suck up accountability. Purchasing decisions were left to local managers, as were many issues about staffing and store layout. The magic of the formula was the "expert in the aisle"—the sort of person who would have been treated as a clerk in other retail environments was hired for expertise in plumbing, wiring, and so on and given great latitude to serve the customer. The company lost its way when a former CEO centralized accountability but has thrived in recent years by returning to the original vision.

6. **Think of business units as guests, not family.**
   Develop an acquisition engine, and match it with an equally powerful divestment engine. Our research indicates that as much as 40 percent of value destruction occurs not as a result of entering doomed opportunities but by staying in businesses, geographies, or products long after the competitive advantage has waned.
   Novo Nordisk, the huge Danish pharmaceutical company, has actively managed its product mix through acquisitions and divestitures. Between 2010 and the end of 2013, it acquired more than 50 companies, and it has been almost as active in divesting. For instance, it spun off an IT consulting business it had developed internally and has sold businesses devoted to anticoagulants, certain cancer drugs, and more.
   Tata Consultancy Services, one of our superaccelerators, adopts a similar attitude. As Natarajan Chandrasekaran, the company's CEO and managing director, told us: "Our approach has been not to get pinned in the trap of a portfolio approach. We believe that every business, every area we work on, must have agility so it can grow. Everything we do should be a growth business."

Mobilize: Clarity

7. **Articulate an audacious objective.**
   Avoid the gravitational forces of lower aspirations. Galvanize the organization behind an aspiration that attracts. Ensure that objectives

are aligned to an integrated set of strategic capabilities. Don't allow distractions. Always assess whether a team decision takes the organization closer to or away from achieving its objective.

Emulate Google, which looks for opportunities that will increase its business by 10 times, not 10 percent.[8]

Through 11 maxims, Nike has, as always, taken an audacious approach that it communicates to employees. Codified in 2000, following a rough stretch at the company, Nike's core beliefs are the following:

1. It is our nature to innovate.
2. Nike is a company.
3. Nike is a brand.
4. Simplify and go.
5. The consumer decides.
6. Be a sponge [as in, be receptive to new ideas].
7. Evolve immediately.
8. Do the right thing.
9. Master the fundamentals.
10. We are on the offense. Always.
11. Remember the man [cofounder Bill Bowerman, still renowned at the company for his creativity and for his knowledge of athletes].

Senior executives travel around the world to discuss the maxims with every employee and have found them to be crucial anchors as Nike tries to reinvent itself every 90 days and keep up with its market.

Ajay Banga, president and CEO of MasterCard, told us that it motivates his employees to think about driving toward an efficient, cashless society. "My employee base used to be 9 percent millennials the year I joined. It's now 40 percent millennials, and cause-based marketing excites them. And this cause is directly embedded in the business. Therefore, it's sustainable."

8. **List your priorities on one hand.**

Spend time and energy on the few critical priorities instead of on the many urgent ones. Stop or delay projects that are not the most critical ones. Finish existing projects before starting new ones. Engage in rigorous debate about how to apply existing resources to new purposes. Use milestones and performance metrics to inform the evaluation and adjustment of priorities. Large organizations are complex and have multiple goals, but creating simplicity out of complexity starts with a stunningly simple articulation of the key priorities.

While this may be simple, it may also be difficult. Many businesses create an Escherian maze that they can never escape. As the great visionary and art critic John Ruskin warned, "It is far more difficult to be simple than to be complicated."[9]

But making a dedicated effort to be simpler can reap big rewards. One CEO who took over a global retailer immediately disbanded 1,000 teams and turned a massive amount of complexity into three key initiatives, allowing everyone to focus on the turnaround program. Shareholder value, customer satisfaction, and employee retention all increased dramatically by the end of the first year.[10]

Similarly, Connie Ma, vice president of human resources at TSMC, one of our superaccelerators, told us that organizing around a clear statement of values known as ICIC has been crucial for the semiconductor giant. ICIC stands for "integrity, commitment, innovation, and customer trust." These values have kept TSMC on the cutting edge of technology, crucial in a business like semiconductors, and have also kept the company away from the temptation to compete with customers as lucrative markets emerge. "At TSMC, customers come first," said Ma. "Their success is our success, and we value their ability to compete as we value our own."

9. Use purpose as your fuel.

As we've said, we disagree with Milton Friedman when he said that business needs to do well, not do good. Instead, we think Peter Drucker was right when he said that the sole aim of a company should be filling customer needs. In fact, companies can often thrive by going beyond Drucker's basic goal and pursuing a greater good.

We all want to be connected to something meaningful. Creating a strong sense of purpose, tied into doing something good, gets people off the fence and encourages them to act urgently. These purposes should not be turned into the long, boring (and generally meaningless) vision and mission statements of previous decades. Truly accelerating companies can tell you what they do and why they do it and get you excited, in just a few words, about the company's "true north."

For example, John Hammergren, the CEO of McKesson, gave his employees at the pharmaceutical distributor and health care information company a higher purpose by emphasizing that, eventually, everyone will become a patient. Employees personalized their work by imagining their loved ones, or even themselves, on the receiving end of McKesson products and services. Medtronic had employees visit hospitals to see the company's technologies helping patients.[11] For his part, David Cordani, the president and CEO of Cigna, the global health insurance company, emphasizes that his organization's purpose extends far beyond merely processing insurance payments. "We exist to improve the health, well-being, and sense of security of the individuals we serve," he told us. "And we want that fact to be absolutely front and center in the minds of all our employees."

Monster.com announced its noble purpose with a Super Bowl ad that carried a "When I Grow Up" theme. It featured children saying what they wanted to be when they grew up—for example, "I want to be a yes-man or yes-woman" or "I want to claw my way up to middle management." The ad ended with the question: "What did you want to be?" and a kicker: "There's a better job out there." The job-posting site became one of the 20 most-visited sites on the Internet, but then a new CEO, Sal Iannuzzi, took over and declared that all he wanted to do was create shareholder value. The stock sank 93 percent under his stewardship, before the board fired him in 2014. The company is now recovering.[12]

Neuroscientific research concludes that we are motivated by a greater good to try harder, work faster, persevere longer, cooperate better, and control our least-productive impulses. Research has found, for instance, that the morale of call center employees at a university rose when they were read letters from students who had benefited from scholarships at the school, and that the quality of food in a restaurant increased when the cooks could see those they were serving.[13] Making a personal connection with others builds purpose and creates meaning. Imagine the productivity of an organization if hundreds or thousands of people are united by a shared purpose? Neuroscience also tells us that meaning from a shared purpose reduces stress and improves health.

A company's purpose defines its existence and contribution to society. Underlying it is a set of values and beliefs. Purpose is as fundamental to a corporation as our purposes, values, and beliefs are to us as individuals. A company purpose operates on four major planes—a covenant with customers, a reciprocal human contract with employees, mutuality of interest between society and the firm, and the desire to contribute to human betterment. Purpose is the indispensable means to create a corporate culture of integrity, which is crucial to business success.

Table 7.1 sets out six categories in which we have found that companies can organize their purpose, along with associated values. These categories are not exhaustive but rather demonstrate the range of what purpose can be.

TABLE 7.1 A range of possible purposes

Type	Definition	Underlying values	Possible issues	Examples
Distributive	Everybody deserves the same products/ services.	Fairness Equality	How do you maintain your purpose when you have achieved it?	IKEA: "To create a better everyday life for the many people."
Exploratory	There are lots of places where nobody has gone before.	Entrepreneurialism Curiosity	How do you know when you have reached your destination?	Tesla: "To accelerate the advent of sustainable transport by bringing compelling mass-market electric cars to market as soon as possible."
Exemplary	We can be the best at what we do.	Pride Drive	Is that goal inspiring enough to a lot of people?	Apple: "To bring the best personal computing experience to students, educators, creative professionals, and consumers around the world through innovative hardware, software, and Internet offerings."
Human	We work with and for humans.	Humanity Solidarity	How profitable can this be?	Starbucks: "To inspire and nurture the human spirit—one person, one cup, and one neighborhood at a time."
Sustainable	We need to preserve the integrity of our ecosystem.	Environmentalism Systemic view of the world	How real is the goal?	Patagonia: "Build the best product, cause no unnecessary harm, and use business to inspire and implement solutions to the environmental crisis."
Disruptive	To turn everything upside down.	Curiosity Drive	How sustainable is this goal?	Uber: "Transportation as reliable as running water, everywhere, for everyone."

97

The payoffs of purpose are increasingly measurable. Operational performance improves, innovation increases, and the cost of capital falls. Recruitment, retention, and motivation of employees all increase, while industrial relations become less adversarial.

Firms need to demonstrate in concrete terms what purpose means to them—and how they can credibly commit to it, particularly when under financial pressure.

The achievement of purpose requires both committed leadership and widespread buy-in at every level of the firm. Techniques include promoting executives who have shown commitment to the purpose, making public commitments, piloting experiments, and signing up for international and national initiatives. Getting buy-in demands that deeds align with words.

Execute: Simplicity

10. **Halve the number of metrics you use.**

Organizations are able to collect any piece of data they want these days. All could potentially be used to make decisions in one way or another. This abundance of data, instead of helping companies make better decisions, is stifling their ability to react quickly and smartly to events as they unfold. Pick a limited set of metrics for your scorecard. Understand your reasons for picking those metrics and how the metrics affect your business. Make decisions based solely on those metrics, and remain open to always questioning the applicability of the metrics to the changing realities of your business. These metrics can be like the rather modest number of traffic laws that guide millions of people around a nation's roads. The metrics can represent the dominant logic rather than making everyone rely on the equivalent of case law when making decisions.

Danaher's metrics reflect the company's focus on shareholders, customers, and people. Core growth, operating-margin expansion, working-capital returns, and return on invested capital are the four shareholder-facing financial metrics. The two customer-facing metrics are on-time delivery, measured against when the customer wanted the company to deliver something (even if that was yesterday), and external quality as a broad measure of every dimension of a customer experience. Finally, there are two human-capital metrics: internal fill rate (the percentage of managerial positions filled with internal candidates) and retention. According to CEO Thomas Joyce: "Every Danaher business uses those eight metrics to answer the following question: Are we winning?"[14]

11. **Reduce layers.**

Simplify your structure. Have no more than five to seven layers between the CEO and the front line, depending on the scope of your organization (global versus local). If you have leaders who cannot cope with the necessary number of direct reports—usually 10 to 15— then change your leaders.

Apple's hierarchy might remind you of a small business. The late Steve Jobs liked to keep management simple. He did not like layers of high-level people. It was Jobs's contention that having layers of management took the focus off of the task at hand, and that task, in his opinion, was designing and building the best products on the planet. Even after his death, much remains the same at Apple. Simplicity has to start with a simple product shelf: While some companies have product incontinence, spewing products everywhere, Apple has 19 products. The company runs one P&L.[15]

TSMC, likewise, has just one P&L. "It's a function-driven organizational structure," Ma told us. "We share the success. We are accountable for one organizational goal together."

For Comcast (one of our superaccelerators), creating an organizational structure that puts leaders in physical proximity to frontline employees "is essential to the quality of the operation of the business," noted William Strahan, executive vice president of human resources at Comcast Cable. It has an added benefit as well. "The derivative effect," said Strahan, "is a constant tamping down on any one person's ego, which helps keep people from taking themselves too seriously."

12. **Let "simple," "consistent," and "scalable" be your watchwords.**

Large organizations are by nature complex, and, over the years, circumstances have conspired to add layer upon layer of complexity to how businesses are structured and managed. Well-intended responses to new business challenges—globalization, emerging technologies, and regulations such as Sarbanes-Oxley, to name a few—have left us with companies that are increasingly ungovernable, unwieldy, and underperforming. In many companies, more energy is devoted to navigating the labyrinth than to achieving results. Accountability is unclear, decision rights are muddy, and data is sliced and diced time and again, frequently with no clear idea of how the information will be used. Many companies have more political intrigue than czarist Russia.

Thyagi Thyagarajan, an independent director at Tata Consultancy Services, a superaccelerator, tells us, "If you can't execute every day, every minute, across all geographies—then you're a goner." He says execution "has been the core DNA of TCS; they execute better than anybody else."

Complexity is the cumulative by-product of organizational changes, big and small, that over the years weave complications (often invisibly) into the ways that work is done. Structure becomes more convoluted. So do processes, after being repeatedly reengineered and redesigned. The product portfolio spreads in reaction to market demands and a periodic refreshing of offerings. Managerial habits produce a cascade of reporting work, often to cope with the complexities in structure, processes, and product offerings. When a company introduces new layers of management, for instance, an executive may naturally ask for more reports and e-mail updates, but the request turns into a habit that adds to the vicious cycle of complexity.

For example, Deutsche Bank, which in 2016 announced a radical restructuring plan that includes cutting 35,000 jobs, has, according to the *Financial Times*, "more than 100 different booking systems for trades in London alone and has no common client identifiers. It has even been unable to retrieve some of the data requested by regulators—which contributed to its failure in this year's U.S. bank stress tests."[16] It uses 41 computer operating systems, which the bank has vowed to reduce to 4.

How valuable can simplicity be? Instagram was bought by Facebook for $1 billion when it had just 13 employees. Facebook bought WhatsApp for $22 billion (more than the value that Sony and its 130,000-plus employees carried at the time) when it had 55 employees.

Not all complexity can be designed out, of course. Interactions between humans are inherently complex, and a concept known as Dunbar's number suggests that humans really aren't built to work in huge groups. Evolutionary psychologist Robin Dunbar studied primates' brain size and social group size and extrapolated his findings for humans, proposing that people could manage in a group of only about 150 through social relationships and face-to-face interactions. Beyond 150, bureaucracy and coercion were needed, which is why groups of hunter-gatherers, Roman army units, Neolithic villages, and so on all tended to be smaller than 150 people.[17]

Still, complexity can at least be countered by integrating four reasonably simple elements into a multidimensional strategy:

1. **Prune products, services, and features**. Take a hard look at the products and services the company offers. Are there too many of them? Which are profitable and have the greatest growth potential? How well do offerings match customers' needs? Which have run their course? One way to get some answers is to periodically do a classic portfolio review.

2. **Build disciplined processes**. Once products have been streamlined, turn your attention to processes. They have to be examined

and rewired (or eliminated) one at a time. Again, simplification has to become a continual activity. Engaging employees across the organization in process simplification, particularly at the grassroots level, can be powerful. People at all levels then become more likely to step up and correct a problem before it gums up the works. At Nortel, employees made 3,000 recommendations for improvements, put 900 of those recommendations into effect, and saved the company $14 million.[18]

3. **Streamline the organizational structure.** Managers should periodically adjust structure so that, while serving the business strategy and market needs, it is as simple as possible. Whether you're centralizing functions or shifting reporting relationships, the point is to think of organizational design as a dynamic, continuing, and organic process instead of a one-time exercise in engineering,

4. **Improve managerial habits.** If managers are serious about reducing complexity, they need to identify how their own (often unintentional) patterns of behavior complicate matters and to make a personal commitment to simplification. Making your organization simple and keeping it that way take a lot of hard work. This requires an explicit strategy and vigilance.

Be careful as you consider these elements. Applying one separately may actually worsen the problem. For example, many companies have found that simplifying processes through large-scale enterprise systems—without addressing organizational structure, product offerings, and work behaviors—often leads to diminished rather than enhanced productivity. One-off efforts may interrupt established relationships, introduce unanticipated roadblocks, and create confusion over decision rights.

Talent can also help tackle complexity, which stems from the wrong mix of sophistication and capability. If someone has a very low capability at baking, then anything to do with baking seems complex. If someone is a master baker, then most things involving baking are simple. To reduce complexity, you need to think about having not only less sophisticated approaches but also more capable people. The economy runs on people.

Execute: Ownership

13. **Develop a culture of commitment.**

Companies often make decisions far too slowly. They need to develop the muscle to move faster, always asking, "Why can't we make this decision sooner?" and working to remove roadblocks. Companies must, if you will, eliminate cognitive overhead.[19] Then, once a commitment is made, bank it. Leaders must be intolerant of renegotiation, unless important new information appears. Ruthlessly hold each other and the team to account as a normal part of "how we do things around here." This culture of commitment needs to empower people to lead.

Allison Joyce, vice president of talent management at Comcast, said she has been surprised in her five-year tenure to see "how fast we get to 'yes.' This is not an organization where you generally go to a meeting with a pretty good idea and someone says, 'Well, let's convene a committee.' The response is more like the line from the film *Jerry Maguire*: 'You had me at hello.' Then the question becomes 'How fast can you go get that done?' That speed of decision making, I think, drives people to sweat the details before they bring up an idea, because they know they're so likely to be told, 'Yes, now go do it.'"

14. **Exit people who don't live your values.**

In an uncertain and volatile business environment, an organization's values are the anchor that keeps the organization solidly positioned in the marketplace. People who are unwilling or unable to live those values will only produce drag. Once you have aligned your values with META, you need to establish mechanisms to quickly identify those people who are not living the values—particularly after a change in values—and exit them from the organization in a way that is not disruptive but sends an important message to internal and external stakeholders.

After employees joined Comergent, a supplier of e-business software applications acquired by AT&T's Sterling Commerce in 2006, they were continually reminded that the company's values of dependability, dedication, and self-motivation were more than just words. The top team used these values as a metric when designating stock, bonuses, and raises. Even deciding whether to let someone go was influenced by values. "I can work with someone who needs more coaching or training, but when it comes to our core values, I have to be intolerant," CEO Jean Kovacs explained in 2002. "That's what ensures the strength of our culture."[20]

15. **Place big people in big jobs.**

Know your people and know your jobs, and make sure that the best people get the big jobs. This ensures that you keep your best people engaged and interested and also that the rest of the organization learns from those who do things better. Putting the best people in big jobs also sends signals to the market about the seriousness of your organization.

By breaking with traditional thinking about credentials, the Pittsburgh Steelers have put the best people in the big jobs and have been the most successful franchise in the modern era of American football. The team had been a laughingstock for four decades before it identified Chuck Noll as a talent and made him the youngest head coach in league history in 1969, at the tender age of 37. He won four Super Bowls for Pittsburgh before retiring at the end of the 1991 season. The Steelers named a 34-year-old head coach to replace Noll, and he won a Super Bowl in his 15 years with the team before stepping aside in favor of another 34-year-old, who has also won a Super Bowl with the Steelers. While roughly a quarter of the head coaches in the league turn over every year, the Steelers have had only three in nearly half a century and have won more championships in that stretch than any other franchise. The team has broken with tradition and focused on talent in other ways, too: It had the league's first African-American starting quarterback, first African-American assistant coach, and first African-American coordinator, and its current head coach is African-American. Indeed, the team's practice of interviewing diverse candidates for important jobs was made league policy in 2003 and is known as the "Rooney Rule," after the team's owner, Dan Rooney.

Execute: Winning Capabilities

16. **Be a talent magnet.**

    Scan the world for the very best, starting at the top and working all the way through the front line, so that the company is a preferred place to work at every level. The difference between good and great talent is orders of magnitude. Poor talent huddles together. Once you tolerate having second-best people for their roles, the best will leave.

    Starbucks is known for its highly knowledgeable employees. They are the main assets of the company, and they are provided with great benefits such as stock options, retirement accounts, and a healthy culture. This effective human-capital management translates into great customer service. Starbucks was rated 94th in the 100 best places to work by *Fortune* magazine in 2013. The company attracts exceptional talent and retains frontline employees, and this in an industry known for high turnover.

    Scott Pitasky, executive vice president and chief partner resources officer at Starbucks (one of our superaccelerators), told us that "the company has a deep and enduring belief in our mission, values, and purpose—and at the center of that is the relationship we have with our partners [what Starbucks calls its employees]. We talk about performance through the lens of humanity, and that's the expectation we're always trying to meet. Our focus is on our partners, on our coffee, and on the experience that we create in the store for our customers."

17. **Become distinguished for your investment in people.**

    Continually develop your talent. Provide regular feedback, and act as a coach and mentor. Once you hire people with growth mind-sets, invest in all forms of learning and development—coaching, stretch assignments, self-initiated training—not just traditional "courses." Push out complacency by making it clear that learners are the only ones who get ahead. Use partnerships, joint ventures, acquisitions, and talent-attraction mechanisms to quickly obtain the required capacity and capability.

Recognized as one of the firms that invests the most in the development of its workforce, Google focuses on hiring "learning animals" and generalists as opposed to specialists. The main reason is that, because of the dynamics of the industry, where conditions are changing fast, things such as experience and the way you've done a role before aren't nearly as important as your ability to think and be developed.

"We're in a space that's moving fast," said Matt Brittin, president of EMEA business and operations at Google (Alphabet, its parent company, is one of our superaccelerators). "Technology is changing very fast, and what's possible is changing very fast. We're constantly changing the organization's shape, size, and structure to choose priorities and the growth areas to think about."

18. **Break free of hierarchy; align resources with opportunities.**

Sever the link between organizational structure and resource ownership. Match resources to opportunities. Mix and match team members to best fit roles, and move them as the organization's needs change. Build governance rhythms and mechanisms that drive increasingly effective execution. Encourage rapid iteration to surface new perspectives. Draw on a diverse set of ideas, information sources, and technical elements to help you course-correct in the face of changing circumstances.

At Infosys, budgets are adjusted on a rolling four-quarter basis. The company prides itself on being able to reallocate resources very quickly, and it does. Business units make it obvious when they do not need as many resources as have been allocated to them. In fact, it is not unusual for businesses to call the corporate planning department to give back some resources they could not support in a specific quarter. High-quality data and total transparency help sustain this approach.

Transform: Innovation

19. **Protect the space to innovate.**

Create incubators and nurseries to enable growth. Create a culture in which it is safe to fail and learn fast. Bring outside ideas in. Track how often new ideas are adopted from the external world, and improve on that record. Leverage differences of perspective. Build routines and rituals that call forth a range of insights and ideas. Constantly look for and challenge biases in framing and gathering intelligence and coming to conclusions that may reinforce the status quo.

Procter & Gamble uses open-innovation networks to solve design problems and tests products with online user communities so it can be sure of a friendly reception before completing a full rollout. In 2008, 10 employees created 10,000 designs to test, reducing to hours a process for innovation that previously unfolded over a period of weeks.[21]

Google's Matt Brittin told us, "We try to have a culture that allows for bottom-up innovation, so we don't have a strategy department. We hire people and encourage them to come up with projects and product ideas that they want to build. The result is a bottom-up internal market for innovation. Our engineering functions, for example, allow people to come up with a project and say, 'Hey, I want to work on this.' If other people get excited about the project, then it's hard to stop the momentum. As we've grown, we've moved away from having a thousand flowers bloom, but at the same time we know that giving people flexibility is great for innovation. So we're aiming for more coherent bouquets. We're organizing our teams into a set of groups where they're working on similar things. Now they're dedicated to a project, whether that be to the cloud and infrastructure, or Android and devices, or huge video, or apps. We're pointing people in a direction and providing just enough organization around them to allow them to move forward in a coherent way."

Innovation carries an enormous premium, when you get it right. Although the movement of manufacturing jobs to China has been of concern for a long time, especially given the 2016 presidential election in the United States, manufacturing accounts for only 5 percent to 7 percent of the cost of an iPhone, while Apple has profit margins of 30 percent to 60 percent. Consequently, the value per employee that Apple generates eclipses that of its manufacturing partners. An employee at Foxconn, the manufacturer of the iPhone, creates value of an average of $2,000 a year, while an employee at Apple creates value in excess of $640,000 a year.[22]

20. **Invest with courage.**

Encourage disruptive thinking. Go with instinct first, and then back it up with empirical data that includes an assessment of the risks and assumptions underlying the choices made. Use healthy and growing sources of cash and a stable platform to launch disruptive forays into the unknown. Measure innovations achieved. Target and track the introduction and impact of new products, services, processes, markets, customer interactions, and improvements for employees.

GM showed not only technical foresight when it launched its OnStar telematics system in 1996 but also the ability to invest with courage. Many inside the company wanted OnStar to be available only as an option, to limit the downside if OnStar proved unpopular. Many others wanted OnStar to be available only on luxury GM brands, viewing OnStar solely as a way to sell more cars. But management felt that OnStar needed to have critical mass to have a chance and installed it as standard equipment across much of the product line. Analysts say OnStar now accounts for a significant portion of GM's $46 billion of market value.

GM is showing similar courage with aggressive investments in driverless cars, even though they could represent a threat to its long-standing business model because the cars would likely be bought and operated by fleets, not individuals.

Another company that typifies this approach is Comcast, which is willing to invest heavily when it identifies "move the needle" opportunities. As Comcast Cable's William Strahan put it: "We solve our problems more with our balance sheet than with our income statement."

21. **Emphasize speed to adoption.**

Push the rate at which great ideas spread across your organization. Establish the systems, processes, and culture that enable good ideas to be scaled quickly. Pinpoint those who have a stake in the initiatives, and communicate intentions clearly, early, and continually.

One key to making this possible: You must have "a single source of truth." A lack of agreement about numbers, or even a common lexicon, slows organizations, as marketing feuds with finance, finance argues with product development, and so on.

Chinese Internet company Tencent uses simultaneous product development and rapid "launch-test-improve" cycles to speed innovation in business models, effectively harnessing user feedback to rapidly improve the quality and functionality of its products after they are launched. Tencent developed WeChat, which added mobile payments in 2013; Facebook didn't announce an online payment system until 2015. WeChat allowed users to set up online stores in 2014; Facebook added a feature that allows retailers to sell from Facebook pages in 2015.

Transform: Challenge

22. **Speak truth to power.**

Encourage straight talking. Value those who speak up. Celebrate the art of giving and receiving difficult messages. Remove the poor performers quickly. Rupture and repair. Enable conversations that have heat and energy. Encourage team members to tussle hard with difficult topics, and build the skills to repair relationships.

Rosabeth Moss Kanter, the prolific author and former editor of *Harvard Business Review*, tells a story that shows both the value of speaking truth to power and how hard it is to set up the right environment. She says an executive joined the top team at a fabric maker that was looking for major innovations. At a meeting, he said he was interested in any ideas that factory workers had. Afterward, someone with a heavy accent approached him tentatively with an idea for ending a long-standing problem that had yarn breaking during production, creating a competitive disadvantage. The idea worked. Asked how long he had had the idea, the worker replied: "Thirty-two years."[23]

23. **Harness the power of doubt.**

Measure yourself and the organization not against the past but against challenges not yet known. Embrace paradox. Challenge yourself to go beyond linear thinking. Reframe the problem, and find solutions to seemingly conflicting priorities (e.g., winning today and investing in the future; executing in the core business while transforming and investing in the future). Mine for conflict. Work hard to understand, name, and tackle power dynamics and hidden issues. Put an end to team meetings characterized by artificial harmony or outright aggression. Accept that it's okay to be wrong at the start as long as you are right at the finish.

A global pharmaceutical company had a few major drugs going off-patent, and every part of the organization was under pressure to innovate. The corporate strategy team and the product team brainstormed in ways that brought all sorts of doubt to the surface. The strategy team asked, for instance: "What is 'known' in the industry that may not be true? If we were CEO for a day, what three things would we do to our brands to set them up for major growth?" The questions initially quieted the room, but everyone soon got excited, and creativity was unleashed.[24]

24. **Draw the red thread to value.**

Make sure that you and your organization understand what the sources of value are for your company, and direct all of your activities to focusing on those. Avoid wasting energy and resources on things that are not directly related to the sources of value, and design mechanisms to alert you and the organization when this is happening.

When Xerox was facing bankruptcy in 2001, CEO Anne Mulcahy drew a red thread to value by first taking stock of all the critical decisions that the company routinely made. Using clarity and simplicity as her guideposts, she then reorganized the company based on where those decisions should reside. For example, while global teams organized by industry verticals had made pricing decisions, she moved the responsibility to local sales teams. She increased local account-ability while taking out several layers of middle management and nearly $1 billion of cost. Mulcahy also concentrated responsibility for the shift from analog to digital technology, simplifying the decision-making process for that crucial transition. Reorganizing based on where key decisions should be made was critical to Mulcahy's turnaround of Xerox.[25]

Alan Mulally took the same approach when he arrived as CEO at Ford in 2006 and began one of the greatest turnarounds in business history. The company had been steadily losing market share and des-perately needed change, but he didn't start with a reorganization. Instead, he focused on the key decisions that needed to be made and worked on making them better and faster—meeting with his team every week to track progress. Drawing the red thread to value allowed Mulally to establish global product platforms, for instance, which had been attempted but had failed previously, and the eventual reorganiza-tion flowed naturally from the emphasis on key decisions.[26]

Transform: Collaboration

25. Be one firm.

Profits are moving around these days, and companies need to hunt for them as a pack would, not as a bunch of disorganized individuals wandering in the woods. The music industry is the poster child for moving profits, given that profits quickly shifted from big record labels and physical distributors selling songs packaged in albums to, more or less, Steve Jobs's pockets as tracks were sold digitally and separately. For many recording artists, their songs may now just as well be ads to sell their concert tickets.

An even broader trend is now taking shape, where companies are being paid based on outcomes, not on the products they sell. We met a textbook publisher in Davos that is now being paid for students' results on exams, not for textbooks. Kimberly-Clark increasingly wants to be paid for customers' health and wellness, not for paper towels and other products.[27] Aviva Investors wants to be paid for meeting clients' life financial goals, not for outperforming its competitors on investment returns. Cisco now may get paid for optimizing customers' operations, not specifically for its equipment.

With the location of profits so fluid, you can't have, say, the text-book division insisting that it will price its products to generate profit when the profit has moved elsewhere. Everyone must contribute to the success of the whole firm, not just their function or business unit. Teams must collaborate.

To achieve that unity of purpose requires a "one firm" approach that goes well beyond culture and ends the Balkanization that afflicts so many companies today. The approach requires a set of concrete management practices consciously chosen to maximize the trust and loyalty that members of the organization feel both to the institution and to each other. Intercontinental Exchange, one of our superaccelerators, goes to great lengths to integrate everyone into the fabric of the firm, to the point of putting different sodas on different floors, so that you may have to go a distance to get your favorite—and bump into some colleagues along the way.

Elements of this approach include the following:

- Highly selective recruitment;
- A "grow your own" people strategy;
- Intensive use of training as a socialization process;
- Rejection of a "star system" and related individualistic behavior;
- Selective choice of services and markets, so as to win through significant investments in focused areas rather than through many small initiatives;
- Compensation based mostly on group performance, not individual performance;
- High investments in research and development; and
- Extensive internal communication, with broad use of consensus-building approaches.

The one-firm approach aims to achieve the highest levels of internal collaboration and mutual commitment in pursuing ambitious goals. Loyalty depends primarily on a strong culture and clear principles rather than on personal relations or the stature of individual members.

Everyone knows the values they must live by and the code of behavior they must follow. Everyone is trained intensively in these values and protocols. Everyone also knows that, if an individual is in trouble, the group will expend every effort to help him or her.

The one-firm approach contrasts with a more common approach, the "star-based" or "warlord" approach, which emphasizes individualism through internal competition, entrepreneurialism, distinct profit centers, and decentralized decision making. In extreme warlord firms, senior members operate as chieftains presiding over their own territories, coordinating occasionally but fundamentally without a commitment to the institution or each other.

Leadership in companies that operate as one is consensual. This does not mean that there are no differences of opinion among the members of the top team; however, the one-firm approach does require that, once a consensus has been reached, everybody will stand by it.

A one-firm company commonly will "grow its own" young talent. Professionals hired directly from school invariably have the strongest emotional ties to each other and to the firm. Young hires also tend to be nimble and energetic and embrace the teamwork culture and core values.

Acting as a one-firm company also improves the relationship with customers and other external stakeholders. Customers have access to all the resources in the organization because employees, rewarded through the overall success of the enterprise, are more comfortable bringing in other parts of the firm.

The one-firm approach makes it easier to survive market downturns. In such (inevitable) circumstances, members of a loyalty-based firm pull together and take pride and pleasure in doing so.

The approach can, however, be fragile in prosperous times. Executives can grow impatient with management's reluctance, for example, to hire willy-nilly to staff all the new opportunities. There is also a temptation to allow investments such as training to take a backseat to getting the work out the door. Only adherence to the firm's principles and values prevents opportunistic behavior that may have short-term benefits but long-term detriments.

WPP shows how powerful a one-firm approach can be. Martin Sorrell built the company into the largest advertising agency in the world through a series of audacious acquisitions of far-larger competitors but sometimes had trouble managing all the growth and complexity. He says that, in the 1990s, he began using a concept he calls "horizontality" to get all parts of the firm to work together. He has accelerated his emphasis on this centralized structure over the past decade in order to give clients access to resources from across WPP's various agencies and has found it greatly enhances results for customers. He writes that, for WPP's largest clients, "We've essentially created an agency within WPP—one that draws not only on ad agencies . . . but also on public relations people . . . and on market researchers and data specialists." He says 38,000 WPP employees now work for these very large accounts and generate $7 billion of revenue a year.[28]

26. **Build winning teams.**

Things slow when egos collide. Teach your people how to work in fluid, output-oriented teams. Drive toward shared values and diverse thinking. Fully harness the power of diverse thinking through robust dialogue.

David Cordani—the president and CEO of Cigna, one of our super-accelerators—gave us great insights into the value of dialogue. He says he spends a lot of time outside his office so he can get a direct read on people, face-to-face. When he talks to employees, he says, "The insights I take away from their comments and questions are telling: For example, are they thinking and acting like owners—or renters? Are they looking forward and setting the bar higher, or looking backward and trying to justify what happened in the past? Seldom do you come away with a singular 'aha' moment. But you can get a lot of pearls, and when you string them together, you have a lot of value."

27. Celebrate net exporters of talent.

Punish information hoarders. Stop providing incentives that encourage lone-hero behavior. Remove blockers. Make information transparent. Having the data and insight into drivers and outcomes for each team player prevents second-guessing, mistrust, and game playing.

"We don't have time for people who hoard insights or data," noted Comcast Cable's William Strahan. "When [organizations] inadvertently create incentives to squirrel away information and treat it as a personal asset—as opposed to a corporate asset—that's where things go sour."

In the interest of making information transparent, Whole Foods Market, the popular American supermarket chain, gives every employee access to company-wide salary information. Similarly, managers are required to post their store's sales data each day, along with regional sales each week. Once a month, Whole Foods sends each store a detailed report on its profitability and sales. The company's unique emphasis on transparency is in the interest of avoiding certain abuses that often occur under typical corporate structures. Co-CEO John Mackey introduced the open policy six years after founding the company, to foster a culture of "shared fate." He states, "If you're trying to create a high-trust organization, an organization where people are all-for-one and one-for-all, you can't have secrets."[29]

Bridgewater Associates goes even further. The hedge fund records every meeting (unless proprietary client information is involved) and makes the recordings available to everyone in the organization. If someone is mentioned in a meeting, that person is likely to be made aware of this, so he or she can review the recording.[30]

Agility: Foresight

28. Develop an early warning radar.

Systematically track what is going on outside and inside the organization to foresee what is going to affect the organization in the near future and how. Ensure that this foresight is shared across functions so that you can prepare for what's coming. Maintain communication channels with competitors, industry associations, and academics; keep a close eye on the rhythm of your workforce (which is getting both older and younger, with the arrival of the millennials and with the gray hairs working longer). Ensure that there is accountability for sensing and acting on weak signals by making unconventional connections among disparate events. Put your most creative people to work on "guessing the future."

Ping An Insurance Group has separated itself from its competitors in China's insurance industry through an early warning system that has allowed it to consistently be a pioneer. Ping An was the first to launch individual life insurance, the first to have an international auditor and international actuary, the first to have foreign capital, and the first to introduce an audit-claim system.

29. Think like a (good) activist.

Take responsibility for thinking ahead, before being prompted, to create a compelling value case for investing in the company's future. Shape the environment, culture, systems, and processes around you rather than being constrained by them. While activists aren't always popular, the best of them can push companies to look honestly at their businesses and unlock trapped value.

F. William McNabb III, chair and CEO of Vanguard, the world's largest mutual fund company, says the best boards think like activist investors. In his February 27, 2015, letter to independent directors, he wrote: "We've observed that the best boards work hard to develop 'self-awareness' and seek feedback and perspectives independent of management. They ask the right questions to understand how their company may be different than [their] peers and whether those differences are strengths or vulnerabilities."[31]

Without that challenge, executives can become complacent or overconfident in their belief that existing conditions will persist. Intel executives, for example, acknowledge that, even though they could see that devices would get smaller, they stayed in denial about the industry move toward tablets in recent years, simply because Intel's PC business was so profitable.[32]

30. Assume uncertainties.

Do not let the unknown slow you down. Assume that what you don't know for sure will happen, and develop contingency plans to be able to deal with whatever is thrown at your organization, minimizing disruption to the business rhythm and allowing for resources to be deployed quickly and seamlessly to address the emerging situation.

In July 2016, less than a month after the United Kingdom's EU membership referendum and during a period of both considerable political and economic uncertainty, Japan's SoftBank announced its planned acquisition of ARM Holdings, a U.K. chip designer with a keen interest in the burgeoning Internet of Things (IoT) industry. Masayoshi Son, founder and CEO of SoftBank, a superaccelerator, saw the shift toward the Internet of Things as outweighing the uncertainty surrounding Brexit. "I did not make the investment because of Brexit. I decided [to view] the paradigm shift as the opportunity," Son told reporters. "I would have made this decision at this time regardless if Brexit happened or did not happen."[33]

Agility: Learning

31. **Systematically learn from mistakes; fail fast with confidence.**

   Implement mechanisms that prevent disruptions from causing extreme malfunction or catastrophic collapse. Conduct a postmortem on every mistake so that the organization can quickly adopt what worked and avoid what did not. Codify what you learn, and make it readily available to everybody in the organization so that the learning becomes part of doing business. Do not punish those who fail. On the contrary, invite people to fail, but fast and with conviction so that the organization does not waste resources pursuing ideas that are doomed to fail in the end. Make deliberate "mistakes" as part of the innovation process—for example, try an ad that you don't think will work or hire some people you don't think meet your criteria, to see if you learn something new or gain a new perspective.

   The idea of learning while failing fast has become the order of the day in Silicon Valley. Seemingly every company talks about coming out with a "minimally viable product," which gets to market far faster than products traditionally have but which is expected to fail. The idea is to give customers just enough to react to so the producer can figure out how to improve quickly in the next version and the one after that and the one after that.

   Intuit shows how to make sure that people know it's okay to fail. It tried a marketing campaign aimed at young adults that would let them get tax refunds as gift cards to retailers. The campaign generated almost no interest—but also cost almost no money. The company founder gave the team an award for generating learning and said, "It is only a failure if we fail to get the learning."[34]

32. **Implement rituals for regular learning and adapting.**

   The organization as a whole has to have rituals in place for people to regularly learn so that they can adapt their ways. Encourage sharing of experiences and learnings through as many media as you can. Make sure that your technology platform supports a learning environment so that people can constantly adapt the way they work to the things they are learning. Ensure that people can unlearn as fast as they can learn. With things changing so fast, it is becoming increasingly important to be able to let go of what we know in order to embrace totally new approaches.

The American Medical Association (AMA) is trying to reinvent medical education in the United States through a series of pilot programs at medical schools that regularly share information on best practices. Students complain, for instance, that it no longer makes sense for them to memorize reams of data on dosages when they can look up the dosages on their smartphones, so schools are experimenting with revised curricula. The AMA notes that it takes more than 15 years for something settled as scientific fact—such as the benefit of taking a daily aspirin to reduce the risk of heart attack—to be put into practice through the medical community, so the AMA is also working on continuing education that will help doctors unlearn things they "know."

33. Live on the learning edge.

Learning never stops. Encourage your organization to always be on the lookout for new things that people can learn to improve the company's operations and the way it satisfies its customers' needs. Ask employees to question what they know, and hire them as much for their ability to learn as for their ability to unlearn what they know and learn something completely different.

Intel, despite its decades of success, is not immune from making mistakes and spends considerable time trying to learn from what it got wrong. The board looked into a series of venture investments that, from the outside, had generally been seen as neutral to positive and found them wanting. The board developed procedures that led to additional reviews. For major initiatives, the board came up with what it called "half-baked" ideas—the notion being that CEOs generally bring only "fully baked" ideas to a board, which means the board can only vote yes or no and not provide much input; instead, the Intel board instructed the CEO to bring forward ideas when they were only half-baked, with the assurance that the resulting discussion would be in the spirit of exploration and that no one would accuse him of a lack of preparation.

Remember that just because you're living on the learning edge now, or you aren't, this doesn't mean that you'll always stay in that position. Dell's manufacturing agility made it the toast of the technology world in the late 1990s and early 2000s, but it has lost its luster. Meanwhile, IBM, dominant for so many decades, lost its way in the PC era, found it again when the tech world moved toward software and services, and is now facing challenges again.

Agility: Adaptability

34. **Improve or atomize the corporate center.**

    The corporate center must remain an important part of the business but only if it helps the company achieve its acceleration objectives. Although centralized roles such as the CFO and the chief human resources officer (CHRO) will always be crucial, if the corporate center is slowing things down due to increased bureaucracy and control, organizations need to find a way to improve it. Atomizing the corporate center is one way to ensure that there is not too much concentration of power.

    Haier, China's largest appliance maker, with more than $30 billion in annual sales, decided that its corporate center was getting in the way of its diverse businesses, so it eliminated 2,500 jobs there and now operates as a confederation of businesses. Haier has just 15 people at the corporate center.

    Gary Hamel and Michele Zanini argue that the U.S. economy alone would grow by $3 trillion if bureaucracy could be whacked away. They cite Haier as an exemplar, along with Handelsbanken, which has only three tiers of management, and GE, which has an aviation plant in North Carolina where one manager oversees 300 employees. Hamel and Zanini say there are 12.5 million unnecessary managers and administrators at U.S. companies, along with 8.9 million "paper-pushing subordinates" whose posts could be eliminated.[35]

35. **Maintain an immutable core, and make everything else around it flexible.**

    As most people know, the key to maintaining flexibility in your body is to have a strong core. The same is true of organizations. To become truly agile and accelerated, organizations need to pinpoint those elements that will remain immutable at the core so that they constitute the strength that will support flexible parts of the organization. Without a strong core, flexibility becomes wobbliness and organizations can't accelerate.

    Manufacturers are having to show great flexibility these days. While it was once a no-brainer for companies in, say, the United States and Europe to move manufacturing offshore to take advantage of low wages, companies now think in terms of ONO—offshoring, nearshoring, and outsourcing. Changes in customer expectations have forced many companies to be able to respond faster to new demand than is possible if manufacturing is done in, say, China. A backlash against free trade has created uncertainty about trade agreements. Energy prices have tilted in favor of the United States, where fracking has lowered costs for manufacturers, but the future is highly uncertain. In this sort of environment, companies need to know what they stand for and stay flexible on the who and where of manufacturing.

36. Develop digital dexterity.

As digital technology takes over our lives, digital skill sets must continually be refreshed to keep up not only with information technology in general but also with 3-D printing, cognitive computing, ubiquitous sensors and cameras, the Internet of Things, and all the other opportunities that keep appearing. Otherwise, skill sets can rapidly become as obsolete as an old Nokia flip phone.

For instance, 74 percent of consumers now rely on social media to influence their purchases,[36] and 71 percent say that, if they receive a quick response from a company on social media, they are likely to recommend the brand to others.[37] Secure cloud technologies are also creating opportunities to deliver an enhanced customer experience. Companies in industries as diverse as utilities, automotive, and airlines have started recognizing the importance of understanding their end users better. They know they must merge the digital and analog worlds—because their customers already have.

State-of-the-art digital skill sets are essential—from embedding technology in products to harvesting business solutions from massive data sets. A new breed of digital talent is urgently needed to deliver on high customer expectations.

Take Tesla. Through technological sophistication, Tesla has radically outperformed its competitors. Tesla's cars are built with wireless networking devices to deliver real-time customer data to the company, and Tesla attributes its high levels of customer satisfaction to its relentless attention to the analysis of this data. The wireless connection also lets Tesla send software updates to its cars overnight.

Paresh Sukthankar, deputy managing director at HDFC Bank, one of our superaccelerators, says, "We have fully embraced the digital revolution. We leverage data analytics and straight-through processing to enhance customer convenience and speed up turnaround times. For example, we have a product called the 10-second loan. Eligible customers can apply for personal loans on the bank's Internet platform, and while the customer is still in the NetBanking session, the loan would be approved and disbursed into the account. We seek to be the easiest and most trusted bank in the world to do business with."

To become a truly digital organization, companies need to go beyond disruptive business models and digital technology platforms. They should also focus on creating a digital culture and a widespread understanding of the relevance of digital dexterity. Domino's Pizza, for instance, has gone digital to the point that someone can order a pizza via an emoji in a text. "You can order on your Apple Watch," says Russell Weiner, U.S. president of Domino's. "You can order on your TV.

If something exists that's a platform, you can order Domino's pizza on it."[38] You can also track the order from the time you place the call until it arrives at your door.

The following is a list of possible actions that your organization can take to increase its level of digital dexterity:

1. Use a single frame of reference to coordinate a digital agenda and strategy for all business activities.
2. Have flat hierarchies to enable greater flexibility of work and fast decision making.
3. Establish a digital manager responsible for coordinating the implementation of the digital agenda across the whole company.
4. Experiment with digital business ideas via spin-offs, incubators, and purchases of start-ups.
5. Extend functional digital skills, especially in technology, project management, and marketing.
6. Support flexible networks within the company as well as external interaction with digital companies; promote the exchange of know-how.
7. Establish a culture of adaptive experimentation and learning.
8. Establish a culture that permits mistakes (i.e., making mistakes as part of a flexible, iterative approach).
9. Digitize the HR department (e.g., by creating a digital HR agenda, by training HR people on digital skills and improving the overall digital understanding, and by improving HR tools and administrative processes).
10. Review the digital skill set in the organization, define gaps, and build appropriate training programs.
11. Use digital technologies, e.g., in recruiting and onboarding.
12. Adapt performance management, compensation and benefits, and so on to new requirements in digital times.

There are signs of progress. In 2013, in a survey of executives, 57 percent of respondents said their CEO advocated for digital; that number surged to 71 percent in 2014 and climbed again, to 73 percent, in 2015. Interest in digital has spread throughout the organization: Today, 68 percent of technology spending flows from budgets outside of IT, way up from 47 percent in 2014.[39] But the progress must continue.

Agility: Resilience

37. Recover quickly and on the move; don't stop or reduce pace.

It is a natural tendency when something "bad" happens to slow down, take some time to think about what just happened, learn from it, regroup, and then start again. In a volatile and unpredictable world, however, recovery has to happen on the go. If an event is so traumatic that you absolutely have to stop or reduce pace, minimize the way the slowing down affects the organization by isolating the situation and dedicating resources to solving it as quickly as possible. Set local rules of interaction, and identify how successes and failures can be shared with the broader organization.

SpaceX, which launched the first-ever commercial spaceflight to dock with the International Space Station, had a series of initial failures but continues plunging ahead because a loss of momentum could ruin the company's prospects. SpaceX iterates rapidly to recover from failure and solves its problems, quite literally, on the fly. It has now landed rockets on land and on platforms in the ocean, milestones that will allow it to send rockets into space and then reuse them, drastically reducing the cost of space travel.[40]

38. Keep your people healthy.

The physical, mental, and emotional state of your people determines their ability to win the race. Be in tune with their mood so you can appreciate and support them to be successful. Good benefits are table stakes these days; you need to free people to enjoy their lives outside the office while fully committing to their work.

Pharmaceutical company Allergan is deeply committed to the health and financial and personal well-being of its employees. The company offers an incredible array of benefits that people can choose from to ensure that they are taking care of their health and well-being, including expansive volunteer benefits. The design of these benefits is clearly aligned with the ways things are done in the organization: They are easy to use and have a direct impact on the staff.

UBS has created a program for its investment bankers called "take two" to improve work-life balance. Bankers, known for a workaholic culture of all-nighters and high stress, are allowed to take at least two hours of personal time a week. Similarly, JPMorgan Chase recently began encouraging its investment bankers to take weekends off "unless they're working on a major deal."[41]

39. Lean in.

Use stress not as a source of anxiety and retrenchment but as an opportunity to galvanize the organization, generate energy, and lean in to keep going. You need to establish coping rituals that will allow people to accept setbacks while avoiding the loss of momentum that a bad moment may bring with it. But you also have to learn whatever you can from setbacks, avoiding the corporate amnesia that afflicts so many.

Virgin Group's charismatic founder, Richard Branson, epitomizes how to keep an organization moving despite setbacks. He's had some big ones, too. The most notable was an attempt at a cola that would displace Coke, which he unveiled by driving a tank into Times Square in New York City. Others have included a chain of bridal shops that also failed. He helps the organization cope by continuing to move forward, showing zero loss of confidence. He mocks his failures—for instance, taking out a full-page newspaper ad after an attempt to set the speed record for crossing the Atlantic by boat ended with the boat sinking and the crew needing a rescue 300 miles off the coast of the United Kingdom; the ad showed the hull sticking out of the water and carried the caption, "Next time, Richard, take the plane." He says his nickname is "Dr. Yes," because he's always approving new ideas.[42]

■ ■ ■

Each industrial revolution has given us a new approach to organization. The first, started by James Watt's steam engine in the 1700s, led to the factory, among other innovations. The second, in the late 1800s, driven largely by electricity, led to much larger businesses (including Sloan's General Motors) and to command-and-control structures. The current revolution, driven by disruptive digital technologies, is leading us toward more distributed management structures, where information, values, and certain rules are centralized but where decisions are increasingly made at a corporation's edges, near the customer. As a result, strategy and organization are increasingly intertwined—an effective organization is an effective strategy, and vice versa. While the current revolution can't yet be characterized in as simple of terms as "factory" or "command and control," these 39 actions will move you toward whatever the breakthrough model turns out to be and will deliver a lot of value along the way.

Notes

1. Some academics think that the sort of A/B testing that has become common among start-ups—where they rush "minimally viable products" to market and then see what works and what doesn't—can help in organizational structures as well. For more, see Ethan Bernstein, "The Organization Lab (o-Lab): How might we create the next iteration of our organizations?" Harvard Business School Digital Initiative, March 15, 2016, medium.com.
2. Lambert Walsh, "Transforming Adobe's customer experiences," *Adobe*, June 21, 2011, blogs.adobe.com/conversations/2011/06/transforming -adobe's-customer-experiences.html.
3. Phil Wahba, "Target has a new CEO: Will he re-energize the retailer?" *Fortune*, March 1, 2015, fortune.com.

4. Martin Reeves, Knut Haanaes, and Janmejaya Sinha, *Your Strategy Needs a Strategy: How to Choose and Execute the Right Approach*, Boston: Harvard Business Review Press, 2015.

5. First Round Review, "Letting go of efficiency can accelerate your company—here's how," *People & Culture*, January 21, 2015, firstround.com/review.

6. Tony Hsieh, *Delivering Happiness: A Path to Profits, Passion, and Purpose*, New York: Grand Central Publishing, 2010.

7. James H. Gilmore, "The uncommon practice of common purpose," *strategy+business* April 2, 2010, strategy-business.com.

8. Chris Outram, *Digital Stractics: How Strategy Met Tactics and Killed the Strategic Plan*, London: Palgrave Macmillan, 2015.

9. John Ruskin, *Modern Painters*, New York: Bryan, Taylor & Company, 1894.

10. Robert H. Miles, "Accelerating corporate transformations (Don't lose your nerve!)," *Harvard Business Review*, January–February 2010, hbr.org.

11. Adam Grant, *Give and Take*, New York: Viking, 2013.

12. Lisa Earle McLeod, *Leading with Noble Purpose: How to Create a Tribe of True Believers*, Hoboken, NJ: John Wiley & Sons, 2016.

13. Daniel H. Pink, *Drive: The Surprising Truth About What Motivates Us*, New York: Riverhead Books, 2009.

14. George L. Roth and Art Kleiner, "Danaher's instruments of change," *strategy+business*, February 8, 2016, strategy-business.com.

15. Gillian Tett, *The Silo Effect: The Peril of Expertise and the Promise of Breaking Down Barriers*, New York: Simon & Schuster, 2015.

16. Martin Arnold, "Deutsche Bank to rip out IT systems blamed for problems," *Financial Times*, October 26, 2015, ft.com.

17. Gillian Tett, *The Silo Effect: The Peril of Expertise and the Promise of Breaking Down Barriers*, New York: Simon & Schuster, 2015.

18. Ron Ashkenas, "Simplicity-minded management," *Harvard Business Review*, December 2007, hbr.org.

19. Dave Girouard, "Speed as a habit," *Management*, July 22, 2015, firstround.com/review.

20. Patrick M. Lencioni, "Make your values mean something," *Harvard Business Review*, July 2002, hbr.org.

21. Martin Reeves and Mike Deimler, "Adaptability: The new competitive advantage," *Harvard Business Review*, July–August 2011, hbr.org.

22. Lynda Gratton and Andrew Scott, *The 100-Year Life: Living and Working in an Age of Longevity*, New York: Bloomsbury Information, 2016.

23. Rosabeth Moss Kanter, "Innovation: The classic traps," *Harvard Business Review*, November 2006, hbr.org.

24. Lisa Bodell, "10 disruptive questions for instant innovation," *Forbes*, October 4, 2013, forbes.com.

25. Marcia W. Blenko, Michael C. Mankins, and Paul Rogers, "The decision-driven organization," *Harvard Business Review*, June 2010, hbr.org.

26. Marcia W. Blenko, Michael C. Mankins, and Paul Rogers, "The decision-driven organization," *Harvard Business Review*, June 2010, hbr.org.

27. Amanda Setili, *The Agility Advantage: How to Identify and Act on Opportunities in a Fast-Changing World*, San Francisco: Jossey-Bass, 2014.

28. Martin Sorrell, "WPP's CEO on turning a portfolio of companies into a growth machine," *Harvard Business Review*, July–August 2016, hbr.org.

29. Alison Griswold, "Here's why Whole Foods lets employees look up each other's salaries," *Business Insider*, March 3, 2014, businessinsider.com.

30. Robert Kegan and Lisa Laskow Lahey, *An Everyone Culture: Becoming a Deliberately Developmental Organization,* Boston: Harvard Business Review Press, 2016.

31. F. William McNabb III, letter to the independent leaders of the boards of directors, Vanguard, February 27, 2015, about.vanguard.com/vanguard-proxy-voting/CEO_Letter_03_02_ext.pdf.

32. Amanda Setili, *The Agility Advantage: How to Identify and Act on Opportunities in a Fast-Changing World,* San Francisco: Jossey-Bass, 2014.

33. Arjun Kharpal, "Brexit, weaker pound didn't influence $32 billion bid for ARM: Softbank CEO," *CNBC*, July 18, 2016, cnbc.com.

34. Martin Reeves and Mike Deimler, "Adaptability: The new competitive advantage," *Harvard Business Review*, July–August 2011, hbr.org.

35. Andrew Hill, "Business: How to topple bureaucracy," *Financial Times*, April 14, 2016, ft.com.

36. ODM Group, "The business of social media," infographic, November 3, 2011, odmgrp.com/blog/2011/11/03/infographic-the-business-of-social-media.

37. See Lisa Wirthman, "Why businesses should listen to customers on social media," *Forbes*, August 8, 2015, forbes.com.

38. "One million pizzas a day: How Domino's keeps it fresh," interview with Russell Weiner on the *Knowledge@Wharton* show on Wharton Business Radio, June 30, 2016, knowledge.wharton.upenn.edu.

39. Juan Pujadas, "Why a CEO's digital IQ matters," *strategy+business*, June 26, 2016, strategy-business.com.

40. Loren Grush, "SpaceX successfully lands its rocket on a floating drone ship for the first time," *The Verge*, April 8, 2016, theverge.com.

41. Anjuli Davies and Pamela Barbaglia, "RPT-UBS tells bankers 'take two' in bid to get the balance right," *Reuters*, June 2, 2016, uk.reuters.com.

42. Rod Kurtz, "Richard Branson on dealing with setbacks," *Entrepreneur*, January 21, 2013, entrepreneur.com.

CHAPTER 8

Accelerating Teams
Capability Equals Ability Minus Ego

From 2012 to 2016, the chief operating officer (COO) of the U.K.'s Nationwide Building Society, Tony Prestedge, built and led one of the most successful leadership teams in its 170-year history. It wasn't always easy. It wasn't always pretty. But with resilience and determination, he followed an orchestrated and thoughtful program of team development, and it paid off.

At the time of this writing, in the first quarter of 2016, Nationwide was ranked number one for customer service satisfaction among its peers. Nationwide has assets of around £210 billion (about $279 billion), making it larger than the remaining 44 British building societies combined. In 2016, Nationwide appeared third in *The Sunday Times'* "Best 25 Big Companies to Work For" poll. For the 2015–2016 year, profits rose 23 percent.

What Prestedge accomplished at Nationwide underscores our premise that organizations are a collection of teams and that teams are the engines of the organization—the performance of an organization critically depends on teams at every level. In today's new normal of constant disruption and fleeting competitive advantage, performance depends on the ability of teams to accelerate. They must mobilize around a simple set of strategic priorities efficiently, harness resources, experiment, and innovate ahead of the market. Teams must also spot opportunities and threats and pivot faster than their competitors. But—and it's a big but—many teams struggle.

As we described in Chapter 4, our research found that acceleration is not a naturally occurring phenomenon for most teams—only 13 percent of the teams we studied could be defined as accelerating, whereas roughly 27 percent were lagging or outright derailing.

Lagging and derailing teams experience many if not all of the drag factors for teams, which are listed in Figure 8.1.

However, when teams get these factors right, our analysis found that being an accelerating team, as opposed to a derailing team, explains 13 percent variance in performance. Across all the teams we studied, accelerating

FIGURE 8.1 Drag factors for teams

Mobilize

Internal focus	Unclear goals	Competing agendas	Confusion
No shared ownership for resolving service failures	Misalignment Confusion about the team's contribution to the organization	Too many priorities Too many conflicting personal agendas	Unclear long-term strategic direction Overly focused on today's problems

Execute

Loose composition	Unclear accountabilities	Unreliability	Poor commissioning
Key gaps in the team's skills and experience Difficulty attracting and retaining talent in the team	Failure to address the performance of team members who are not pulling their weight	Inefficient use of the team's time Gap between what the team says and what it does	Getting involved in activities that should be delegated to others Moving from one distraction to another

Transform

Unaligned stakeholders	Overconcentrated leadership	Aggression	Biased decisions
No real insight into the wants and needs of stakeholders Inability to influence stakeholders effectively	Tendency for the team leader to micromanage or manage team members individually	Outright hostility or artificial harmony, undermining the team's effectiveness	Specific team members dominating conversations and distorting decision making Date-free decisions

Agility

Hindsight	Immunity	Inflexibility	Frailty
Not enough time given to exploring the big issues Resistance to new ideas	Failure to change things that aren't working Frequently repeated mistakes	Changing direction, reprioritizing, and testing new ideas too late	Highlighting the negatives Victim mentality

teams, on average, had an economic impact 22.8 percent higher than that of derailing teams. Higher-performing teams get the drive factors of acceleration, shown in Figure 8.2, in place and working for them.

To understand where teams are working well and where there is room for improvement, we designed the TAQ to measure the 16 drive factors that our research has shown are critical to team acceleration and that align with the META framework (Figure 8.3).

FIGURE 8.2 Drive factors for teams

Mobilize

Customer first	**Unique commission**	**Shared purpose**	**Clear direction**
Creation of value for customers at the center of what the team does	Deep understanding of the expectations of the team's stakeholders, and the stakeholders' backing to achieve those expectations	Clear purpose with mutual commitment from team members to deliver the team's priorities	The team sets, and prioritizes, an inspiring vision and strategy for the organization

Execute

Tight composition	**Explicit accountabilities**	**Uncompromising standards**	**Focused grip**
Fit-for-purpose structure, made up of team members with the necessary mix of skills and experience	Clear performance metrics aligned with strategy, reinforcing individual and collective accountabilities	Strong principles and values Unrelenting focus on professional standards	Rigor in how the team contracts with the organization and matches critical resources to the biggest opportunities

Transform

Stakeholder influence	**Distributed leadership**	**Robust challenge**	**Disciplined decisions**
Proactive shaping of the external environment through building, maintaining, and engaging key strategic relationships	Leader ensures full team participation Members take on challenges on behalf of the team	Climate of support and trust that enables team members to be candid and challenge each other	Clear decision rights and responsibilities Seamless information sharing and governance mechanisms

Agility

Foresight	**Learning**	**Adaptability**	**Resilience**
Scanning the environment for fresh ideas Anticipation of changing circumstances Rethinking of assumptions	Capability building for the future Quick absorption and implementation of new learnings	Quick responses to changes in circumstances Experimenting and failing fast to move with speed	Risk taking and energizing the team to attempt ambitious goals Overcoming barriers to delivery

For each team we work with, the TAQ provides a "heat map" set of scores showing where the team is on all 16 factors, on each of the four components of META, and on overall team performance (Figure 8.4).

Each score lets a team know if they are accelerating, advancing, steady, lagging, or derailing. This set of scores gives such a clear picture that a team can focus on the key set of interventions needed to shift the dial on the performance of their team and construct a journey to suit the industry context, the organizational strategy, and the team ambition.

FIGURE 8.3 The TAQ model

FIGURE 8.4 A sample TAQ heat map

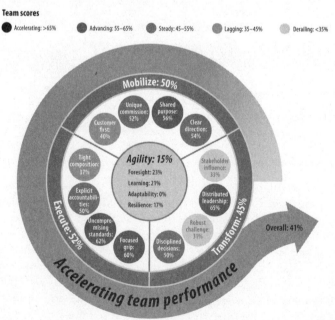

Each team is unique, and which actions will provide the greatest impact need to be considered in light of the TAQ heat map. But, working with teams across all industries and levels, we found that each of the 16 drive factors is underpinned by two actions that in most situations will make the biggest difference (Figure 8.5).

FIGURE 8.5 Differentiating actions for teams

Mobilize

Customer first	Unique commission	Shared purpose	Clear direction
Have a "seat at the table" for your customers	Be clear on who measures the team and how they measure it	Ensure the team's purpose is clear and aligned with that of the organization	Ensure an agreed-upon, focused, and coherent direction
Start first with customer metrics in the team scorecard	Align the team's priorities with the expectations of its stakeholders	Ensure enterprise-wide thinking and accountability	Work on what only the team can do; delegate the rest

Execute

Tight composition	Explicit accountabilities	Uncompromising standards	Focused grip
Mix and match team members to best fit roles	Have only the right skill and will in the team	Be single minded in the pursuit of priorities and execution rhythms	Be transparently clear on what is required from whom
Get good at onboarding and offboarding team members	Eliminate gaps and overlaps in accountabilities	Be ruthless in how you manage the team's time together	Match critical resources to your biggest opportunities

Transform

Stakeholder influence	Distributed leadership	Robust challenge	Disciplined decisions
Manage your stakeholders as if they were customers	Speak with one voice	Ruthlessly hold each other to account and stretch each other's thinking	Ensure total transparency on who gets to decide what
Create a compelling call to action and build partnering skills	Make sure decisions and actions happen at the right level	Understand each other as people as well as colleagues	Assess and manage risk to maximize performance

Agility

Foresight	Learning	Adaptability	Resilience
Find and leverage difference of perspective	Use the power of doubt and curiosity to continuously develop the team	Implement rituals for testing assumptions and questioning fact-free optimism	Find ways to actively manage the energy of the team
Red-circle time to fully explore the big issues	Evaluate the team's performance from many points of view	Build the team's capability to experiment and fail fast	Reframe setbacks and challenges as opportunities for growth

So let's use the journey of Prestedge and his team over the last four years to explore the differentiating actions—from each META drive factor—that made the most difference.

At the start of the process, the TAQ showed that the Nationwide team was far from perfect. Even in 2015, the picture was mixed. Six of the drive factors were in the accelerating range and three in the advancing category, but the other drivers were weaker.

Prestedge is a very strong leader, intelligent, and extremely quick to make decisions and act but also quick to impatience. At times he favored a directive leadership style; he had worked on this issue for the four years of the development program, but it remained a work in progress. Without coaching and space to lead, it was unlikely his team members would be able to step fully into a distributed leadership model.

In addition, there had been enormous amounts of core operating transformations to pull off and cost challenges to meet from 2011 onward. This full-on delivery mandate meant that heads were down; people were focused on pulling off minor miracles, not on building team performance.

In many ways, productive conflict has been the archnemesis for this team throughout its development—not being brave enough to name issues or provide challenge, not being skilled enough to challenge well or to handle challenge without defensiveness, and not being able to repair when team ruptures occurred.

With the status quo understood, the Nationwide team turned to the first step in META: mobilize.

Mobilize

When teams mobilize, they are aligned and inspire those they lead to act in line with a compelling purpose and a clear set of strategic priorities.

Customer First

First, teams need to be able to put the customer—and, more important, the creation of value for the customer—at the center of everything they do. The team must gear its measurement systems to continuously anticipating its customers' changing needs. Accelerating teams immerse themselves in the customer experience and often engage in co-innovation with customers.

Thyagi Thyagarajan, an independent director at Tata Consultancy Services, says TCS employees "have no fear of being fired by the company. There's fear of being fired or rejected by the *customer*. If the customer is unhappy, that's what employees fear."

In contrast, poorly performing teams don't align their internal processes and metrics with customer needs and take little heed of customer feedback. They worry about financial targets and internally focused key performance indicators (KPIs), which can distance them from their customers. And when service failures or spikes in customer attrition occur, low-performing teams tend to deflect responsibility.

We have found in our research that the further a team is away from the customer, the harder that team must work to accelerate its performance. Teams that have their purpose for existence "in their faces"—that is, customer-facing teams—are 1.4 times more likely to be within reach of their goals compared with internally focused teams. In addition, customer-facing teams score significantly higher on 14 of the 16 drive factors of acceleration. So finding ways to bring customers into the room for those senior teams that do not naturally face the customer becomes even more important.

Unique Commission

Second, mobilizing cannot happen if the team doesn't also have a deep and common understanding of the expectations of its stakeholders and have their backing to deliver what it is being asked. A clear commission is a foundational element supporting a team's ability to accelerate, and the power base such a commission provides can be instrumental in helping teams anticipate and dismantle potential roadblocks.

Shared Purpose

Third, the team needs a shared understanding of why it exists. Of course it exists to deliver customer experience, revenue, margin, growth, and so on, but you could put five different leadership teams at the top of an organization and find that the purpose for each is very different. Given that purpose drives us individually and taps into our discretionary effort, teams need to do the work to ensure that all team members have a shared purpose. Otherwise, team members may go into the parts of the organization they lead and drive toward their individual purpose, which may well be at odds with the purpose held dear by their colleagues. This is a surefire way to dissipate effort and confuse people with conflicting agendas.

Lack of shared purpose also encourages the pursuit of individual—not team—priorities. Indeed, 49 percent of the 3,000 teams we studied cited "allowing priorities to pull in different directions" as getting in the way of acceleration.

Yet when teams enjoy a strong sense of shared purpose, they are more likely to focus on collective goals. Thyagarajan says that TCS benefits because "the senior team has all grown up together. They don't second-guess each other. There's a lot of freedom given to people to run the business, and there's a lot of trust in their ability to make decisions on the spot. They see that collective success is more important than individual success. The competitiveness is not bitter, personal, one guy trying to take the other out. It's quite a remarkable thing that they've been able to have that culture for so many years."

Clear Direction

Finally, the team needs to be very clear in the direction it pursues. Becoming caught up in "troubleshooter" mode is one of the most common constraints on acceleration. Instead, teams should focus tightly on doing the work they (and only they) are best placed to do—and delegate away the rest.

Insights from Nationwide

Busy schedules, long task lists, and pressures to perform all mean that, at times, teams are busy spinning their wheels but not stopping long enough to understand where they are trying to go, so they have trouble with shared purpose. The situation can be very much like the A. A. Milne picture of Winnie-the-Pooh: "Here is Edward Bear, coming downstairs now, bump, bump, bump, on the back of his head, behind Christopher Robin. It is, as far as he knows, the only way of coming downstairs, but sometimes he feels that there really is another way, if only he could stop bumping for a moment and think of it." Teams need to spend time away from their offices, to-do lists, and phones to have productive discussions about their stakeholders and their expectations, the purpose of the team and what it wants to be known for, how the team would decide what not to do as well as what to focus on, and so on. This is even more important in a team with new members.

Many senior team leaders and CEOs will recognize the following phenomenon: The team sits around the table making key decisions, everyone apparently nodding their assent; to any observer—including the team leader—everyone leaves the room in alignment. Team members then go out into the organization and do the complete opposite of what has been agreed upon. This is the "nodding dog syndrome." At its root is often a lack of quality time spent on aligning the team and ensuring that its purpose has a strong and clear red thread to the strategy of the organization.

Prestedge and his team focused on shared purpose and excelled at it. In 2012, they were a semi-"greenfield" team, with some members stepping up to new roles and with new members being recruited from very different organizations and industries. Investing in himself and in the performance of the team were the twin pillars that Prestedge established to deliver on his strategy and objectives.

The first two-day off-site meeting of the team was dedicated to ensuring a common understanding of the company strategy and context and identifying and aligning around a purpose for the team. That purpose was to "Deliver great service and execute the group's operational strategy at optimal cost." Underneath that headline were five accountabilities of the group operations team. Underneath those accountabilities were seven objectives, including a shared-services model for the back office that would integrate an offshore center and deliver much greater agility. And that was just 2012–2013.

Over the following four years, Prestedge continued to drive for pace and impact as he, among other things, reinvented the operating model. In off-site sessions and in regular governance meetings, the critical work of focusing on shared purpose was constantly front and center.

Execute

Mobilizing, by its very definition, is getting ready for something. But that's only the start.

Tight Composition

The first of the four drive factors of great execution is tight composition. Teams that get this right have a fit-for-purpose structure, made up of team members with the necessary mix of skills and experience to deliver the agenda at pace. Getting this team in place and quickly is key to acceleration. Because life never stands still, and neither do the organizations we work within, being able to regularly restructure the team to deliver on new challenges, priorities, and opportunities is essential.

Meg Whitman, CEO of Hewlett Packard Enterprise and former CEO of eBay, says it in a nutshell: "You can always move faster than you think you can to get the team in place. . . . I wish I had moved faster." She adds, "At eBay, someone who was perfect when it was a $40 million company was not quite so perfect when it grew to $4 billion."[1]

In practice, this means the leader needs to keep moving team members into different roles but also has to be up to the task of closing key gaps through adding members or removing those who no longer are the right fit. To benefit from this drive factor, a team must do everything it can to attract and retain talent. Organizations often go wrong on the talent issue because they don't understand top talent well enough. A study of 20,000 people identified as top performers at more than 100 organizations found that, even though companies had identified them and tried to nurture them, 1 in 4 expects to leave within a year; 1 in 3 admits to withholding effort; 1 in 5 has personal aspirations that diverge significantly from the company's; and 4 in 10 have little confidence in their colleagues and even less confidence in senior management.[2] While emerging stars have great talent, they also have huge ambitions—and plenty of opportunities at other companies. So senior leaders have to get personally involved in developing talent and in ensuring that high performers stay engaged.

Even when the talent is right, team composition sometimes goes wonderfully right and other times horribly wrong. Friction causes drag in physics, and the same is true on teams.

Geoffrey Colvin's story on Michael Eisner shows how the former CEO of Disney wound up at both ends of the spectrum. Colvin writes, "For the first ten years of his reign at Disney, he and COO Frank Wells formed one of corporate America's great teams. On their watch, Disney revived its glorious animation tradition, and the movie business flourished." This partnership ended when Wells died tragically in a helicopter crash in 1994. Eisner then formed one of the most famously disastrous teams, bringing in Michael Ovitz as president. He lasted only 14 months. Colvin describes how Ovitz wanted to pursue ideas that Eisner saw as off-strategy. Ovitz also spent $2 million giving his office a makeover. The result was a very expensive team failure in terms of both money and reputation.[3] This partnership ended in a letter from Eisner to Ovitz in which he listed all of Ovitz's shortcomings and concluded with the following sentences: "It cannot work. And I want it to end as soon as possible. I want you to direct your energies to how to exit, not how to cure."[4]

Explicit Accountabilities

The second driver—explicit accountabilities—is a close cousin to tight composition. Most progress charts are splattered with more red than the scene of a murder. People need clarity on what they are to deliver if they are to have a half-decent chance of delivering it. The team leader must design the team, including composition, structure, roles, and accountabilities.

Clear performance metrics for the team collectively and individually for its members need to be aligned with the strategy, and decisive actions need to be taken on an ongoing basis to reinforce accountabilities, eliminating gaps and overlaps. Many teams suffer from performance metrics that have grown over time and that have ended up being overly complex. This needs to get sorted out and quickly.

Matt Brittin, Google's president of EMEA business and operations, told us: "I'm often saying to our teams: Act like an owner, and win as a team. Acting like an owner is saying that nobody knows your area at Google better than you do, so you should be the person saying, 'This is what we must do.' That might apply whether you're managing our operations in Italy or whether you are building some innovative app around image recognition and photographs. You should know your stuff better than anybody else. And you should think, 'Well, what would I do if I was Larry Page? What would I do if I was the owner?' The converse of that is that nobody can bring all of the resources of our organization to bear on that problem. Therefore, we also need to have a culture that really encourages collaboration. You want people to ask for help, and you want a culture where offering help is the norm. By doing these two things—acting like owners and winning as teams—I think we can really try to keep that innovative start-up–style spirit but also combine it with the resources and the capability of a much larger organization. It's very easy, otherwise, for companies to get bogged down with complexity."

Uncompromising Standards

Third, a team must live up to uncompromising standards, established in a clear set of principles. A core enabler of this driver is being ruthless in how the team's time together is used and being rigorous in the pursuit of priorities. In contentious situations, participants may quickly become protagonists, so excellent execution rhythms need to be adopted.

One of these principles needs to be speaking truth to power. Adam Grant writes in his book *Originals: How Non-Conformists Move the World* that out of almost 1,000 scientists at the U.S. Food and Drug Administration, more than 40 percent feared retaliation if they raised safety concerns publicly. Half of the 40,000 employees at a technology company were afraid to express disagreement at work. A broader study of employees in consulting, financial services, media, pharmaceuticals, and advertising companies found that 85 percent had chosen not to speak up about an important issue.[5] Teams—and, ultimately, the whole organization—can't function without truth.

Focused Grip

Finally, a team is not an island. Every leadership team needs to be rigorous when contracting for work to be done by the organization it heads and relentless in driving for impact through its leadership of others. It's not easy to commission work well and be transparent on what is required from whom, but it is crucial. Focused grip requires constantly scanning for big opportunities and matching critical resources to them. Going from one distraction to another is all too common, as is a lack of follow-through.

Insights from Nationwide

Our research found it is crucial to be rigorous in the pursuit of priorities and execution rhythms. The last thing you need as a leadership team is a gap between what the team says and what it does.

Michael Watkins advises team leaders to differentiate between the three types of meetings that leadership teams generally hold—strategic, operational, and learning—so they can set up their meetings for success by designating the right amount of time, the right place, and the right agenda and stimuli for each. He observes, "When teams try to jam all these activities into a single recurring meeting, operational urgencies tend to crowd out strategic and learning discussions."[6]

Prestedge's operational meetings were a thing of beauty. Tightly managed, they enabled an unflinching focus on the priorities that the team had set for itself. This focus on priorities was reinforced through a joined-up team story that went something like this: "At Nationwide, we've always done the right thing for the 15 million members who own us. But the financial world in which we operate has changed forever. So we must reinforce and transform our business to create a sustainable future. And we're being trusted with a once-in-a-lifetime £1 billion investment to do it."

That story led to a series of deliverables, including balance sheet protection, reductions in the cost-to-income ratio, and strategic investments.

A shared story on the need for big change in customer service, its cost base, and so on led to another series of deliverables: deeper relationships with members along with a need to drive for pace, efficiency, and quality, while not putting the current business at risk.

A key part of the execution rhythms for this team was the adoption of an action cycle methodology based on the work of Fernando Flores,[7] where the team identified necessary actions and for each action there would be one customer and one supplier. An overt and explicit request was made, and, after discussion to clarify the request (and sometimes a counteroffer and negotiation), a commitment was given to do something within an agreed-upon time frame. The commitment was considered as delivered only after the customer declared satisfaction.

So far, so good . . .

Transform

A team that mobilizes and executes well is an asset to any organization. It's fabulous for the steady state, but the steady state is pretty atypical at the moment and likely to remain so. As a result, teams need to transform both the organizations they lead and how they lead them. The rate at which a team can reinvent the business is strongly influenced by the team's ability to focus outwardly to leverage deep stakeholder relationships and inwardly to build trust, full team participation, robust challenge, and the ability to rupture and repair quickly. Teams that transform rapidly share information seamlessly and have clear mechanisms and decision rights in place to enable efficient decision making.

Stakeholder Influence

Being great at stakeholder influence is a critical first driver. Stakeholders need to be managed as if they were customers. It's not unusual, however, for teams not to give the time and attention needed for this crucial activity. Often, stakeholders are an afterthought, or it is assumed that the team knows what stakeholders are thinking, or their support for the team's transformation is taken for granted. Stakeholders can be supportive, rally the support of others, and provide resources and great input. Or they can passively or overtly dismiss, build distrust for, criticize, or even block the team's efforts.

Actively managing complex and ever-changing stakeholder landscapes needs to be a team sport, yet teams often leave it to one individual who is seen to be "good at internal politics" or who "can handle difficult people." Great stakeholder relationships are thought about by the team, planned, nurtured, reported on, and kept alive on a continuous basis.

Our research has shown why teams cannot afford to rely on their own view of how the team is doing and need outside perspectives. Teams consistently had a rosier picture of their performance than their stakeholders did. Team members' average scores were significantly higher than the scores of the team leader, the team leader's boss, and key stakeholders on 11 of the 16 drive factors.

Distributed Leadership

The second drive factor of accelerated performance through transformation is distributed leadership. When this goes well, the leader ensures full team participation. The team has a collaborative mind-set, and members take on challenges on behalf of the team.

Silos appear all too easily in team dynamics—different takes on the world, different focuses for team members' deliverables, and incentive structures that discourage collaboration drive tensions and factions. Silos mean a lack of collaboration, and collaboration is a necessity if complex transformation agendas are to be achieved. Sometimes it's not even silos causing the problem; it's just not knowing each other as team members that leads to a lack of distributed leadership. The U.S. National Transportation

Safety Board found that 73 percent of the incidents recorded in its database took place during the first day a crew flew together, before crew members had the opportunity to form a cohesive team. According to a NASA study, tired crews with experience flying together made about half as many mistakes as well-rested crews who were working together for the first time.[8]

The other necessity is absolutely no micromanaging by the team leader. Directing deliverables and ways of working is a surefire way of shutting off energy, creativity, and accountability. The Japanese proverb states, "None of us is as good as all of us." The days of the "lone-hero leader" being able to deliver through a directive leadership style just won't work for the agendas of most teams.

Robust Challenge

Robust challenge is the third transformation drive factor. Team leaders know this is in place and doing well when there is a climate of support and trust that enables the team to be candid. Holding oneself accountable to the team, holding each other to account, and holding the team as a whole to account is part of this package. Those teams that get this right rupture and repair from conflict quickly.

The kind of trust that Patrick Lencioni describes is in place when team members have confidence that coworkers have their best interests at heart, that no one is out to get them, and that they can share ideas without fear they will be dismissed or personally attacked.[9] This kind of trust is critical for teams in stretching each other's thinking and driving dial-shifting outcomes and is built through knowing each other as people as well as colleagues. Deep trust is even more important, given that the best-performing teams have a diverse range of perspectives, which are a fertile breeding ground for miscommunications and assumptions and can lead to cliques and scapegoats.

Disciplined Decisions

The final drive factor for teams to be able to transform is disciplined decisions. To avoid confusion during times of transformation, decision rights and responsibilities need to be clear, information needs to be shared seamlessly, and streamlined mechanisms need to be in place. Decisions about risk are a particular subset of decisions that need to be managed well. Too risk-averse, and opportunity is left on the table. Too risk-"loose," and risk is managed poorly, with potentially disastrous outcomes.

As outlined in Chapter 6, decision making is fraught with difficulty and peppered with all kinds of potential bias. Team decision making is no different. Consider optimism bias—our research has revealed that derailing teams are almost (5 percent variance) as positive about the performance they will deliver in one year's time as are accelerating teams. In practice, the likelihood is remote.

Insights from Nationwide

Our research found that a key differentiating action within robust challenge is to ruthlessly hold each other to account and stretch each other's thinking. Accelerating teams engage in high-quality debate, embrace paradoxes, and exchange supportive and frank feedback. Poorly performing teams are often mired in groupthink and a culture of consensus or, at the other extreme, meekly take their cues from a domineering leader.

To counter tendencies toward artificial harmony or unchallengeable leadership, you can institutionalize dissent by creating a devil's advocate role that rotates among team members. Form an independent "red team," as the U.S. intelligence community does, to act as a surrogate enemy and to challenge unexamined assumptions. Insist on alternatives, as Alfred P. Sloan famously did when he was chair of General Motors. "Gentlemen," he said to the top team gathered around the table, "I take it we are all in complete agreement on the decision here." When they all nodded, he said, "Then I propose we postpone further discussion of this matter until our next meeting to give ourselves time to develop disagreement and perhaps gain some understanding of what the decision is all about."[10]

Team capability equals ability minus ego. You can even write that as a formula: TC (team capability) = A (ability) − E (ego). No matter how bright a team is, if ego prevents all the team's ability from being used, there is a discount on its performance. William Strahan, executive vice president of human resources at Comcast Cable, told us, "As we've hired people at the level of president of a division, we have at times passed on what is obvious and demonstrated skill, success, knowledge, and executive talent because we could see that the person was just not going to fit in from an ego perspective." Strahan regards the company's insistence on a lack of obvious ego at the senior level to be an accelerant for the business.

In addition to keeping egos in check, teams must be able to name the elephants in the room. Nadler Advisory Services cites four such examples: distribution of power between the team leader and the team; the question of who will succeed the leader; relationships among team members; and the possibility of failure. Keeping quiet risks serious consequences: "In time, the failure to confront creates an implicit conspiracy of silence." Such teams ignore important issues and don't resolve major concerns. Problems fester.[11]

The key to openness is trust because a lack of trust produces a fear of conflict and a lack of challenge and debate. What helps foster trust?

We can learn from Google and the research it started with hundreds of teams—Project Aristotle—in 2012 to understand how to build the "perfect team." Researchers analyzed their data using concepts from a 2010 *Science* study, that found that great teams generally shared two behaviors. First, members were given roughly the same amount of time to speak. Second, members were adept at sensing their colleagues' feelings based on the tone of voice, expressions, and other nonverbal signals. These behaviors created "psychological safety," which Google's data indicated was the most crucial component of successful teams.[12] Google found that there was a 38 percent difference in performance between its high-achieving teams and low-achieving teams.[13]

An advantage that Prestedge's team had with regard to holding each other to account and stretching each other's thinking was that team members fundamentally liked each other—and a disadvantage was that they fundamentally liked each other.

The team spent a lot of time getting to know each other. In off-site sessions, the team employed various activities that deepened the team members' connections by getting them to share moments that mattered in each of their lives. Team members got to know why each might operate in the business in the way that he or she did. They developed an agreement, a charter, for team behavior.

In high-energy, experiential sessions, the team set targets and planned the timed execution of a series of indoor and outdoor tasks, learning, in the process, how they interacted with each other. For each meeting, a team member took on the role of the observer of team behavior and held up the mirror to the team. The observer named the elephants in the room, commenting on behaviors from individuals that helped or hindered the team, using the agreed-upon behavioral charter as a benchmark.

The team learned stage by stage to give each other feedback using various techniques and facilitated sessions. For instance, members would finish the following sentences: "The thing you do that most contributes to the team is . . ." or "The thing you do that most hinders the team is . . ." Members shared with each team member what the person needed to stop doing, start doing, or continue doing to enhance the performance of the individual and of the team.

All of these activities helped the team have conversations that were franker than most teams get to have. The goal was to offer lots of support but also to challenge each other. And all of this improved—like a fine wine—the team over time.

But what eluded the team right up to 2016 was the ability to ruthlessly hold each other to account and stretch each other's thinking. There were many reasons: an, at times, dominating and parental style by Prestedge, who occasionally flew off the handle with impatience and closed down discussion;

an unwillingness on the part of the team to call him out on his behaviors and an inclination to protect him from anyone trying to do so; a lack of effort by team members to walk into each other's offices and join forces to tackle cross-divisional issues; and a fear of and lack of capability with conflict and challenge. A cycle developed where challenge was served up cold and without skill. The challenge would be met with robust defense, and then silence would ensue as tumbleweeds drifted through the meeting room.

There were two saving graces. First, Prestedge took on the role of challenger on behalf of the whole team—not an ideal situation but better that he did than he didn't. Second, because the team genuinely liked each other, it didn't hold grudges or let the moments of unproductive conflict seep into the everyday work.

The missed opportunity? Rather than step into enterprise-wide responsibility and accountability, the team sometimes didn't come to the optimal answer and relied too much on Prestedge to lead the way.

Agility

The final set of four drive factors essential for team acceleration fall under the heading of agility. Teams never stand still. Team members come and go, organizational contexts and industry drivers shift, and stakeholders change. Teams that are agile create energy, attempt the ambitious, and overcome barriers to delivery. Teams enable the organization under them to be more agile, creating the necessary culture and leadership practices that allow the organization to pivot when required and execute and transform where the strategy demands it.

Foresight

First in this set of drive factors is foresight. Teams that practice the art of foresight scan the external environment for fresh ideas, anticipate changing circumstances, and readily rethink assumptions on what is required for future success. Without having a view of what might be coming down the road, a team has no chance of figuring out in which direction it might need to pivot.

At Comcast, for example, senior management discussions about the changing nature of competition led to investments in a new change-management capability supported by a common training approach. "What we realized," noted Comcast Cable's William Strahan, "was that we would have to adapt and pivot, not just execute faster and quicker and better. And I think the string of those [management] conversations was an important factor."

By contrast, failing to create the time to fully explore the big issues prevents many teams from developing foresight, as does a resistance to ideas that challenge conventional wisdom. One way teams can overcome these failings is to institutionalize ways of finding and leveraging differences of perspective.

Learning

Learning from the past, present, and future is a second key drive factor. Teams that are blocked in their ability to learn fail to actively change things that aren't working. Teams should do "aftercasts," just as they do forecasts, to see what they've learned. On the other hand, agile teams seek feedback, preemptively invest in building capabilities for the future, and absorb and implement new learning at pace.

The future cannot be predicted. Scenarios can be explored, but for sure the future will never be exactly as anticipated. So having the ability to learn rapidly and continuously is essential for any team wishing to navigate the future as it emerges. Leveraging the power of doubt and harnessing curiosity serve a team well. We found that teams in accelerating companies are almost twice as likely as others to be willing to fail fast and learn at speed and that more than half of the teams in derailing companies reported failing at absorbing and implementing new learnings at pace.

Adaptability

Having foresight and the ability to learn is great, but these need to be combined with adaptability. Here, the team responds quickly to changing circumstances, experimenting with new ideas while not being hampered by a fear of failure. A BCG Strategy Institute study titled "The Adaptive Advantage Index" found that adaptive teams "generate powerful economic and financial gains" for their companies and "consistently outperform their industry peers during periods of market volatility."[14] Yet our study of hundreds of organizations found that 70 percent of teams in derailing companies struggle with adaptability.

Resilience

The final drive factor is resilience, and it's easy to understand why this is needed. Mobilizing, executing, transforming, developing foresight, learning, and adapting take energy. Resilience is about managing the energy of the team to ensure that there is enough appetite to take risks, attempt ambitious initiatives, and overcome barriers. Resilience is also about reframing setbacks and challenges—inevitable in our increasingly intense world—as opportunities for growth.

Teams wanting to create energy should watch out for any tendency to focus on problems the team cannot influence and a critical outlook that highlights the negatives rather than identifying the positives.

Insights from Nationwide

Our research found that a key differentiating action within the foresight drive factor is to find and leverage differences of perspective. Martine Haas and Mark Mortensen argue that "diversity in knowledge, views, and perspectives, as well as in age, gender, and race, can help teams be more creative and avoid groupthink."[15]

Differences of perspective are hard to achieve, though, due to the prevalence of unconscious bias. Neuroscience research confirms that human beings are constructed so that bias is built in, meaning we can end up being less inclusive than we want to be or than we realize we are being.

Katherine Phillips shows how building diversity into our teams can help to overcome the impact of unconscious bias and make us smarter. She says: "Simply interacting with individuals who are different forces group members to prepare better, to anticipate alternative viewpoints, and to expect that reaching consensus will take effort . . . leading to better decision making and problem solving." She adds that diversity can increase profit and even produce breakthrough innovations.[16]

Business professors Cristian Deszö of the University of Maryland and David Ross of Columbia University studied the effect of gender diversity on the top firms in Standard & Poor's Composite 1500 list. They found that, on average, "female representation in top management leads to an increase of $42 million in firm value." They also found that companies with a focus on innovation experienced greater financial gains when women were represented among the senior leadership.[17]

If we need any more evidence, in 2012 a team at the Credit Suisse Research Institute published the results of their study of 2,360 companies globally from 2005 to 2011. They found that when companies had at least one female board member, they saw greater average returns on equity, lower net debt to equity gearing, and higher average growth.[18]

Teams with a very stable membership risk a deterioration in performance over time should members become too similar in viewpoint. Let's look at the story of Lego. Lego was founded in 1932 by Ole Kirk Christiansen, a master carpenter in a small village in Denmark. In 1958, the company patented a plastic brick system, revolutionizing the construction toy market. In 1980, Lego got onto an unprecedented path of growth for the next decade. In the 1990s, it hit a growth plateau amid unforeseen market shifts, including declining birthrates; an expired patent that led to the market being flooded with cheap Chinese imitations that snapped right onto Lego sets; and the shift to audio, video, and online entertainment. Lego failed to see the key market shifts because it was so insular—based in a small village in Denmark, where it was by far the largest employer. Lego even missed its first chance to partner with George Lucas on *Star Wars*–licensed Lego products. Lego should have been monitoring the full range of market forces—in particular, customer preferences, competitors, and social trends. A more diverse team would have helped. In 2008, Lego began its turnaround—not least through a partnership with *Star Wars*. According to Jonathan Ringen, "In the last 10 years, Lego has grown into nothing less than the Apple of toys: a profit-generating, design-driven miracle built around premium, intuitive, highly covetable hardware that fans can't get enough of."[19]

At Nationwide, the operations leadership team was not a paragon of virtue on some dimensions of diversity. Over the years, out of a team that ranged from 10 to 12 members, there were always 3 or 4 women, but the team was always British and white.

Prestedge found other ways to bring in diversity of perspective. He made sure that some team members were from very different organizational backgrounds, and there has always been a younger member or two. Nor was he shy about onboarding and offboarding team members to ensure the composition of the team was right. He himself went to Harvard for a six-week leadership program and to INSEAD in Abu Dhabi to stretch his thinking. Right from the very beginning, he brought in external thinkers to team sessions to stimulate insights, challenge assumptions, and generate learning. Guests included an expert in operating-model construction, psychologists deeply trained on team dynamics, world-class innovation experts, and, more recently, a business school lecturer in the six disciplines of strategic thinking.

Assumptions about the dominant ways of thinking were surfaced and challenged. At off-site meetings, he posed questions for the whole team (and himself), such as, "How do we allow people to pursue their own personal ambitions without it being competitive or disruptive for the team?" and "How do we balance what we need to deliver this year while positioning ourselves for future years?"

Team members were encouraged to sit as nonexecutive directors for other organizations outside of the industry as well as join national bodies and interest groups within financial services. And Prestedge has invested in a Silicon Valley joint venture to explore opportunities for an emerging future.

Caution for Senior Teams

Becoming an accelerating team is not rocket science, and our research and investigations have made the path to accelerating clear. Be warned, though, if you are a top team, as it's much harder and the potholes are deeper and disguised.

The Nationwide team showed how to avoid the acceleration trap. Rather than succumb to a crude call to just do everything more quickly, Nationwide accelerated where it was important, even when that meant "going slow to go fast." It also didn't forget its strengths.

Senior teams need to know that they tend to be the least likely to be categorized as accelerating among all teams in the organization. Indeed, our research found that junior teams were 1.6 times more likely to be accelerating than were director-level teams and above. In addition, we found that senior teams rate themselves lower on 13 of the 16 drive factors than do the members of junior teams. This finding aligns with previous research by Heidrick & Struggles and the University of Southern California's Center for Effective Organizations; in a survey of 60 top human resources executives from *Fortune* 500 companies, only 6 percent of respondents agreed with the assertion that "the executives in our C-suite are a well-integrated team."[20]

Why is it worse at the top? While junior teams are generally organized by geography, department, or product line, teams at the top of the organization are, by definition, doing quite different things: One person runs marketing, another runs manufacturing, another runs finance, and so forth. At the senior level, the challenge is to integrate a portfolio of activities into a coherent whole, and we think the explanation behind the data is that too much energy at this level is consumed in dealing with ego problems driven by instincts for self-protection: "I want more power than you," or "I will agree with your proposal if you agree with mine," or "I'll stay off your turf if you stay off mine." Furthermore, senior team members have invested a lot in their careers by the time they've risen to the top of an organization, and they are vulnerable. If they fail, they have a much longer way to fall.

In other words, the senior team is the most critical but the least likely to be able to quickly build and change momentum to perform. Thus, organizations must make their most senior teams the top priority. The upside is the sheer scale of opportunity for organizations to train and coach their senior teams to improve.

For CEOs who are reflexively inclined to respond, "Not us. Not my team," research offers this note of caution: "CEOs have a rosier view of senior management's performance than other top team members do." As our colleague Rich Rosen reports, a global survey of 124 CEOs and 579 other senior executives found that 52 percent of the non-CEOs on top teams said the teams had problems in critical areas such as thinking innovatively and leading change, while only 28 percent of the CEOs reported such problems for the team. The CEOs gave an average rating of 5.39 for the top team's effectiveness, where 7 is the top score, but the non-CEOs gave an average rating of only 4.02. "Statistically, these ratings are worlds apart," Rosen and his coauthor wrote, "and it seems that CEOs are the executives who need a reality check."[21]

Any CEO seeking to strengthen his or her top team should not only seek ways to improve along the performance dimensions we studied but also be tuned in to signs of excessive optimism, as this could itself be symptomatic of underperformance. All teams and team members in our study were inclined to suffer from a bit of self-delusion (stakeholders who weren't team members tended to rate them lower than they rated themselves), but it was the worst-performing teams that were the most optimistic about their future performance. If you are currently not performing as you would wish, there is at least a 50 percent chance that you are suffering from excessive optimism in your self-ratings and that the odds are against you in achieving your goals. The best way to test this? Hold up a mirror. Involve multiple outsiders in evaluating your team. In addition to providing a dose of realism, your stakeholders' views are critical because they will decide whether they support your team's actions, allocate it adequate resources, and open doors—or not.

Finally, remember that business competition can be like a sport. Consider two athletes. One is a 125-pound female table tennis player who is quick as lightning. The other is a 250-pound male heavyweight boxer. They're both healthy and incredibly skilled. However, their pattern of acceleration—how they build and change momentum to perform—is completely different, requiring different strategies, muscles, and reflexes. If the table tennis player gets in the boxing ring, she risks injury, and if the boxer competes in table tennis, he will likely be defeated. Athletes must be more than just healthy; their training must be appropriate to the task at hand.

Final Insights from Nationwide

In June 2016, when we analyzed the top U.K. banks, Nationwide came in second and was in the advancing category. None of the banks we tested were in the accelerating category. Four were in the advancing category, one in steady, three in lagging, and three in derailing. When the Nationwide team's results were compared against its earlier assessment on the 16 drive factors of team acceleration, most of the drive factors either had remained consistently high or had improved.

Having come so far, what's next for the organization?

Nationwide, like many financial institutions, is faced with threats. Financial technologies ("fintechs"), the "blockchain" potential for disintermediation, and the move toward a cashless society and open banking are just a few of the exciting and worrisome trends. As Bill Gates has said, "We need banking but we don't need banks anymore."[22] In the face of that prospect, as this book goes to press, Nationwide is undertaking a strategic review, with Prestedge leading it.

The strategic review is likely to lead to a change in operating model and, with it, the call for a new evolution of the team. In response, the team needs to enter a new period of development with multiple strands. With the advent of a new chair, David Roberts, and a new CEO, Joe Garner, whose leadership style is to engage wide and deep with the organization, the need for improving the team's ability in stakeholder influence moves up the agenda more than ever before. While the team has been focused on operational delivery for the last four years, the team now needs to find mechanisms that force it to lift its head and see further and wider and develop the skill of foresight. The team needs to learn to develop its people to free itself up to enable a more effective use of its most critical resource—time for strategic leadership.

As we leave Prestedge and his team, these are the ambitions they hold for the team, whatever form it takes in the future:

- To improve how we ask questions,
- To interpret data and trends better to make higher-quality decisions,
- To move away from admiring great ideas and into execution,
- To hear and receive challenge more constructively,
- To move from following others' ideas to leading the pack with our own,
- To be able to think and act strategically, and
- To develop courage to lean into and face the future.

■ ■ ■

As more and more companies organize through teams, think about your own team challenge. The challenge can be especially great these days, when a drive for cost reduction and wage arbitration may mean your compliance function has been moved offshore from London to Nashville; your application development is in Pune, India; your processing is in Kraków, Poland; and your IT shop is in Shanghai. The reality of today's virtual organizations makes team skills critical. And, as we said at the outset, our research shows that as much as 22.8 percent of alpha is on the table—the difference between the economic benefits provided by an accelerating team and a derailing one.

What would it take to capture that value for your organization?

Notes

1. Adi Ignatius, "'We need to intensify our sense of urgency': An interview with Meg Whitman," *Harvard Business Review*, May 2016, hbr.org.
2. Jean Martin and Conrad Schmidt, "How to keep your top talent," *Harvard Business Review*, May 2010, hbr.org.
3. George Colvin, "Why dream teams fail," *Fortune*, May 31, 2006, fortune.com.
4. Michael Cieply, "In 1996 letter, Eisner confronts Ovitz: 'You . . . manipulated me.'" *Los Angeles Times*, February 26, 2004.
5. Adam Grant, *Originals: How Non-Conformists Move the World*, New York: Viking, 2016.
6. Michael D. Watkins, "Leading the team you inherit," *Harvard Business Review*, June 2016, hbr.org.
7. David Walden, "Using the methods of Fernando Flores: An interview of Jack Reilly," *Center for Quality of Management Journal*, Spring 1997.
8. Diane Coutu, "Why teams don't work," *Harvard Business Review*, May 2009, hbr.org.
9. Patrick Lencioni, *The Five Dysfunctions of a Team: A Leadership Fable*, San Francisco: Jossey-Bass, 2002.
10. Peter F. Drucker, *Management: Tasks, Responsibilities, Practices,* New York: Harper & Row, 1974.
11. Nadler Advisory Services, *Teamwork at the Top: Designing and Leading Effective Executive Teams*, nadler-leadership-advisory.com.
12. Charles Duhigg, "What Google learned from its quest to build the perfect team," *New York Times Magazine*, February 25, 2016, nytimes.com.
13. Mark Thompson, "Google discovered these 3 factors make a 38 percent difference in team performance," *Inc.*, July 6, 2016, inc.com.
14. Roselinde Torres and Nneka Rimmer, "Winning practices of adaptive leadership teams," Boston Consulting Group, April 3, 2012, bcgperspectives.com.
15. Martine Haas and Mark Mortensen, "The secrets of great teamwork," *Harvard Business Review*, June 2016, hbr.org.
16. Katherine W. Phillips, "How diversity makes us smarter," *Scientific American*, October 1, 2014, scientificamerican.com.
17. Katherine W. Phillips, "How diversity makes us smarter," *Scientific American*, October 1, 2014, scientificamerican.com.
18. Katherine W. Phillips, "How diversity makes us smarter," *Scientific American*, October 1, 2014 scientificamerican.com.
19. Jonathan Ringen, "How Lego became the Apple of toys," *Fast Company*, January 8, 2015, www.fastcompany.com/3040223/when-it-clicks-it-clicks.

20. Richard M. Rosen and Fred Adair, "CEOs misperceive top teams' performance," *Harvard Business Review*, September 2007, hbr.org.
21. Richard M. Rosen and Fred Adair, "CEOs misperceive top teams' performance," *Harvard Business Review*, September 2007, hbr.org.
22. Emmanuel Amberber, "'Banking is necessary, banks are not'—7 quotes from Bill Gates on mobile banking," *YourStory*, January 22, 2015, yourstory.com.

CHAPTER 9

Accelerating Leaders

The Leader Sets the Pace

When Microsoft CEO Steve Ballmer announced in 2013 that he was stepping down, the board faced a fundamental choice about his successor. Was it going to go for a radical change in strategy to chase Apple, Google, Amazon, Facebook, and some of the other technology companies that had challenged or even eclipsed Microsoft during Ballmer's 14 years at the helm? Or was the board going to bet that a new style of leadership could unlock the talent that still clearly resided at Microsoft?

The board bet on a new leader and has reaped the benefits.

That new leader, Satya Nadella, stepped into a fraught situation. The computing world had passed Microsoft by as users moved away from desktops and laptops to tablets and smartphones and away from software packages to apps and the cloud—Microsoft's share of all computing devices had been 90 percent in 2009, but that number had plunged to 20 percent by the time Nadella took the CEO job in 2014.[1] And in the world of technology, there is almost never a second act. Look at what happened when Digital Equipment Corporation missed the move to personal computers; when Compaq, Gateway, and others didn't react quickly enough to online ordering of PCs; and when Motorola and Nokia were slow about smartphones and then BlackBerry missed the move to smarter, sleeker phones.

In addition, Nadella was stepping into a war zone in the executive suite and boardroom. Ballmer and Microsoft cofounder Bill Gates, the CEO for the company's first 25 years, stopped speaking for a time when it became clear that Gates had lost confidence.[2] The two had been the closest of friends since their days as undergraduates at Harvard together, but Microsoft's stock price hadn't budged during Ballmer's tenure, even as some others in the tech world saw their prices shoot into the stratosphere. Ballmer defended himself in his trademark loud style. After all, net income had more than tripled while he was CEO, and Microsoft was earning a mind-boggling $23 billion a year when Ballmer left. Gross margin was north of 70 percent.[3]

Still, the board was so disheartened by the loss of competitiveness that many barely even considered the possibility of an internal candidate—but also couldn't agree on a choice from the outside. Eventually, Gates made it clear that he wouldn't support the external candidate the board was leaning toward, and the job went to Nadella, a 20-plus-year veteran of Microsoft who had begun to make the company's cloud hosting business a success.[4]

The soft-spoken Nadella, just 46 years old at the time, calmed the waters by being respectful toward the prior regime rather than throw Ballmer under the bus. He also convinced Gates to begin spending time at the company again to lend his still-considerable cachet to Nadella's plans—Gates agreed to spend 30 percent of his week on Microsoft work despite the demands of his charitable foundation. Nadella focused on getting his top team in line, partly by spending four hours a week in a meeting with them. (The meeting expanded to eight hours once a month.) He also focused on a message and began communicating it relentlessly to the organization. He had three concentric circles labeled "concepts," "capabilities," and "culture." He felt Microsoft was doing well with the outermost circle, concepts; it was spending 11 percent of revenue on research and development and was staying on top of technological possibilities.[5] Nadella also felt Microsoft was fine on the middle circle, capabilities, because it was still attractive to top talent. Where Nadella felt Microsoft needed an overhaul was in the innermost circle: culture.

Microsoft had become hidebound as executives running hugely profitable businesses protected their fiefdoms. Under Ballmer, Microsoft had actually spent heavily to develop a tablet computer, but the groups that produced software for desktop and laptop computers wouldn't share some key technology. Microsoft abandoned its tablet right as Apple introduced its phenomenally successful iPad. Much the same happened with e-readers. Microsoft worked and worked but couldn't get its existing businesses to play nicely with the start-up effort—then watched Amazon steal the show with its Kindle.

Nadella had shown that cooperation was possible. He had made his name in the cloud business largely by getting others to share key technology with his efforts. As CEO, he institutionalized his approach.

Ballmer had recently reorganized the business to make it much flatter, but Nadella took out even more overhead, to encourage sharing of resources. While Ballmer had defined Microsoft broadly as a software and products company (to add hardware to the company's mission), Nadella went even further. He said Microsoft was in the business of increasing workers' productivity—notably leaving out any claim that workers would have to use only Microsoft products; he was going to fit into workers' world rather than continuing the attempt to make them fit into Microsoft's. Nadella named a chief customer experience officer. He created environments in which customers could experiment with products that Microsoft is considering and began to iterate product development and to incorporate customer feedback rather than spend years on a big piece of software that is unveiled all at once (and sometimes flopped, as Windows 8 did). All the while, Nadella kept communicating his vision for change.

He generated some early wins, notably with the service that lets companies host their computing in a cloud that Microsoft manages—Microsoft was in grave danger of falling irretrievably behind Amazon, Google, IBM, and others in a competition that will define a big part of the computer industry for years to come. He used the wins to bolster momentum, and the whole mood about the company has now changed. The stock price, after 14 years of vibrating in place, is up more than 40 percent since Nadella became CEO, increasing market capitalization by more than $100 billion and making Microsoft the third most valuable company in the world (after only Alphabet and Apple). Although we've said that we don't think market cap is the best way to keep score, the market is certainly signaling that investors expect Microsoft to finally break out of its holding pattern and do some very useful things for customers. The company's recent announcement that it is buying LinkedIn, the social media platform, suggests that Microsoft is listening.

As Nadella shows, while teams are the engines of organizations, leaders set the pace of those teams and therefore of the organizations they lead. He also demonstrates the two most important aspects of META for leaders— adopting strict execution rhythms and developing the right mind-sets— which we will explore in this chapter.

How to Accelerate a Leader's Performance

Based on an approach we developed in 2014 to assess leaders (described in detail in the Research Appendix), we found that watching an accelerating leader at work is like watching a great, three-act play titled META.

In the first act, the leader mobilizes the organization around a compelling strategy and purpose. This act has three scenes, corresponding to the three drive factors that we have identified. The first scene shows a leader anticipating market volatility, change, and competitive threats—all while interpreting the impact that these changes may have on the business and *shaping its strategy* accordingly. The resulting strategic priorities for the company provide absolute clarity on the critical factors for success, while not hampering the company's ability to be flexible and agile.

In the second scene, the leader *puts customers first*—spotting how to create distinctive value for customers, deeply connecting with them, and shaping their changing needs before competitors have the opportunity to do so.

The final scene of the first act unfolds with our leader *inspiring and influencing* others to help them find meaning in their work. Our protagonist engages and energizes colleagues and aligns key stakeholders on the organization's most critical priorities.

The second act is where the heart of the action takes place: execution. The leader *builds talent and teams*, strengthening organizational capability and bandwidth. The leader *drives for results*, continuously improving and streamlining the core business and, when necessary, adapting at pace.

In the third act, transformation, there are two main scenes. In the first, the leader *disrupts and challenges* conventional ways of looking at the business and the marketplace as he or she explores opportunities for disruptive change (including disruptions to the company's own business model, if necessary). In the second scene, the protagonist *leads innovation,* finding ways to experiment and test new ideas, breaking down silos to harness cross-discipline creativity and rapidly scaling up those ideas that promise a material impact.

Throughout the play, the characters demonstrate agility. We see them developing *foresight, learning,* constantly *adapting* to changing contexts, and drawing on their *resilience.*

We have captured the essence of this play on great leadership in the accelerating leadership framework (Figure 9.1).

FIGURE 9.1 The LAQ model

Our research shows that the factors we've identified for accelerating leaders match up with business results. Just as for the development of strategy, the transformation of organizations, and the leading of teams, individual leaders either drive accelerating performance or create a drag effect through how they mobilize, execute, and transform and whether they do those things with agility.

In a world where capital is effectively priced at zero, value creation resides in the leadership process of harnessing and implementing ideas better than competitors. Leadership alpha is the significant untapped potential to be found, captured, and leveraged. Leadership is estimated to be up to 30 percent of bottom-line performance. Yet most companies state that their leaders reliably get only 50 percent of the full potential of their people.

We have found through years of working with, assessing, and developing leaders that some of the most talented senior and high-potential leaders—just like actors in a play—have clear strengths, areas that require development, and potential derailers. But leaders can be forgiven if they're bewildered about how to work their way through the vast array of skills they're told they need to develop. One such list includes the following: the ability to motivate, domain knowledge, the ability to listen, decisiveness, financial literacy, a sense of humor, reliability in a crisis, frugality, delegation, adaptability, and bravery.[6] And there are many other, similarly detailed lists.

What we do know is that leaders need to be both fast and effective. For example, research into 360-degree evaluations of 50,000 executives narrowed the list to the 5,711 most successful and found that fully 95 percent were judged to be both particularly fast and exceptionally effective. The researchers defined "fast" in three ways: the ability to see problems or trends early, to respond to problems quickly, and to make changes quickly. Only 2 percent were seen as fast but not effective, and only 3 percent were evaluated as being highly effective but not especially fast.[7]

So how do leaders find that holy grail? Our research with thousands of leaders found two constants for success. First, successful leaders have a superb sense of timing, every bit as good as the best actors; their execution rhythms are excellent. Second, successful leaders have a core set of accelerating mind-sets.

Execution Rhythms

Successful leaders typically execute based on five golden rules: (1) Put the right team in place; (2) set only three to five strategic priorities and initiatives; (3) plan properly; (4) put rigorous rhythms and processes in place; and (5) generate energy.

Put the Right Team in Place

You can never move the needle on your own, so your team must include people who think systematically, adopt an 80-20 approach, self-organize rigorously, and follow through relentlessly. Move people out of the team quickly if they are not performing or are not a good fit, and develop capabilities of team members as quickly as possible.

Kevin O'Connor, cofounder of Graphiq and previously cofounder of DoubleClick, offers two useful pointers: You have to empower people to make decisions without moving everything up the hierarchy, and "seniority is evil"—all responsibilities need to depend on merit.[8]

Set Your Strategic Priorities

The most important thing is to work out what three to five things you and your team can do that will move the company forward. Get them right, and you have a natural energy to execute. Get them wrong, and you get confusion. How do you get them right? Get inspiration from visits with key customers and from marketing. Mix external input with the views of internal people who really understand what's going on and are successful. Identify strategic priorities based on data, and then create a vision of what they will look like when achieved. Link those priorities to the purpose of your organization and to what your people care about.

Following are four tips: (1) Remember that setting priorities is iterative; (2) don't take more than six months to determine priorities; (3) make sure that the business case is right; and (4) engage your wider leadership team in the process. Ask yourself, "Will setting this priority grow the business faster and more profitably? Does it improve our competitive position? Is it putting our customers first?"

Plan Properly

Take time to develop a good execution plan, set measurable and clear key performance indicators (KPIs), allocate responsibilities and accountabilities, set a regular operating rhythm for delivering, constantly measure against the plan, and communicate the plan to all stakeholders.

When Alan Mulally became CEO of Boeing Commercial Airplanes in 2001, a time when the division of Boeing was having trouble executing, he set a rhythm of one plane a day. If Boeing could get one plane a day out of manufacturing and off to a customer, the business would thrive. Mulally then set up a meeting of his top team every morning to discuss what they needed to do to remove any obstacles to achieving that rhythm. That meeting became the means for accountability. There was no going off and studying something for days or weeks; if you promised to do something, you had to face your colleagues again the next morning and report on what you had done. Mulally got the rhythm he needed.

Adopt Rigorous Rhythms and Processes

Jeff Sprecher, founder and CEO of Intercontinental Exchange, a network of exchanges and clearinghouses for financial and commodity markets that is one of our superaccelerators, tells us he's found great success with a rhythm that he discovered by chance. "I met a junior person at Goldman Sachs, and then a few weeks later I met the chief executive. The CEO referred to my first meeting and said, 'You know, I understand you've met [the junior person] and that you two were talking about such and such.' I was incredibly impressed that there was such a high level of communication between the more junior person and the chief executive.

"So I brought that idea here. We created a management committee that meets for four hours a week. We go around the table, and every person talks about the issues they're dealing with, what their proposed solution is, and what they are working on over the next week. We have a rule that anyone can talk and challenge anything. And it's a rule that you must tell everyone what your problems are—the point is not to merely reward people and congratulate them. Then, as a group, we decide where things are going to go. If we can't come to a decision, I can be the tiebreaker. But whatever we decide in that meeting is the decision of the company. There's no calling somebody up after the meeting and saying, 'Let's redo this.' There's no backstabbing. There's no crying that something was mishandled or misdirected. We have a rule that all of that bellyaching has to be done in the meeting. When we leave, we leave with unity and a plan, and we move forward.

"And then each of these people holds a similar meeting, and we try to move that type of management up and down the organization every week. The risk is that you give even junior people a lot more information than they specifically need for their individual job. If they were to be recruited away, they would take a lot of your business plan out the door. But the flip side is that we feel that if we empower people with information about what the company is doing at the top, they'll make better decisions. They'll also be less likely to leave.

"It may seem like a weird management style, but it's worked for us."

Even if you don't go as far as Sprecher has, you need to set up very strict rhythms and processes, adopt a fit-for-purpose rhythm of meetings, and map out your annual calendar of meetings and *never* miss one. If someone can't come to a meeting, insist on a fully briefed alternative. Start (and end!) on time and have only people on the call or in the meeting who need to be there. Use these meetings to be in control of execution, to troubleshoot problems, and to challenge, support, and coach. Be sure that you are one of those leaders who does less telling and more asking.

Generate Energy

Our research found that leaders who could sustain energy and optimism by managing stress levels were much more evident in accelerating companies than in derailing companies. We've all been around leaders who we refer to as "mood Hoovers"—people who suck the energy out of a room or the people they work with. You feel tired after five minutes around these leaders. On the other hand, as we can see just from looking at leaders around us, those who manage their energy and point it in the most useful direction accelerate the creation of value. Energetic leaders have authenticity, a clear purpose, passion for that purpose, discipline, and excitement around possibility and opportunity. The energy of a leader spins out into an organization from the most senior levels through to the front line and across internal and external organizational boundaries. It's viral. It creates a social movement within organizations that infuses customers, stakeholders, regulators, and opinion formers. Leaders who create energy prepare for every moment, meeting, and conversation in which they can bring energy into the organization. This contributes significantly to acceleration. This is how the leader sets the pace.

Kevin Kruse offers some pointers based on thousands of interviews with ultraproductive people such as billionaires, Olympic athletes, and straight-A students. They include the following:

1. **Setting daily priorities.** They identify their most important task and work on it for two hours every morning.
2. **A focus on energy, not time.** They maximize their energy to maximize their productivity by focusing on sleep, diet, exercise, and short breaks throughout the day.
3. **The 80-20 rule.** Eighty percent of outcomes come from only 20 percent of activities, so they identify the 20 percent and ignore the rest.

Think about this: In any one day, there are only so many minutes that really matter. How many of those are there for you in a day? Fifty? One hundred? Two hundred? Execution exemplars identify the moments that really matter and channel their energy accordingly.[9]

We think of the goal here as exothermic, not endothermic, leadership—in other words, leaders who produce more energy than they consume. There is no acceleration without energy.

Natarajan Chandrasekaran, CEO and managing director of Tata Consultancy Services (a superaccelerator), puts it this way: "We want our company to be a platform in which [all our employees] can build their dreams. We want to create a very high level of belonging here, because that translates into high performance. We believe very strongly that realizing the potential of every employee translates multifold in terms of realizing the potential of the company."

Core Mind-Sets

You can't know what the future will hold. However, building the discipline of adopting and maintaining accelerating mind-sets enables leaders to meet full on and with dexterity the ever-changing contexts and requirements within which they galvanize and lead those who follow them.

Think of yourself as sitting in a swivel chair—you can swivel between multiple different systems to make sense of things rather than having straight-through, simple processing. At the core is your ability to be agile as change erupts all around you. Research by Paul Brown and Brenda Hales concluded that there is a need to create "the conditions under which [people] can use all their own adaptive capacity to get to the goals they are after."[10] We found that the ability to learn in this way was twice as likely to be present in leaders of accelerating companies than in those of derailing ones.

We set out to answer the following question: What are the few compelling shifts in mind-sets that enable leaders to be agile in this way and, in turn, to set the pace in today's ever-changing landscape? Our answer can be found in Table 9.1.

TABLE 9.1 Shifting to an accelerating mind-set

Derailing leaders' mind-sets	Accelerating leaders' mind-sets
I need to know the answer.	*I need to constantly discover patterns and connect the dots.*
These are my resources.	*My job is to optimally match resources to opportunities.*
It's either/or.	*How do I dissolve the paradox?*
I have the power and authority.	*Working through a traditional hierarchy takes too much time.*
I need to know.	*Doubt is powerful.*
It's okay to be grumpy.	*I'm on 24/7, and what I do impacts every second.*
I don't have enough time to be a good leader.	*Creating leadership is my goal.*
I know myself well.	*Feedback is a gift.*

The first four mind-sets are so important that we cover them in great detail in Chapter 14 ("Ripple Intelligence"), Chapter 15 ("Resource Fluidity"), Chapter 16 ("Dissolving Paradox"), and Chapter 17 ("Liquid Leadership"). Here we explore the other four mind-sets to help both you and others around you accelerate.

I Need to Know versus *Doubt Is Powerful*

Leaders do well when they exercise the power of doubt. Our conversations with and studies of CEOs found that senior leaders must routinely make tough decisions, yet many CEOs worry that they don't have the right information—or enough of it. Our interviews with more than 150 global CEOs suggest that the key to this dilemma is to embrace uncertainty and doubt by focusing on the feeling side of decision making and not just the thinking side.

The Persians used to make decisions twice: once while sober and once while drunk. If the decisions agreed, they proceeded. If not, they deferred a decision. We're not recommending drinking at the office, but the Persians certainly had a good run, ruling the known world for some 300 years, by combining their thinking and feeling sides.

CEOs who combine the two dimensions can get more comfortable with discomfort, better distinguish constructive doubt from disruptive second-guessing, and better select the appropriate decision-making strategies that help minimize risk and maximize opportunity.

It's Okay to Be Grumpy versus *I'm on 24/7, and What I Do Impacts Every Second*

Daniel Goleman and his colleagues found that the leader's mood and its attendant behaviors are both the most important and the most surprising to leaders themselves. They write: "The leader's mood and behaviors drive the moods and behaviors of everyone else. A cranky and ruthless boss creates a toxic organization filled with negative underachievers who ignore opportunities; an inspirational, inclusive leader spawns acolytes for whom any challenge is surmountable."[11] Add the findings of the *Gallup Business Journal*—that 25 percent of employees would fire their bosses if they could, and that 75 percent report that the single most stressful aspect of their job is their immediate line manager—and we see how potent leadership mood is.[12] The economy runs on people, and leaders set the pace in organizations.

Pause for a moment and think through those grumpy leaders who you've come across in your career and the impact they've had on those they lead and the ability of the organization to operate at pace. Now think about those moments when you, too, have been guilty of the same, knowing it but not having the discipline to catch yourself and course-correct.

Author Gary Hamel summed up the warning message that Pope Francis sent to potential grumpy leaders within the Roman Curia: "Leaders are susceptible to an array of debilitating maladies, including arrogance, intolerance, myopia, and pettiness. When those diseases go untreated, the organization itself is enfeebled. To have a healthy church, we need healthy leaders."[13]

For good or bad, leadership is contagious. A core skill in any leader's tool kit is to be able to change his or her internal state to ensure that the contagion he or she is spreading is positive. There are no two ways about it: How you work, your imprint, and your shadow of leadership make the difference. As our colleagues at Senn Delaney say: When you go into the office, decide what floor of the mood elevator you want to get off on and be here now. At best, the shadow of the leaders in your organization can be a competitive advantage; at worst, it can be a significant drag.

Jeff Sprecher, founder and CEO of Intercontinental Exchange, tells us, "I'm a terrible manager. I am just a terrible manager. And so you say, 'Okay, how does a terrible manager manage an organization?' The only thing I could come up with is to lead by example, to run my own behavior the way I would want my employees to run their behavior, and do it in a way that is quite obvious and transparent and hope that people will try to emulate the leader."

I Don't Have Enough Time to Be a Good Leader versus *Creating Leadership Is My Goal*

Think of leadership as fire, not water. It's not a limited resource such as water but a spreading process such as fire. Not all leadership needs to come from the top.

Many articles and books talk about how organizations are prone to getting stuck in the middle of the hierarchy. Midlevel leaders are variously named "permafrost," "the marzipan or clay layer," or "the missing middle." These are all ways to describe the difficulty of engaging middle managers and creating leadership throughout the organization. How important is this middle layer? For four years, a team of researchers at Stanford studied the performance of more than 20,000 frontline workers, such as airline check-in staff, call center workers, and supermarket checkout personnel. An analysis of six million data points showed that productivity was increased by 12 percent if someone who had a poor manager was given a strong one.[14]

The recent development of organizational ecosystems brings another twist because of all the contractors and freelancers who have to be led. Apple, for example, has 45,000 employees worldwide but another 180,000 people outside the company who earn their living developing apps for Apple's iOS. A whole different kind of leadership is required now.

According to neuroscience, the degree to which a leader engages others is the degree to which the leader inspires trust and excitement.[15] It is feelings, not thoughts, that dominate how we make decisions. It is this energy from feelings that can inspire accelerated performance.

We see lots of organizations striving to engage their people by trying to tap into their emotions through value statements, even though most people's organizational life is not the espoused values or mission and vision statements. The objectives, tasks, KPIs, and outputs required of them are the things we measure and, therefore, the things we pay attention to. But these things don't motivate people to apply their discretionary effort. Only things that shape and elicit people's feelings can do that, and only leaders are capable of creating those things. The creation of a motivational culture is not an outcome of accident or coincidence. How you make decisions, how you have conversations, how you direct the actions of those you lead, and how you behave generate a chain reaction in those you lead.

Look no further than Howard Schultz of Starbucks to see the value of leadership. The company thrived during his first 15 years at the helm, lost its way when he stepped away from the CEO position for 8 years, and has gone gangbusters again since he returned in early 2008, so much so that it made our list of superaccelerators. Scott Pitasky, executive vice president and chief partner resources officer, told us that there is an emotional component to the business: "It's about the relationships that we have with our partners [what Starbucks calls its employees], and their relationship with customers. That creates a unique environment that is the core of our business. You can't have a great relationship with your customers if you don't have a great relationship with your partners. It won't work. It's a strategy that binds us, and an emotional commitment. A couple years ago we had an investor day here in Seattle with a group of investment bankers, and Howard started out saying, 'I want to talk about love.' That felt a little awkward as a way to begin a discussion about how we are doing as a company, but that's a pretty good way to describe what we do. And I haven't seen that in other places I've worked."

Business leaders need to learn, as politicians have, that even if you govern in prose, you must still campaign in poetry.

I Know Myself Well versus *Feedback Is a Gift*

Accurately gauging how we impact others can be very difficult indeed. We will never forget working with one leader who was certain of his ability to be empowering. When asked how he knew his people were empowered, he replied (with no trace of irony), "Because I told them to be."

Leaders need to find time and ways to reflect on their behaviors and their impact on others, identify what drivers shape their behaviors, and determine how, with discipline, to adjust their behaviors. Feedback is critical. Goleman and his colleagues found that an alarming number of leaders suffer from "near-total ignorance" about how they are perceived within the organization. "It's not that leaders don't care how they are perceived; most do. But they incorrectly assume that they can decipher this information themselves. . . . They're wrong."[16]

There is a further stage to be conquered. Something must be done with the feedback. But we humans inherently resist change. We can talk a good talk, but actually making a significant change generates fear in the best of us, and we find incredibly inventive ways to avoid change. We have to own up to needing to do things differently, which can bring feelings of shame, guilt, and incompetence. And any behavior change can be clunky, feel strange, and backfire on us as we try to develop new ways of acting. It's easy to revert to old patterns when we don't get the change right the first time. Change requires grit and determination. Change requires curiosity about one's own resistance to change, coupled with an understanding of the processes going on in our brain. Realizing this can release us from fear.

Shifting Mind-Sets

How do we shift our limiting mind-sets and embrace those that facilitate accelerated performance? What can you do to create mind-set shifts in your leaders?

The change cannot be imposed. You need to truly engage the individual. Individuals need to "unfreeze" existing learned ways of looking at things and the habits that go with them and shift their personal leadership behavior.

The "technology" that we have found to be most helpful incorporates three stages: awareness building, unlocking processes, and reinforcement and embedding activities.

Awareness Building

Build deep insight into the current state of thinking. Create experiences that help your leaders see that what they think of as reality is, in fact, their own personal experience of events, created by their own filters, thoughts, and feelings—so they can examine the experience rather than be subject to it.

We label things to make our world manageable; otherwise, we would overwhelm our senses with information. But the labels we give things create "blinders" and assumptions that benefit from being shaken, challenged, and remolded. We need to be able to recognize the difference between what we know and what we are making up, to know when our stories are just that—stories.

Practicing the art of curiosity and encouraging your leaders to be curious about themselves and others is central. Curiosity raises questions, and questions can lead to a feeling of vulnerability. Therefore, it is important to create a safe environment for people to share their vulnerabilities and experiment in order for them to question and test what can be fundamental and long-held beliefs about how the world operates and how they fit within it.

Add to this mix a heavy dose of straight, two-way communication—the clear communication of observations, thoughts, feelings, and wants.

Unlocking Processes

Stretch your leaders physically, emotionally, and intellectually to enable growth. Provide experiences that offer some discombobulation, a tiredness that enables freedom from how we normally operate and that requires a reorienting of how one sees the world. Ensure that you take your leaders out of their business environment to enable them to become detached from hierarchical labels. Ways of working with the body can be used to release emotions and create new insights and perspectives. A certain amount of intensity needs to be created to provide the conditions for change—an intensity that takes us out of our comfort zone but not into the panic zone!

For these unlocking processes to have a fighting chance of being impactful, leaders need to be able to be fully engaged and present in the moment. A mind busy on the challenges of delivering the next report, juggling the children, or working out how to locate that "just right" birthday present for a loved one has no capacity for unlocking processes.

Teach your leaders tools and techniques to try on new opinions and experiment with new behaviors. This is not about theory input but more about learning from experiences and anecdotes. It is the act of experimentation that opens up worlds of possibility never considered before.

Reinforcement and Embedding Activities

Ensure that your leaders get dedicated self-reflection time—the space to reflect, ponder, and decide what mind-sets and behaviors to adopt into their everyday world and how they are going to make that a reality. Provide tools, techniques, and processes for individuals to draw on when back in the business so they can continue the learning by themselves.

Just as important is to use social reinforcement through creating leadership groups and networks. Tap into the capacity for collective mind-set shifts being reinforced through the group dynamic. We are social creatures, so create programs that provide shared experiences.

Finally, make sure that you use skilled leaders and coaches who know how to open up, facilitate, and close down development safely. There is an art to creating new perspectives that enable new possibilities in others, and there are too many horror stories of badly run sessions and interventions. If you need to go outside of the organization, ask those you trust, do your research, and find the right people with the right credentials. If you want to build capability internally, don't do it lightly. It takes years of learning and development to help others grow in this way, so invest fully and ensure that your internal resources have the supervision and support they need. Anyone who helps your leaders do this work needs to be a role model and keep doing this work on themselves as well.

■ ■ ■

The sum of our advice to leaders and those who build leadership capability in their organizations is to rigorously implement execution rhythms and ruthlessly adopt accelerating mind-sets. These twin disciplines enable leaders to set the pace of their organizations.

Once you see the gilded cage within which you sit, it no longer has the power to hold you, and it's easy to step outside it into high-growth, high-performance leadership.

Notes

1. Bethany McLean, "The empire reboots," *Vanity Fair*, November 2014, vanityfair.com.
2. Bethany McLean, "The empire reboots," *Vanity Fair*, November 2014, vanityfair.com.
3. Dividend Sensei, "Microsoft earnings: Here are the four most important takeaways for dividend investors," *Seeking Alpha*, July 26, 2016, seekingalpha.com.
4. Bethany McLean, "The empire reboots," *Vanity Fair*, November 2014, vanityfair.com.
5. Jessi Hempel, "Microsoft in the age of Satya Nadella," *Wired*, February 2015, wired.com.
6. Luke Johnson, "Animal Spirits: The anatomy of a true leader," *The Sunday Times*, July 12, 2015, thesundaytimes.co.uk.
7. Jack Zenger and Joseph Folkman, "You have to be fast to be seen as a great leader," *Harvard Business Review*, February 26, 2015, hbr.org.

8. Kevin O'Connor, "Nine ways great companies organize their teams for success," *Fast Company*, August 21, 2012, fastcompany.com.

9. At the risk of giving you too many things to focus on, here is a list we generated after working with thousands of leaders. These are 10 things every leader can do that do not require talent, special gifts, or resources but instead just require you to be aware, self-disciplined, and focused: (1) Work hard; (2) use positive body language; (3) be prompt; (4) be clear on what you want from a meeting; (5) seek feedback; (6) give feedback; (7) convey passion; (8) bring energy; (9) say thank you; and (10) keep specific, achievable, and prioritized action lists. We encourage you to scan this list and give yourself a score, from 1 to 10, for each. How did you do? What was your score out of a maximum of 100? It's a good list to keep handy as you go through your working day and week. Ask two or three people who frequently interact with you to give you some impromptu feedback on how you did on these 10 things at the end of meetings or projects.

10. Paul Brown and Brenda Hales, "Neuro-science for neuro-leadership: Feelings not thinking rule decision making," *Developing Leaders: Executive Education in Practice*, Issue 6, 2012.

11. Daniel Goleman, Richard Boyatzis, and Annie McKee, "Primal leadership: The hidden driver of great performance," *Harvard Business Review*, December 2001, hbr.org.

12. For more, see Jennifer Robison, "Turning around employee turnover," *Gallup Business Journal*, May 8, 2008, gallup.com; and Bryant Ott and Emily Killham, "Would you fire your boss?," *Gallup Business Journal*, September 13, 2007, gallup.com.

13. Gary Hamel, "The 15 diseases of leadership, according to Pope Francis," *Harvard Business Review*, April 14, 2015, hbr.org.

14. Bill Snyder, "Researchers: How much difference does a boss make?" Stanford Graduate School of Business, September 27, 2012, gsb.stanford.edu.

15. Paul Brown and Brenda Hales, "Neuro-science for neuro-leadership: Feelings not thinking rule decision making," *Developing Leaders: Executive Education in Practice*, Issue 6, 2012.

16. Daniel Goleman, Richard Boyatzis, and Annie McKee, "Primal leadership: The hidden driver of great performance," *Harvard Business Review*, December 2001, hbr.org.

How to Start

Now it's time to start thinking about how to put into action all the data we've provided on how to accelerate your strategy, your organization, your teams, and your leaders.

Chapter 10 explains how to find the right recipe. It's not possible to carry out all the differentiating actions we identified in the previous four chapters. It's not even advisable to try, because you'll wind up focusing on lots of issues that just don't matter much for your organization. Instead, you need to pick your battles by choosing the right recipe of actions to take. We lay out four recipes that, in our experience, work best. One centers on understanding the customer intimately, one on attracting the best talent, one on becoming expert at managing a portfolio of businesses (for instance, by quickly moving capital to the best opportunities), and one on executing at a world-class level. We describe the six threshold actions necessary for any recipe to succeed, as well as the four anchor actions that are specific to each of the four recipes. We also provide a series of acid tests, so you can tell whether you're succeeding. For instance, if you capture a 20 percent price premium, that indicates you're intimate with your customers. You are a talent magnet if your unplanned (or regretted) turnover is half the norm in your industry and you need 30 percent less time than the norm to fill a position. And so on.

Chapter 11 describes how to get people to embrace all the changes that will come with implementing your chosen recipe. The change model covers five steps, each consisting of three parts. First, you can't just talk to people about the coming transition; you have to engage them in honest dialogue as you communicate the need to change. Then you have to realign the organization to support them and teach them new skills. You also have to role-model the new behavior for employees and hold yourself and others to account against the new standards. This is hard. The tendency is to be forgiving. But holding to account is crucial. The biggest piece that leaders miss in trying to effect change is that they don't give people enough space. You can't force someone to change. People have to choose to do so, and you have to give them the ability to think about things, to experiment, to decide what they want to do. Change management has traditionally been about pushing change onto people, but it needs to shift to a "pull" model, where the employee draws on whatever resources he or she needs for the change to occur.

Chapter 12 focuses on the fact that your organization still needs to change, whether individuals decide they want to or not. As the chapter title says, you have two options: You must either "change the people or change the people." In other words, you have to move out those who are unwilling or unable to come with you on the new journey and replace them with those who want to join and who are capable of doing so. We focus on the CEO and the top team, because they have the most leverage in the organization, and draw both on our research and on Heidrick & Struggles' extensive experience with executive placement. We describe, for instance, the seven archetypes of the people who likely won't be up for change and list the seven factors that are most important in determining whether a new hire is likely to succeed. We also explain the four steps to follow when you have to exit a senior employee, both to handle the unpleasant task as smoothly as possible for all concerned and to learn as much as you can to go through the process less often in the future.

That discussion on replacing senior executives leads into Chapter 13, on the board as a catalyst. Our research turned up some surprises. For instance, boards at superaccelerator companies tend to be smaller than boards at others, with less representation from outside the industry and younger members. We also found that there are four types of effective boards, roughly matching up with the four recipes for successful acceleration that we describe in Chapter 10. We conclude with a list of five things that every board should do, even if they do nothing else. Chief among them: Be willing to fire yourself. The truth is that the days of "professional directors" are over. You can't just coast as a director, enjoying a reward for long and distinguished service. Directors need to be all in, or they need to be gone.

CHAPTER 10

Finding the Right Recipe

Bluefin tuna, Kobe beef, Alba white truffles, Coffin Bay king oysters, kopi luwak coffee, bird's nest, and saffron are among the world's most expensive and prized ingredients—but you wouldn't put them all in the same dish. In the same way, as you sort through all the actions we've shown that can lead to acceleration and that you should consider, you shouldn't attempt all of them at once. Instead, you need to come up with a sort of recipe that will let you blend the right ingredients in the right proportions so that you wind up with something that could be served at an Alain Ducasse restaurant and not a tuna/beef/truffle/oyster/coffee/bird's nest/saffron stew.

In fact, our research did not find any company that attempted all of the actions that can turn drag into drive at the four levels (strategy, organizations, teams, and leaders). Instead, we found that accelerating companies successfully selected a subset of actions based on aspirations and an understanding of the company's competitive advantage and culture. We found very strong evidence of what academics call "complementarity." That is, virtually all of the actions we recommend are much more powerful when combined with others from the same winning recipe. The inverse is also true. Actions that are implemented without a coherence to their selection lose their power markedly.

Our work has some parallels with Professor Michael Porter's work on strategy, where he insists that companies have to make a hard choice among cost, value, or differentiation, rather than "get stuck in the middle." One of his most famous quotes is: "Strategy is about making choices, trade-offs; it's about deliberately choosing to be different."[1]

In other words, strategy isn't just what you do but also what you don't do. The same is true for organization acceleration. Doing too many unconnected actions will likely slow you down, not speed you up.

In our research, we identified four recipes (combining actions from different drive factors) that companies have used to successfully pursue acceleration.

The recipes are Customer Intimate, Talent Magnet, Portfolio Investor, and Execution Engine (see Figure 10.1). Each has four anchor actions; these are the actions that you must get right. In addition to the anchor actions that are specific to each recipe, there are six threshold actions that are common to all recipes.

Choosing a recipe helps organizations to focus among the 39 possible actions that we laid out in Chapter 7 ("Accelerating Organizations"). Each recipe

FIGURE 10.1 Recipes, actions, and acid tests

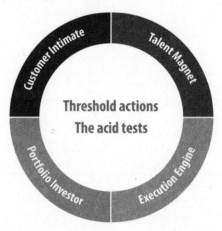

Foundational elements for each recipe

Threshold actions
- Use purpose as your fuel
- Role-model urgency
- Reduce layers
- Place big people in big jobs
- Exit people who don't live your values
- Develop digital dexterity

The acid tests
- Purpose mentioned by top 20 leaders at least once a month
- Ratio of managerial costs to other costs <80% of what competitors experience
- Top 10 improvement projects directly affect 80% of top 100 managers
- Destination employer for top talent
- 90% of decisions supported by big data analysis

Recipe: Customer Intimate

Anchor actions
- Immerse yourself in the customer experience
- Co-innovate with customers
- Be one firm
- Gear your measurement systems to start with customers and end with finance

The acid tests
- Customer churn under 10%
- Sunset more products each year than new ones are introduced
- Customers' interfaces with the organization's multiple units reduced to less than 3
- Capture a 20% price premium

FIGURE 10.1 (*Continued*)

Recipe: Talent Magnet

Anchor actions
- Become distinguished for your investment in people
- Build winning teams
- Speak truth to power
- Celebrate net exporters of talent

The acid tests
- Listed toward the top of the list of companies people like to work for
- ROI in training and development above 100%
- Unplanned turnover at half the normal rate; planned turnover at double the normal rate
- Time to fill a new open position 30% below local benchmark

Recipe: Portfolio Investor

Anchor actions
- Think of business units as guests, not family
- Invest with courage
- Protect the space to innovate
- Break free of hierarchy; align resources with opportunities

The acid tests
- No annual budgeting process; zero-based budgets every two years
- High variability in portfolio configuration
- Ability to innovate hardwired into formal processes (e.g., performance evaluation, compensation)
- As many initiatives are abandoned each year as are started

Recipe: Execution Engine

Anchor actions
- Let "simple," "consistent," and "scalable" be your watchwords
- List your priorities on one hand
- Emphasize speed to adoption
- Systematically learn from mistakes; fail fast with confidence

The acid tests
- Small top team with daily interactions
- Adoption and cascading of new processes take less than half the time they take competitors
- No more than 7 signature processes adopted across the whole organization
- Cost per unit falling by 2% each year or more

includes a single coherent set of actions to take in order to build an organization that can help create value in a way that is consistent with the company's strategy.

Most successful organizations we have seen tend to choose just one recipe to pursue. Just as Usain Bolt and Serena Williams are both successful in their chosen sport and yet are very, very different athletes, focusing on their own unique actions to succeed, so it is with the recipes. Choose your recipe and excel at it, rather than trying to get the best of both worlds and ending up good at two things but vulnerable to a competitor who is great at one.

This is arguably one of the reasons for restructuring Google, which follows a Talent Magnet recipe, into a holding company, Alphabet. Alphabet pursues a Portfolio Investor strategy—and Google carries on being a great Talent Magnet.

In fact, we've seen very few companies that have successfully pursued two recipes simultaneously. They tend to be very successful companies, overrepresented among our superaccelerators. Tata Consultancy Services, for example, with its relentless focus on revenue and margin growth, as well as on customers, appears to be an example of a company that has mastered both the Customer Intimate and Execution Engine recipes. As there are few companies to observe, it is difficult to say this with the certainty that comes with large amounts of empirical data, but TCS seems to have mastered one recipe before mastering the second. The recommended path for most organizations is to choose a single recipe and get great at it.

The Customer Intimate recipe is all about putting the customer at the center of what the company does. The anchor actions ensure that the customer, who traditionally stays outside the confines of the organization, is brought inside and becomes a key ingredient of the business model. As Figure 10.1 shows, the anchor actions draw on four of the drive factors we've identified at the organization level: immerse yourself in the customer experience; co-innovate with customers; be one firm; and gear your measurement systems to start with customers and end with finance.

To create a better customer experience, company executives see and feel it firsthand. The company presents one face to the customer and minimizes the points of contact to avoid confusion. Innovation happens with the customer's input, through customer councils, focus groups, and crowdsourcing. Performance management focuses on customer metrics, relegating financial metrics to a secondary plane.

You will pick this recipe if you are operating in an environment where customers' needs are rapidly evolving, where customer loyalty is hard to gain and easy to lose, and where customer decisions can really make or break your business.

We suggest four acid tests to make sure that you are mastering this recipe. First, your customer turnover will be less than 10 percent—why would people leave if you know them intimately? Second, you will be "sunsetting" more products than you introduce because you will know more about how to target your customers' needs. Third, the interfaces with your customers will be reduced to three or fewer; you don't want customers to have to navigate the complexities of your organization to be able to get what they want. Finally, you will capture a 20 percent price premium.

These acid tests should not necessarily be copied verbatim at every organization. There is scope for customization to suit the industry, the particulars of the business model, or even just available data. However, whatever acid tests your organization chooses should be as ambitious, as edgy, and as measurable as the ones we have outlined.

Exemplars of the Customer Intimate model include Cigna, Shire, and Tata Consultancy Services, whose CEO and managing director, Natarajan

Chandrasekaran, describes the company's goal as "Stay close and stay relevant. Whether you are in the front office, the back office, or the CEO of the company, every employee should know how what they do affects the customer."

The Talent Magnet recipe puts companies constantly on the lookout for the best people available. This recipe also means a huge focus on retaining that talent, offering opportunities for professional and personal development. In their book *An Everyone Culture: Becoming a Deliberately Developmental Organization*, our good friends Robert Kegan and Lisa Laskow Lahey argue that it's possible to build psychological advancement of employees into their jobs and accomplish talent goals organically. This is key for companies following the Talent Magnet recipe. These are its four anchor actions: become distinguished for your investment in people; build winning teams; speak truth to power; and celebrate net exporters of talent.

Talent Magnet organizations create an environment where building teams (and disassembling them) is seamless and provides the best approach to deliver better results. The talent feels empowered because they aren't being micromanaged; they operate in a way that reinforces their sense of ownership of the business and the outcomes they produce. They are not afraid to speak up and are free to craft their own growth trajectory.

You would pick this recipe if the caliber of the people working in your organization represents a competitive advantage. This is often true of knowledge-intensive organizations, but highly operation-based companies can also follow a Talent Magnet recipe.

The acid tests that let you know whether you are a successful Talent Magnet are, first of all, that you are ranked toward the top of the list of companies that people like to work for and that your return on investment (ROI) in training and development is above 100 percent. You also have unplanned (or regretted) employee turnover at half the normal rate and planned (or non-regretted) turnover at double the normal rate. The time required to fill a new open position is 30 percent below the local benchmark.

As we've said, Alphabet's Google subsidiary is an absolute Talent Magnet. So are Starbucks and Cerner.

The Portfolio Investor recipe is all about allocating resources to the opportunities that will drive the company forward. These companies take a more venture capital–based view of their business portfolio, thinking about it in terms of the opportunity it represents and not of tradition.

The four anchor actions, again drawn from the drive factors for accelerating organizations, mean that Portfolio Investors acquire and divest actively (treating business units as guests, not family), make courageous investment decisions, and preserve the space for experimentation and innovation. They ensure that resources are not tied to structures or hierarchy and have mechanisms in place to allocate the best resources to the most promising opportunities—and quickly reallocate them if an opportunity does not deliver on its promise.

You would pick this recipe if you are operating in a particularly volatile environment, where business results are driven by constant innovation and disruption is a daily occurrence.

An acid test for a successful Portfolio Investor is a lack of an annual budget process: The formal budget is much more fluid to allow for faster reallocation, but with zero-based budgeting every two years. In addition, there is a high variability of return in the portfolio. The ability to innovate is hardwired into formal processes such as performance evaluation and compensation, and as many initiatives are abandoned each year as are begun.

Danaher, BlackRock, and The Priceline Group are all prime examples of Portfolio Investors.

The Execution Engine recipe is about a focus on efficiency and effectiveness. Simplicity is the core concept that drives these organizations. The four anchor actions are: Let "simple," "consistent," and "scalable" be your watchwords; list your priorities on one hand; emphasize speed to adoption; and systematically learn from mistakes—fail fast with confidence.

This focus on simplicity means that processes are easy to replicate and scale. Priorities are reduced to a few that are easy to communicate and monitor. Execution Engine companies also focus on continuous improvement and learning, disseminating the best ideas across the organization quickly and learning from mistakes, which encourages a trial-and-error approach to solving problems.

This recipe is appropriate if your focus is on delivering products and services at a low cost, if you are concerned about responding to pressures from the market, and if evolution comes in manageable ways, rather than in huge steps.

The acid tests for success include: The size of the top team is small and interacts daily; the adoption and cascading of new processes take half as long as they take other organizations; there are no more than seven signature processes across the whole organization; and unit costs fall by 2 percent or more each year on a like-for-like basis.

Great examples of Execution Engines include Apple, Gilead Sciences, and Intercontinental Exchange. We've included Apple here, as it has demonstrated mastery through its supply chain management, innovation in manufacturing processes, and ruthless focus on innovation that turned into high-volume consumer products—as opposed to low-volume concept products. There is no doubt that Apple has a strong minor in customer intimacy and could, in time, become a true master of two recipes simultaneously, but Apple is not there yet. The bar for being a master of two recipes is that high.

The six threshold activities—common to all four recipes because they are fundamental—shone through the data. Without a clear purpose, no organization can embark on a journey. People need to know where they are going and why. This purpose has to be communicated clearly and often. Leadership must also signal urgency, so people aren't tempted to think that they are just going through a phase, experiencing "another" transformation that will fade like the ones before it. Structures need to be simple, or the organization becomes stale, bureaucratic, and political. The right people must be in the big jobs. You must exit the people who are going to stand in the way, especially if they have clout. Finally, in this day and age you can't compete if you don't embrace digital. Big data is at the core of a company's better understanding of its people, customers, competitors, strategy, and environment.

The threshold actions also have corresponding acid tests, and organizations should measure how well they are doing. Acid tests include whether the organization's purpose is being communicated monthly by each of the top 20 leaders. The ratio of managerial costs to other costs should be no more than 80 percent that of competitors. The top 10 improvement projects in the organization should directly affect at least 80 percent of the top 100 managers—if not, they won't have impact. The organization should be a destination for top talent and should be making at least 90 percent of its decisions with the support of big data analytics.

Again, these acid test are examples. More important than adopting them wholesale is making sure that whatever tests you do adopt have the same level of ambition and are as easily and regularly measured.

Choosing the right recipe is one of the most important tasks when starting an acceleration journey. Choosing the wrong recipe or a random combination of differentiating actions may not produce the desired outcome. Worse, the choice may backfire and create unnecessary turmoil, resulting in fatigue and wasted resources.

What the Right Recipe Can Produce

Pictures of the Googleplex can make Google look like an adult playground, not a place for work. But Google's success can be attributed to relentlessly following the Talent Magnet recipe. Google has people whose sole job is to keep employees happy and maintain productivity— and, as Paul Krugman says, "Productivity isn't everything, but in the long run it is almost everything."[2]

Each year, Google gets about 2 million applicants.[3] That's more than 5,479 per day and not quite 4 per minute—and Google reviews each one. That's partly because Google wants those who are turned down to still feel good about the process, so they won't bad-mouth the company to those Google does want to hire. Google relentlessly tracks how its criteria for hiring match actual performance and, once it updates the criteria, will go back through applicants who were turned down and offer jobs to some of them.

If Google wants people who aren't looking for a job, it may "acqui-hire" them. For instance, Google acquired start-up incubator Milk in 2012 for a reported $15 million to $30 million to bring on Digg founder Kevin Rose and a few other key people. Google acquired Meebo, an instant messaging service that developed into a toolbar and an ad platform, for a reported $100 million in 2012 to "hire" Seth Sternberg and a few others. Google shut down both Milk and Meebo after the acquisitions.

Google offers incredible perks to its employees. That's expensive, but much less so than having employee dissatisfaction and high turnover. Human resources, or People Operations, is a science at Google. It's always testing to find ways to optimize its people, both in terms of happiness and performance. Almost everything Google does is based on data. Google doesn't view its culture as a "set it and forget it" program.

What a Confused Recipe Can Produce

Sears Holdings Corp. is a company in steady decline. The owner of Sears, Kmart, and Lands' End chose a recipe that had no alignment and, in the end, destroyed value. The principal owner, Eddie Lampert, a hedge fund manager once mentioned in the same breath as Warren Buffett, focused on financial metrics, essentially hoping that the underlying real estate for his stores would more than justify what he paid for the retailers. As a result, his efforts to actually run the stores have been a series of tactical moves that didn't mesh.

Managers have been pressing ahead with initiatives such as a customer loyalty program, a push for a larger e-commerce presence, and celebrity-designed clothing lines. But any strides are overshadowed by the shrinking consumer base. Any initiatives the company implements right now will need at least a year to take hold, and in a precarious economy with fierce competition from nimbler store operators such as Target Corp. and Home Depot Inc., Sears and Kmart stores don't have room for missteps.

The company recently closed its Sears Hometown and Outlet chains and is steadily closing Sears and Kmart stores, while also reducing inventory. The hope is to find a core business that works and stop the downward spiral, but the company has been ignoring customers: Many stores are unkempt, and management has just been paying lip service to merchandise. Sears and Kmart stores need to attract new customers if they want to win over investors and achieve long-term success. But no strategies have worked to date.

How to Find the Right Recipe

Figure 10.2 shows the five factors you need to consider in depth as you build your acceleration agenda.

FIGURE 10.2 Setting the agenda

To sort through your options, start with anticipation, with what the future calls for. How do you expect to win in future market conditions based on major trends and potential sources of disruption? How can you profit from uncertain, unavoidable environmental shocks in the future while challenging conventional wisdom? You'll need to revisit the issue frequently because "strategy" is changing from a noun to a verb in these days of continual transformation.

Next, consider the intent of the organization. What is it you want to create? What do you want to be known for? What imprint do you want to have on the world, and what legacy do you wish to leave? You can't just have a strategic ambition; the hearts and souls, dreams, and ambitions of your people must be in sync to sustain energy.

Then, consider what your brand values are, what you stand for in the marketplace. A company and its products are always involved in a sort of conversation with customers. You can say you stand for something, but you have to get customers to accept what you say. You need to understand what they're thinking and how far you can move them in the hoped-for direction.

Look, as well, at your organization's heritage. There are successes and failures that resonate with people because of your history. There are stories that have passed into lore. You need to take a hard look at where you've been before and the sources of your competitive advantage. This will help you understand where you can go and which of the differentiating actions are most important for getting you there.

Finally, look at the stance of your competitors and decide whether to attack or avoid. As much as we all like to think we control our destinies, we aren't working in a vacuum. There are competitors out there, plenty of them, and we have to understand how and where we can gain an advantage and where we shouldn't try to compete.

Once you've viewed the META framework through the lens of anticipation, your intent, your brand values, your heritage, and your stance against competitors, you may see an obvious choice of recipe. For instance, a large global engineering company with the strategic aim of dominating the market for medical goods and with a 125-year history of engineering excellence that its leaders are very proud of but with a troubled time-to-delivery record is likely to fit the Execution Engine recipe.

The size, scope, and scale of change required to adopt a recipe, however, must not be underestimated. It is not for those without dogged determination. The choice of recipe and how far it takes you from your current path needs to be considered thoughtfully. If the difference between your strategic intent and your heritage is huge, you have an uphill climb.

With your recipe firmly in mind, the next step in the journey is to conduct some diagnostics. The aim is to look for data, patterns, and insights from forensically examining your organization. There are many ways to do this. You can draw on the four accelerator tools that we describe in the Research Appendix—the SAQ, OAQ, TAQ, and LAQ—and correlate the data with what can be seen in your financial, customer risk, and people data. However you choose to diagnose your organization, the diagnostics must give you a thorough understanding of the current state of your organization vis-à-vis the acceleration agenda.

If the diagnostics reveal that you are already in pretty good shape on the threshold and anchor actions for your recipe, you can turn your attention to those actions that are in worse shape. As an example: If your ideal recipe is the one we call Execution Engine and your diagnosis reveals a very complex matrix organization with unclear accountabilities, you obviously need to do something to reduce organizational complexity and clarify accountabilities. If the team diagnostic, the TAQ, shows a very unaligned top team, it may be wise to spend some time creating alignment there, even before you start picking differentiating actions that match the recipe.

The results of the diagnostics will, most likely, reveal issues with the threshold or anchor actions. The threshold ones, in particular, are ones that companies get wrong.

A Journey in More Detail

A global electronics retailer was going through a very rough period. The company seemed to have lost touch with its customers and damaged relationships with key suppliers, as a result of excessive centralization, at a time when consumer tastes were changing, both in terms of the products they wanted to buy and in terms of how they wanted to buy those products. Market share was dissolving even in the most successful markets.

The CEO called his top team together to get everyone aligned on a common strategy and aspiration. To help them decide what kind of recipe they were aiming for, they took stock of where they wanted the company to be in 5 to 10 years. It was clear that they had high aspirations: They wanted to regain their place in the market and the industry. They also reviewed the value of their brand, which has always been about creating a hassle-free environment for customers to find what they are looking for. They reflected on their heritage, on how entrepreneurialism became the key engine for growth in the early years, and how important it was to go back to an environment where people felt ownership of results and of the business. The top team reviewed the competitive landscape, looking at changes in the industry and at concrete threats—cheap manufacturing, shortening of production cycles, and growth of online retailing for consumer electronics.

Based on all the input, the team could anticipate a future that provided big opportunities for the company. Increasing complexity and diversity in product specifications were making it harder for consumers to make purchasing decisions, creating a need for expertise that others in the industry weren't providing. In addition, it seemed likely that there would be a resurgence of smaller, urban, specialized retail concepts across a variety of categories. That change, too, would create an opportunity for more personalized selling that could move products away from the commodity end of the spectrum and reduce the emphasis on selling at the lowest price.

This information pointed toward the recipe we call Customer Intimate (Figure 10.3). The team decided that they needed to do everything in their power to rebuild the relationship they had with their customers and their understanding of customers' needs and concerns. They needed to go back to putting the customer at the center of everything they did.

They completed a self-diagnosis. It was clear that there were some things that required a more deliberate response and were important to address before moving forward; others that seemed easier to fix, particularly

FIGURE 10.3 Customer Intimate recipe

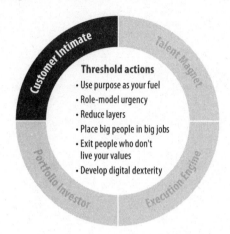

Anchor actions
- Immerse yourself in the customer experience
- Co-innovate with customers
- Be one firm
- Gear your measurement systems to start with customers and end with finance

Threshold actions
- Use purpose as your fuel
- Role-model urgency
- Reduce layers
- Place big people in big jobs
- Exit people who don't live your values
- Develop digital dexterity

based on the company's history; and still others that would be harder to implement but that eventually would reap the biggest rewards for the organization. The self-diagnosis indicated that the company needed to make employees the eyes and ears for the organization, sensing what customers wanted and reporting back quickly in ways that could drive actions. The company also needed to increase its digital capabilities, to facilitate feedback on customers' desires, and to streamline decision making about how to respond. The company needed new measurement systems to gauge how well it was understanding customers, with the idea that those measurements would show up soon enough in the financial measures of success. The company also decided to experiment with ways to work with customers to understand what their ultimate needs were and to coinvent products and processes that would fill those needs, even if that meant going outside normal sales channels.

The recipe worked. The company managed to reorganize itself around the customer and—through the sorts of programs we'll describe in detail in Chapter 11 on how to implement change—drove the new ethos through the whole organization. But the hard work didn't stop there. The company had to keep tinkering with the recipe to get it right, but it was off to a good start toward recapturing its past glory.

■ ■ ■

Recipes don't always work. Soufflés fall. Sauces burn. Difficult ingredients fail to cooperate. But good recipes succeed far more often than they fail. And working without a recipe, tricky enough for even a genius chef in a kitchen of a few dozen people, is a guaranteed way to fail, once you multiply a major corporation's complexity by its size.

Notes

1. Keith H. Hammonds, "Michael Porter's big ideas," *Fast Company*, February 28, 2001, fastcompany.com.
2. Paul Krugman, *The Age of Diminished Expectations*, Cambridge, MA: MIT Press, 1994.
3. Tom Lamont, "How to get a job at Google: Meet the man who hires and fires," *Guardian*, April 6, 2015, theguardian.com.

CHAPTER 11

The ABC of Behavior Change

Alice has an exchange with the Cheshire Cat in Wonderland that ends with her saying that she just wants to "get *somewhere*." The cat responds, "Oh, you're sure to do that if you only walk long enough." Even once you've done all the hard work of determining your recipe, you'll wind up like Alice—*somewhere*—unless you develop a very specific set of actions that will change the behavior of your people.

When you get the behavior change right, the results can be stunning. Former U.S. president Jimmy Carter showed this with his campaign against the Guinea worm, a horrible parasite that afflicted three million people in 1980, as he was leaving office. The worm larvae live in freshwater and can infect those who drink the water. The larvae then turn into worms and grow within the host's body to as long as three feet. There can be several in one person. After about a year, a worm may erupt through the person's skin, and it has to be slowly pulled out; sometimes, an incision is made in the skin with a hot knife to get to the worm. To ease the pain, many infected people jump into the water, releasing larvae and starting the process all over again. But through education, the use of guards around water sites, and other measures, Carter's campaign has almost succeeded in eradicating the disease. The number of cases worldwide has gone from three million to two. Not two million. Two.[1]

Keep in mind that, when transformations don't work, the biggest reason is that bold new ideas weren't implemented quickly enough.[2] Richard Branson says that one of his favorite quotes, from Karen Lamb, is: "A year from now, you'll wish you had started today."[3]

The CEO of a global semiconductor company surely wishes he had moved faster with a transformation program that he rolled out to the company's 50,000 employees around the world. Few even knew how to contribute to the first phase, and he didn't roll out the second phase for two years. The program failed. By contrast, a major retailer took only a few weeks to roll out a transformation to its 40,000 employees. On the first day, executives three levels down from the CEO sat down with district managers, described major initiatives, asked for commitments, and got into details about how the managers could contribute. A week later, the district managers finalized their commitments. Two weeks after that, the district managers took store managers through the same process, and then the store managers repeated the process with their teams. Management finished with a three-hour event for the whole company on a Sunday morning and then opened the 800-plus stores in a very different environment.[4]

Ambrose Bierce wrote in *The Unabridged Devil's Dictionary* that patience is "a minor form of despair, disguised as a virtue."[5] We believe that organizations need less patience and more acceleration.

The "Any Behavior Change" (ABC) model we developed allows you to identify the very specific components you should assemble to drive behavior change and shows how best to combine them.

The "Any Behavior Change" (ABC) Model

Every organization objective is at its core a behavior change. Nothing changes without people in the organization doing something different—interacting with a customer in a different way, taking layers out of a structure, or scanning the environment to more effectively spot trends. All change involves actual people doing something actually different in practice. The key question is how to get thousands, tens of thousands, or hundreds of thousands of people to take actions that accelerate the metabolic rate of the organization.

John Murabito, executive vice president of human resources and services at Cigna, told us the company pulls five levers to shape its culture and values: "mission and strategy, structure that supports, the right people in place, the right processes, and the rewards that reinforce what we're trying to achieve." He further stressed that Cigna "always goes to those five things to try to drive a culture that is supportive of our strategy. People care about the customer, care about each other, are passionate about our business and our business model, and care about development."

We, too, emphasize five arenas of activities that need to be in place to shape culture and drive behavior change, and our approach aligns with the one used at Cigna. The ABC model provides a map of the territory to be navigated (Figure 11.1). First, leaders need to connect with their people through a common and compelling purpose. Next, leaders must align the operating model of the organization to reinforce the behavior change. Third, capabilities must be built—there is no point in asking people to do things differently if they don't have the skills to do so. Fourth, the changes must be role-modeled by leaders; we all know that following the parental mantra of "Do as I say, not as I do" will ruin any chance of colleagues doing what leaders ask of them (although it is surprising how many senior players

FIGURE 11.1 The ABC model

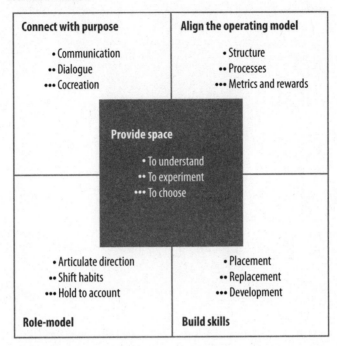

still try to get away with this manner of leading). Fifth, but by no means last, is the need to provide space for people to explore the change being asked of them and to choose whether to adopt it.

Each arena is supported by both traditional and current insight and knowledge from behavioral, psychological, and adult developmental research. Each has three different levels at which it can be applied. Each subsequent level demands more of leaders' skill and time than the last but also provides much greater impact on achieving sustainable behavior change. Let's explore these five arenas in more detail.

Connect with Purpose

Purpose provides a reason to change. If you want people to change, the purpose tells them why. It tells them why continuing to behave in the way they do won't help to deliver on that purpose and why shifting how they do what they do will make a difference. Purpose can engage people and tap into their discretionary effort.

"The need for purpose is one of the defining characteristics of human beings," as Steve Taylor said.[6] Focusing on purpose shields us from the distractions in our heads and in our daily lives. Tying in to a wider purpose helps us feel connected, which allows us to feel safe. Connecting to our organization's purpose may even put us in a state of "flow," where we forget our surroundings and ourselves and can find a sense of well-being and happiness.[7]

So leaders who can inspire will create followership. Peers, customers, and employees all align with a greater purpose under their own steam and not because they are told to.

Let's take you back to 1930. As an employee of Kroger Stores, Mike Cullen wrote a letter to the company's president, Bernard Kroger, in which he suggested a new type of store. He believed that a supermarket—with large square footage, where customers could get consumer goods for low prices, with cash-only sales, with no delivery service, and with lots of parking— could greatly benefit consumers. When his letter didn't get a response, he quit his job and moved his family to Long Island, New York. On August 4, 1930, Cullen took his life savings and opened the world's first supermarket, carrying a range of 1,000 items. Today the family still owns 35 King Kullen stores around Long Island, doing $1 billion in annual revenues. Having a clear purpose as "the world's greatest price wrecker" gave Cullen and his employees the ambition they needed to revolutionize the grocery industry.

Similarly, Ingvar Kamprad had nothing when he started IKEA in 1943 other than a clear purpose: "to create a better everyday life for the many people." The same purpose, more than 70 years on, guides IKEA employees today. Many who comment on the success of IKEA, whose owner in 2015 was estimated by Bloomberg to be personally worth more than $43 billion, cite the adoption of the IKEA purpose by employees and customers as their own.[8]

The first level in the art of connecting with purpose is *communication*. This means describing the rationale to people for behaving differently, in a simple and compelling way. Organizations and people don't resist change; they resist loss. So the message needs to include, "What's in it for me?"

Simon Sinek says that very few people can clearly articulate why they do what they do—what their purpose is and why they pursue the things they pursue.[9] When most companies and people think, act, or communicate, they do so from the outside in—from what to why. Companies try to sell us *what* they do, but we buy *why* they do it. As Sinek explained in a TED talk, if Apple were like every other company, it would say, "We make great computers. They are beautifully designed, simple to use, and user friendly. Want to buy one?" Sinek said that Apple actually says, "Everything we do, we believe in challenging the status quo. We believe in thinking differently. The way we challenge the status quo is by making our products beautifully designed, simple to use, and user-friendly. We just happen to make great computers. Want to buy one?"[10] The same principles should apply when we are "selling" a behavior change. Communicate the why first.

We also need to communicate much more than we think we need to. John Kotter found that change agents typically undercommunicate their vision by at least a factor of 10.[11] As Adam Grant puts the issue in his book *Originals: How Non-Conformists Move the World*, in three months an employee might hear about the vision in "a 30-minute speech, an hour-long meeting, a briefing, and a memo. Since more than 99 percent of the communication that employees encounter during those three months does not concern the vision, how can they be expected to understand it, let alone internalize it?"[12] Change agents miss the need for more communication because they are so familiar with their ideas.

The second level in connecting with purpose is *dialogue*. Issuing one-way messages gets you only so far. As Andy Stanley says, "Leaders who don't listen will eventually be surrounded by people with nothing to say." Dialogue is far more powerful in inciting long-lasting change in others. Dialogue is an authentic process of genuinely seeking others' opinions.

The third level is *cocreation*. Lasting change occurs through insight, not instruction. Cocreating with others allows them to own and understand the results, which may get them to tap into their discretionary effort— the time and talent they don't have to provide you but will under the right circumstances.

For dialogue and cocreation efforts (and compelling communication) to be successful, they need to activate the primary reward circuitry of the brains of those involved and reduce the primary threat circuitry. Based on developments in neuroscience, David Rock's SCARF model provides a handy framework for shaping and implementing dialogue and cocreation. SCARF involves "five domains of human social experience: Status, Certainty, Autonomy, Relatedness, and Fairness." You need to make the effort important (Status), while making people feel they can predict the future (Certainty) and control events (Autonomy) in an environment where they are safe among their peers (Relatedness) and are treated equitably (Fairness).[13]

Align the Operating Model

Your people may well be engaged in the why of the change you want them to make happen. However, if it's a meaningful change, they are likely to need you to provide an operating model that enables them to deliver on that shift.

At the simplest level, this might mean changing the *structure* of the organization. For example, in the pursuit of greater customer intimacy, it is probably better if the company is organized along customer segments than along product lines. Many organizations move boxes and lines on the structure chart as a first step to resolve challenges or exploit opportunities.

On its own, structural change will achieve only so much. The second level is fundamental change to operating *processes*. The way the lifeblood pumps around the organization will help or hinder the organization.

Take a telecom company. It's pretty hard to deliver high levels of quality customer service when a convoluted and siloed process flow means multiple touch points for a customer wishing to buy products, have a fault repaired, or even order a second telephone line for the business he or she runs from home. The multiple handoffs are a recipe for disaster.

Today, the digitization revolution opens up all kinds of opportunity for recrafting processes. Take the simple but sublime customer experience of shopping in an Apple store. Within five minutes, you are served, supplied, and invoiced; payment is taken; and a receipt is sent to your e-mail address. What might have taken you half an hour waiting in line becomes a quick and impressive service that leaves you grateful for the time saved and with a feeling of goodwill toward such a thoughtful company.

The third level in aligning the operating model uses *metrics and rewards*, which classical motivational theorists such as Victor Vroom, B. F. Skinner, and Ivan Pavlov have shown can modify outcomes and which modern practices such as lean and Six Sigma use to drive continuous improvement. So give your people an enabling structure and underlying processes that support the ambitions of a purpose they've bought into. However, if you measure and reward them in a contradictory way, you create a gravitational force that few can resist no matter how compelling the vision. An electrician in a utility company who is paid based on how many jobs he gets through in a day, whether the jobs are finished or not, is less likely to take the extra time needed to finish a tricky job no matter how much he thinks that is the right thing to do for the customer and the company he works for. As Upton Sinclair posits, "It is difficult to get a man to understand something, when his salary depends upon his not understanding it."[14]

Getting metrics and rewards schemes right is notoriously difficult. They often have unintended consequences. It's a bit like managing a blancmange—poke it on one side, and it pops out the other in ways you did not anticipate. The upsides, though, can be fabulous.

Recent insights from studies provide good clues on how to do metrics and rewards well. According to Rock and his SCARF model, the neurological science finds that a sense of inequity hurts the same part of the brain as physical pain, so we need to avoid creating any feelings of unfair treatment. The increasing understanding of the importance of nonmonetary recognition also represents great potential for many organizations. There is an opportunity to involve employees in deciding on the optimum metrics and the best formula for providing rewards. With human capital gaining prominence over financial capital, getting metrics and rewards right is fundamentally important to organization acceleration.

Digitization creates a new world of possibilities for processes, metrics, and rewards. Routine business activities can be automated, creating time for the most important issues. Measurements of work or progress can happen automatically. Digitization also opens up the possibility for new types of rewards, such as through gamification. Hewlett-Packard Company, for instance, wanted technologists to review papers for a global technology conference but always had trouble getting enough people to spend enough time on the work. HP took a gamification approach, creating a dashboard that showed everyone who the top reviewers and review teams were. HP sent automated e-mails to reviewers before and after each weekend—when the reviewing was almost always done—and included a personalized analysis of the person's performance along with a leaderboard. These simple techniques, which focused on positive feedback and didn't chastise even the lowest performers, were enough to generate the greatest amount of review work that HP had ever had.[15]

Build Skills

In the pursuit of your change objective, you now have an aligned and inspiring call to action that your people are engaged with, and you've created an operating model that supports the delivery of that purpose. It's critical, however, to have the right people with the right skills and mind-sets. The levels at play here are (1) *placement*—not only having the key capabilities needed to realize your ambitions and strategy but also ensuring that they are matched to the best opportunities; (2) *replacement*—making the hard decisions to exit players and to recruit for missing capabilities; and (3) *development*—ensuring that any capability gaps are closed as quickly and effectively as possible and that your people are fit for an emerging and ever-evolving future.

Optimum placement requires that you know your resources well—who they are, how good they are, and what potential they have to grow and respond to challenge and stretch. That, however, is only half of the picture. The other half is working from the future back, from the outcomes you deliver to an understanding of the talent demands and supply needs of your organization. You need to develop insights and quantify risks to the business plan to shape the talent agenda and map the talent you have today. If organizations mapped their talent, most would find that they have allocated their stars to operationally critical and high-risk roles rather than to roles that are crucial for creating future value. It is critical to develop the organizational discipline for proper placement.

An interesting placement challenge is that many roles that will exist in five years either don't yet exist or will see their shape dramatically change. Look at the web site Futurist.com's lists of future jobs, such as crowdfunding specialists, corporate disruptors, privacy consultants, and big data doctors.

In the uncertain and ever-evolving world that we inhabit these days, it's easy for today's technical skills to get outdated. This puts a premium on ensuring that those most volatile roles in your organization are staffed with people who are well versed in the agility skills of foresight, learning, adaptability, and resilience.

Matt Brittin, president of EMEA business and operations at Google, told us that the company is "in the process of training 2 million Europeans in digital skills, because most countries have a significant lack of the skills that are needed to exploit these technologies. We've already trained nearly 1.5 million. There is huge demand for these sort of skills. So there's a job to do in helping the world take advantage of this revolution. We're playing our part as a citizen."

Replacement is all about taking people out of roles or out of the organization entirely when the individual has not responded to feedback and coaching. The reason could be a lack of skill (i.e., technical skills and experience), but it could equally be a lack of will (i.e., the mind-sets and ways of operating required for the future). Both types are terrible drags on organization acceleration. But it is extremely common for leaders and organizations to take too long in addressing the issue. Whether it's an individually poor-performing compliance leader when conduct risk is an issue in a financial institution or whether a whole function or division becomes obsolete, the chances are the decision to replace has rarely happened too soon. Leaders all over the world recognize the times when they have put off making that tough decision, to the point where damage is done to the business.

The psychology is all too clear—avoidance of a difficult decision, not wanting to inflict harm, not wanting to be seen as the bad cop, or fear of retaliation. All of these stop us from doing the right thing for our business, for the pursuit of our purpose, and for the people in the business, who often have to work around or compensate for those left in roles that they don't fit. Interestingly, many leaders and organizations find it just as difficult to fill the roles once tough replacement decisions are made. Sometimes, this is a genuine war-for-talent issue. Other times, however, there are more subtle reasons at play—for example, the seduction of a firefighting approach to leadership that is subconsciously reinforced by the amygdala endorphin hit every time a crisis is averted or resolved.

Assuming you have the right talent in place, there will almost always be a need for development interventions to enable the behavior change you want. If people don't have the skills, they just won't be able to deliver, no matter how hard they try.

Today, we know so much more about adult development than we knew even 20 years ago. There was once a belief that, once adults stopped physically growing, so, too, did our minds. But the work by researchers such as Bob Kegan and Lisa Laskow Lahey has shown that adults can indeed continue to develop and grow in more ways than just amassing technical knowledge.[16] Minds of all ages can develop through different stages of sophistication in terms of how we make sense of our worlds—what is known in psychological terms as "vertical development."

Why does vertical development matter? Why do you really want to include actions of this kind in your ABC model when you find capabilities missing? Keith Eigel studied chief executives and high-potential managers from large companies. He found very clearly that vertical development increases the effectiveness of the leader or manager because they can *think* in more complex ways.[17] According to John McGuire and Gary Rhodes of the Center for Creative Leadership (CCL), "People who gain another step can learn more, adapt faster, and generate more complex solutions than they could before. Those at later stages can learn more and react faster because they have a bigger mind."[18]

One word of caution about development interventions. Don't keep trying to develop a capability in someone if that capability is impossible for that person to develop. This takes us back to replacement—you may be able to teach a tortoise to climb a tree, but why wouldn't you just hire a squirrel?

Role-Model

So we have three of the five pieces of the puzzle in play. Always remember, though, that without effective, visible role modeling, it is very unlikely that any change in the organization that you wish to make will take place. Why would it? Why on earth would your people do something that you are not prepared to do yourself?

Although the argument for role modeling is clear, how to do it and what makes the difference when attempting to do it can at times be opaque. The simplest level is to *articulate direction*. You can't expect your people to be mind readers. If you don't tell them how you want them to behave, you can't expect them to behave that way. The second, reinforcing level is to show them how to behave by behaving that way yourself. That means that you and your leaders need to be able to *shift habits* yourselves. Tricky stuff but important. Of even greater impact, though, is the third level: learning to *hold to account*.

With the pace of change accelerating, virtually every organization and team leader must be able to continually articulate direction—where the enterprise is going, why change is necessary, how everyone can contribute, and what their efforts are achieving. If no one is telling them, they will set their own direction—it's easy to imagine 100 staff members going in 100 different directions. Being clear about direction can unleash the talent in your organization and point it true north. Being clear requires describing expectations and responsibilities for every employee, including how their work contributes to the purpose and what outcomes they are responsible for. It takes practice to simplify and clarify direction.

If you are going to be the change you want to see, you must shift habits yourself. Research by neuroscientist Matt Lieberman of UCLA shows that "our minds are less like hermetically sealed vaults that separate each of us from one another and more like 'Trojan horses': letting in the beliefs of other people without our realizing the extent to which we're being influenced."[19] This ensures that we have the same kind of beliefs and values as people around us do, to create the social harmony we depend on. Role modeling allows leaders to create an "in" group with desirable behaviors that they want others to copy. The better those behaviors are seen, and the more they are obvious, the easier it is for others to identify with them.

The work of Stanford psychologist Carol Dweck highlights that knowing how someone behaves is not enough. You also have to understand why they behave that way. Only with the "why" will the behavior be authentic and thus successful. Role models need to be able to describe their purpose and their beliefs and not just their behaviors.

For maximum impact, however, the third level of role modeling—hold to account—is imperative. Embedded deep in the DNA of a European car manufacturer was a drive for consensus decision making, based on the belief that colleagues would automatically do the right thing and on a desire for a working life absent of conflict and robust challenge. Needless to say, because people weren't being held to account, the performance of this enterprise was derailing, with revenue declining year after year and profits eroding. Unfortunately, many managers mistakenly thought they had only one of two unpleasant choices when dealing with the truth: (1) to have a contentious confrontation, or (2) to avoid the situation. Neither promotes a lasting change.

The answer? You need to be able to instill a culture where getting to the truth is more important than feeling comfortable and protecting egos. According to Robert Fritz, "real" truth telling—not a watered-down version of the truth—can add 25 percent to 40 percent capacity to organizations. He describes how for every manager there are critical moments that occur regularly, what Fritz refers to as Managerial Moments of Truth (MMOT). These moments include two distinct events: (1) the *awareness* that there is a difference between what you expected and what was delivered, and (2) the *decision* about what to do with that information. Whatever decision the manager makes, the MMOT has already happened. The way you deal with these moments will lead either to a vicious cycle of limitations that just makes things harder or to a virtuous cycle that enables you to tap into others and have a far greater leadership impact. Fritz offers a four-step approach to handling these moments: an acknowledgment of the truth, an analysis of how it got to be that way, the creation of an action plan, and the establishment of a feedback system.[20] This can be applied at the individual, team, and organization levels.

Ajay Banga, president and CEO of MasterCard, told us, "We've got a saying in the company, which is that 'good news takes the stairs and bad news takes the elevator.' I used to see e-mails at the beginning of every day, and multiple people would be copied on them, and they'd all be congratulating each other. Nobody would e-mail each other about the deal we lost, right? I asked them to stop, because all we were doing was convincing ourselves that we could do no wrong. That doesn't work for me because we all do wrong. So I've told everybody I don't need good news."

Provide Space

Too many models of change start from the premise of influencing others to change. It's seen as a doing-unto-others activity. Whether the change is a new strategy, structure, system, set of behaviors, or culture, a solution is packaged and communicated in ways designed to overcome resistance.

But people have the freedom to choose to not engage, and they exercise that freedom only too often—frequently because of how the change was arrived at and, ironically, how the plan is being implemented.

We pointed out earlier the powerful impact of cocreation on building an inspiring purpose behind which people put their energies. Even more important, however, is the need to provide space. Change management, like training, has traditionally been seen as a "push" model but needs to become a "pull" model, where employees draw what they need rather than having it imposed on them. If you allow your people the luxury of taking time and space *to understand* the change and what is asked of them and the world around them, they are more able to make an informed decision. If you enable them *to experiment* with what the change could look like, feel like, and be like, then their level of comfort with a new reality is more likely to rise. And if you allow them *to choose* to be influenced to change, then they are more likely to adopt the change with greater conviction and energy than if you don't.

As H. P. Lovecraft in the 1920s highlighted, "The oldest and strongest emotion of mankind is fear, and the oldest and strongest kind of fear is fear of the unknown."[21] People need to be able to experiment and to acclimate, or they will push back because of that fear of the unknown.

According to John Kotter and Leonard Schlesinger, "People also resist change when they do not understand its implications and perceive that it might cost them much more than they will gain." They tell of a president of a Midwestern company who set up a flexible schedule for employees, especially those in clerical and plant jobs, to make working conditions more attractive. It didn't occur to him that anyone would resist the idea, but the employees weren't familiar with the concept, and many distrusted the executive in charge of manufacturing. Rumors circulated. One rumor was that employees could be asked to work anytime, including evenings and weekends. It wasn't long before the union "presented the management with a nonnegotiable demand that the flexible hours concept be dropped."[22] Unless leaders build understanding, resistance to change is almost inevitable.

Jeff Sprecher, founder and CEO of Intercontinental Exchange (one of our superaccelerators), told us that he thinks "human beings hate change. Even the most outgoing millennial who says, 'I want to live out of a backpack and walk across India and discover myself'—I honestly believe that person doesn't like change. Fundamentally, we all want to go home tonight and sleep in the same bed that we left this morning." He adds that he finds opportunity in others' distaste for change: "Once we're open about change, maybe we'll be a little less afraid of it than the next guy. We're going to admit it and move faster and with more thought than other people who don't like to recognize change or who resist change. That realization has affected my life, as well as my thinking about business. When somebody walks into my office and says, 'A terrible thing has happened to this company, and we're facing some kind of dire circumstance,' you have to ask yourself, 'Is there an opportunity in here?'"

Building understanding is a good first step in helping people deal with change. Even better is fueling an appetite to step into a new reality, and that comes from allowing people to experiment. The Swiss psychologist Elisabeth Kübler-Ross wrote extensively about the grief cycle, which is still as relevant to changing behavior today as it was when she first wrote about it in 1969 and which lists "bargaining" as a key phase.[23] Similarly, the change curve requires a "testing" phase so people can become acclimatized to the change we are contemplating.

Comfort with the status quo is extraordinarily powerful. Research on the function of the brain shows that resistance is not only a psychological reaction to change but also a physiological reaction.[24] To act in a new way requires more power from the brain, and therefore the physiological reaction when presented with a new way of doing something is to revert back to what the brain already knows. Human beings can adapt their behavior, but it is a painful process—even for the brain itself. Giving people the luxury of being able to experiment with new behaviors reduces that pain and produces the "new normal."

The ABC Model in Action

To see how the ABC model works in practice, let's go back to the client case we introduced in the last chapter. The global electronics retailer chose its recipe—to be a Customer Intimate. The top team did its diagnostics and found that it needed to take some immediate actions on both the threshold activities and the anchor activities and to establish an executive committee to focus on the transformation. Knowing that nothing changes unless behaviors change, the top team used the ABC model to craft a set of actions that would allow it to change behaviors across the organization—by thinking about the right mix of purpose, operating model, skills, role modeling, and actions to create the space needed to concoct interventions that would shift the dial and increase the organization's ability to accelerate. In conjunction with key players from across the organization in a carefully constructed series of working sessions, the team developed ABC maps for each of the core transformation changes it needed to deliver and rolled those detailed maps up into the following overarching ABC map of activities.

Connect with Purpose

The executive team focused on reconnecting with the company's original mission of making the buying experience as painless as possible for customers. The team started with honest and humbling "Time to Talk" sessions of the executive team with staff in a wide variety of settings. These talks were set up to have conversations of a kind that had never been experienced before by employees—adult-to-adult, two-way dialogue that explored how the company had lost its way and what the contribution of the senior leaders was that had led to the current situation. This type of disclosure set the stage for great discussions on the vision for the future and what it would take from everyone to get there. Follow-up working sessions cascaded from the top in a carefully orchestrated sequence that put a spotlight on reconnecting to the original purpose of being customer focused.

Align the Operating Model

There was no way to get close to the customer, with the complexity and bureaucracy that had sprouted over the years. The executive team reduced layers at its stores, even though that was a very painful process, because the organization had never laid anybody off. To complement the thinning out, the executive team fundamentally recrafted the role of the center and the core information and decision-making processes to create greater "servant leadership" and empowerment at the store level, in particular for those interacting daily with customers. Other operational actions included ensuring a "seat" for the customer at every meeting by stress-testing decisions from the customer's perspective and starting an internal "secret shopper" initiative, where employees from one store or part of the business underwent the customer experience in another.

The executive team established a new process to better understand how customer segmentation had evolved, what characteristics of the market segment were most attractive, and how to reshape decisions related to product mix, product development, and store layout.

The top team redesigned its performance scorecard around customer-related metrics. Every meeting at a store, function, or corporate group now started with the revised customer satisfaction levels, which were kept up to date on a weekly basis.

Build Skills

Skill building was critical—at all levels. Effort was put into helping the top team develop the strategic capabilities required to maintain competitive advantage, mainly centered on the ability to read the business environment and translate it into concrete issues for the company to address.

Frontline employees were provided with training not only to truly listen to customers but also to know how to bring that insight back into the organization, to address issues, and to adopt and export good ideas across the enterprise.

Twenty percent of the leaders were changed. These were leaders attached to a command-and-control, hierarchical, and at times almost bullying approach to managing people. These leaders had no interest in adapting their style and often dug in their heels, in some cases even trying to block the desired changes.

New skills were hired. Data was going to be key in the new world and needed to be insightful, relevant, real-time, and, of course, customer-centric. A new analytics center was created and populated by people from data-fueled organizations in other industries.

Role-Model

The small executive committee was established quickly and its purpose communicated widely across the organization. This underscored the importance of the transformation and provided a model for the focus that was expected from the rest of the organization. A "top 100" leadership community was established. For the first time, there was clarity on who were seen to be the leaders of the organization and what the expectations of leadership were. Leaders were provided with development that focused on the core mind-sets needed to deliver the new ambition, and feedback mechanisms were put in place. Feedback was established as a cultural norm and as a "gift" that enabled both course correction and a leveraging of strengths in the service of employees and customers.

Three other core role-modeling actions were taken. First, overdue and marginal projects were cut early on in the transformation process, signaling the need to choose and focus. Then collaboration projects were established to break down long-established silos. Finally, a well-connected network of change agents was identified, trained, and given the remit to be "active agitators" on behalf of the customer.

Provide Space

The senior team encouraged every store and corporate function to create safe spaces for people to air their grievances with the change and to discuss what was working well and not so well. The sessions were facilitated by outside professionals who fed results directly to the executive committee. Adjustments to the program were made based on how people were responding to the change and what elements were resonating. "Volunteering" opportunities were opened up to enable people to choose different ways to contribute to a better future, and nurseries and incubators were created to provide the space to innovate.

The results of the acceleration were significant: The company not only reversed its revenue declines, but revenue showed a hefty increase. Time required for the product development process shrank. Customer defections fell. Decisions at the senior level took half as long as they did previously, setting the company up to continue to respond quickly to changing tastes. Many decisions, such as on store layout and product mix, were pushed out to the stores, to be closer to the customer.

In short, the company followed the dictum from Alan Kay, the principal developer of the personal computer at Xerox PARC, that "the best way to predict the future is to invent it."[25] The company grappled with the entrenched behaviors that had accumulated to produce drag and created an integrated set of actions that accelerated performance.

■ ■ ■

There are three top tips to get the most out of adopting the "Any Behavior Change" (ABC) model to transformation. The first tip is to think of the model as a Russian nesting doll. For each major change you want to achieve, you will need to populate an ABC matrix. Say you want to become the best Customer Intimate organization in your industry, and you've identified that you have to simplify your structure, improve the quality of your leaders, and shift focus to the customer. Each one of these changes will require its own ABC map. The art then lies in reading across all three ABC maps and rolling them up into one overarching, change-transformation ABC map. You manage the change simultaneously at both levels, but in the act of the roll-up you identify domino-effect interventions—those interventions that enable change across several ABC maps. This enables you to implement change with maximum impact and effectiveness but with minimum effort and disruption.

The second tip to successfully leveraging the ABC model is the 4-C checklist. Be robust in your assessment of the quality of your ABC maps and ensure that they meet the following conditions: The actions are characterized by *complementarity* (i.e., they reinforce each other); they are *comprehensive* (i.e., together they will enable the entirety of the shift you want to achieve); they are *coherent* (i.e., they pull together and are in tension with each other); and, finally, they take into account the *capacity* the organization has for change and does not overload it.

The third and most important tip is to ensure that your ABC map has balance. It is critical when you want to implement accelerating change that you act on all five fronts of the ABC model at the same time to ensure that change sticks. Focusing on only one element of the behavior change model will produce subpar results, and the transformation effort will likely fail.

Seventy percent of transformations fail, according to multiple research initiatives, so you need to draw upon every tip, skill, and discipline to make sure that you are one of the success stories.

Notes

1. Leslie Salzillo, "Jimmy Carter & The Carter Center 2 cases away from ending Guinea Worm Disease (from 3 million)," *Daily Kos*, June 8, 2016, dailykos.com.
2. Robert H. Miles, "Accelerating corporate transformations (Don't lose your nerve!)," *Harvard Business Review*, January–February 2010, hbr.org.
3. Jacquelyn Smith, "Richard Branson shares his 10 favorite quotes about embracing change," *Business Insider*, March 13, 2015, businessinsider.com.
4. Robert H. Miles, "Accelerating corporate transformations (Don't lose your nerve!)," *Harvard Business Review*, January–February 2010, hbr.org.
5. Ambrose Bierce, *The Unabridged Devil's Dictionary*, Athens, GA: University of Georgia Press, 2000.
6. Steve Taylor, "The power of purpose," *Psychology Today*, July 21, 2013, psychologytoday.com.
7. Mihaly Csikszentmihalyi, *Flow: The Psychology of Optimal Experience*, New York: Harper & Row, 1990.

8. Jason Jennings and Laurence Haughton, *The High-Speed Company: Creating Urgency and Growth in a Nanosecond Culture*, New York: Penguin, 2015.

9. Simon Sinek, *Start with Why: How Great Leaders Inspire Everyone to Take Action*, New York: Portfolio, 2009.

10. Simon Sinek, "How great leaders inspire action," TED talk, TEDxPuget Sound, September 2009, ted.com.

11. John Kotter, "Think you're communicating enough? Think again," *Forbes*, June 14, 2011, forbes.com.

12. Adam Grant, *Originals: How Non-Conformists Move the World*, New York: Viking, 2016.

13. David Rock, "SCARF: A brain-based model for collaborating with and influencing others," *NeuroLeadership Journal*, Issue 1, 2008.

14. Upton Sinclair, *I, Candidate for Governor: And How I Got Licked*, Berkeley, CA: University of California Press, 1994.

15. Charles Bess, "Gamification: Driving behavior change in the connected world," *Cutter IT Journal*, February 26, 2013, cutter.com.

16. Robert Kegan and Lisa Laskow Lahey, *Immunity to Change: How to Overcome It and Unlock the Potential in Yourself and Your Organization*, Boston: Harvard Business School Publishing, 2009.

17. Nick Petrie, *Future Trends in Leadership Development*, Center for Creative Leadership, 2014, ccl.org.

18. John B. McGuire and Gary B. Rhodes, *Transforming Your Leadership Culture*, San Francisco: Jossey-Bass, 2009.

19. Jan Hills, "How the brain works and the link to good business," *HRZone*, July 1, 2016, hrzone.com.

20. Bruce Bodaken and Robert Fritz, *The Managerial Moment of Truth: The Essential Step in Helping People Improve Performance*, New York: Free Press, 2006.

21. Howard Phillips Lovecraft, *Supernatural Horror in Literature*, Mineola, NY: Dover Publications, 1973.

22. John P. Kotter and Leonard A. Schlesinger, "Choosing strategies for change," *Harvard Business Review*, July–August 2008, hbr.org.

23. Elisabeth Kübler-Ross, *On Death and Dying: What the Dying Have to Teach Doctors, Nurses, Clergy, and Their Own Families*, New York: Scribner, 1969.

24. David Rock and Jeffrey Schwartz, "The neuroscience of leadership," *strategy+business*, May 30, 2006, strategy-business.com.

25. Alan Kay, "A powerful idea about ideas," TED talk, TEDxPuget Sound, March 2008, ted.com.

CHAPTER 12

Change the People or Change the People

Wes, an old friend of ours, managed a branch for a major computer company some years ago and had to let a salesman go. The young man just wasn't producing the numbers, despite numerous attempts at training to address some of his deficiencies. Wes liked the young man but reluctantly ushered him out of the company.

Fast forward two years. Wes was walking down the street in Los Angeles, when the biggest stretch limo he'd ever seen pulled to the curb next to him and stopped. Out jumped the former salesman, who bounded over and gave Wes a bear hug. The former employee said, "Your letting me go was the best thing that ever happened to me. I'd always thought I could be a studio musician, but I never tried until I lost my job. Now, things are going great." He added, "Here, I'd like to introduce you to the singer and the producer on the album I'm working on now." So Wes went over and leaned into the limo, where Michael Jackson and Quincy Jones sat in the backseat.

The unfortunate fact is that, while the last chapter laid out the ABC model for how to change the people and get them to behave differently as part of a transformation effort, there is another form of "change the people" that needs to come into play, too: You have to move out people as soon as you get the sense that they will be drags on your attempts at acceleration and replace them with people who will drive your organization forward. You hope that those who leave will thrive, as Wes's former employee surely did in this admittedly atypical example. But, no matter what, you have to make the hard decisions about changing out people, and you have to do this in a way that reflects the need to accelerate the performance of the organization.

In this chapter, we'll draw on our research and the extensive search experience at Heidrick & Struggles to lay out the principles for both how to exit people and how to find the right replacements. We'll talk specifically about chief executive officers, and then executive team members, because they have the most influence on the organization; but many of the principles apply generally, as well, to all levels within the organization.

When You Can't Change the People, You Have to Change the People

Sometimes, developing accelerating leadership capabilities in your leaders is not enough, and you need to let people go. One of the hardest decisions to make for a board, for example, is to determine when it is time to change out a CEO. The decision can be straightforward if there is illegal or unethical behavior, but more often the issues are nuanced and may include company performance, changing business conditions, or leadership style. For instance, Hewlett-Packard ousted Léo Apotheker and asked Meg Whitman to become CEO after becoming very concerned about performance. Valeant Pharmaceuticals replaced its CEO when the regulatory and market environment changed, becoming extremely hostile to the kinds of price increases the company instituted on older drugs and requiring a reassessment of strategy.

Once you have decided to replace a CEO, you need to begin with three steps. These steps must be taken concurrently and with pace. First, you must focus on legal and regulatory compliance. The board should begin talking with outside counsel as early as possible. Second, if the board hasn't already found a permanent replacement, an interim selection is needed. The most frequent and timely solutions include a board member who can step in temporarily. Alternatively, the CFO—or an Office of the CEO, typically consisting of three people—may step in and continue operating the company while the board searches for a permanent CEO. Third, the board must work with the departing CEO to align on a direct and clear explanation for why the transition is taking place and share that message consistently with employees, customers, capital markets, and any other relevant stakeholders. These three steps will help minimize the impact of the change for all.

Hiring the Right CEO

While each search for a full-time CEO replacement may unfold with its own subtleties, the most successful processes share a number of steps, beyond the normal deep interviews and reference checks.

First, you must achieve strategic alignment. Perhaps the most important factor is ensuring that the board and the organization's leaders spend extensive time at the outset truly understanding the strategic imperatives for the company over the next several years. If board members are aligned on the strategy, they can focus on hiring for the right skill set. The right next CEO needs to be identified and appointed while keeping in mind the chosen recipe for accelerating the organization. Leadership style is important but so is the ability of the CEO to deliver a Customer Intimate or Execution Engine organization. Muhammad Ali was a great leader, but he could also punch.

Second, you must choose the right search committee. Many are either too small or too large. If the board tasks one to two people with the responsibility, the remainder of the board may have little visibility into the process and, at the end of the search, wonder, "Are there better candidates out there?" Alternatively, if the full board, or a large portion of the board, is involved throughout the entire process, the timing slows significantly and the difficulty of arriving at a consensus on an individual increases substantially. The most effective and efficient selection processes are run by a committee of three or four people, with a chair taking the lead. The committee shares updates with the rest of the board (weekly or biweekly) so that they are up to speed but not slowing the process down.

Third, insist that finalist candidates present to the board preliminary thoughts on strategy and how they would approach leading the company. This provides a detailed sense of each candidate's thinking and his or her approach to collaborating with the board. Here, the ability of the potential CEO to be able to energize the organization around the six key threshold actions (purpose, urgency, fewer layers, big jobs for big people, exiting people when needed, and digitization—as outlined in Chapter 10) necessary for any accelerating performance recipe can be surfaced and tested. It's a two-way street: This process also provides the candidate with an opportunity to get a feel for what collaborating with the board will be like, to voice any concerns, and to set expectations.

Finally, you must conduct a thorough background and social media check. Hiring a CEO may be the most important decision a board makes for a company. You don't want any damaging or tricky issues slowing or even potentially halting a successful transition. So you must ensure that the person you are hiring has been fully transparent with you.

What Makes a CEO Successful

In our experience, the best CEOs demonstrate mastery of the characteristics of accelerating leaders (as outlined in Chapter 9). They are stunning at execution, have growth mind-sets, have situational awareness, come in with a low ego, talk to the right people, get up to speed quickly, and are customer-centric. But different CEOs will need to do different things in varying situations to achieve the same performance. One board we worked with had to replace a hands-off CEO, so they hired a CEO to refocus the company on operations and accountability while pursuing an Execution Engine recipe.

Another CEO with extensive industry knowledge joined a company and was quick to recognize that technology was having a big impact; he immediately set up meetings with as many brilliant and disruptive tech minds as possible (pursuing a Talent Magnet recipe). He asked questions, recognized his shortcomings, and got up to speed quickly by being understated and knowing he could learn from others. Yet another CEO recognized that his company had a strong product but had not focused enough on customers over the years. He reinvigorated the company with a strong customer focus (pursuing a Customer Intimate recipe). While these individuals all emphasized different approaches, the characteristics that allowed them to accelerate their organizations were that their skill set matched the circumstances and that they adopted a learner's mind-set.

Getting the Best out of Your New CEO

When you recruit a CEO, you paint a beautiful picture of her future. You describe in great depth and color how awesome it will be for her to accept your offer rather than join that other company she may be considering. That's great. But you need to quickly focus on the seven factors that can determine success or failure: company, scope of role, level of role, culture, location, industry, and function.

The more of these factors that differ in the new role from what an individual has been doing, the more likely an individual is to fail. Let's say a person becomes the CEO of a much bigger company in a new industry. This person had been a successful CFO for five years in a small entrepreneurial company. The job is in a different city but not far from where the person currently lives. The companies have a very different history and culture (one is entrepreneurial, led by the founder for many years, while the other is bureaucratic). Figure 12.1 shows how the larger company could use our

FIGURE 12.1 How to evaluate chances of success: An example

1. Company	Same	Similar	Different
2. Scope of role	Same	Similar	Different
3. Level of role	Same	Similar	Different
4. Culture	Same	Similar	Different
5. Work location	Same	Similar	Different
6. Industry	Same	Similar	Different
7. Function	Same	Similar	Different

seven factors to determine the areas of difficulty this candidate might face in the new role.

To mitigate the chance of failure, the new executive, with the support of the organization, must focus on four critical points:

1. Understanding the strategic agenda
2. Establishing team and management cadences
3. Developing strong stakeholder relationships
4. Building cultural integration

Coaching provides another way to improve a CEO's odds of success. The right coach supports and works with the new hire, the board, and HR to ensure a smooth entry into the organization. The goal is to build on strengths, reduce blind spots, and close any critical development gaps. As a result, there is a greater chance that the new CEO will effectively navigate the new environment and deliver results at an early stage of the transition. Remember, at this stage everyone in the organization will be watching and waiting to take their cue from their new leader. Will they wait to make moves? What do they focus on? What changes do they make or not make? The new leader, supported by a great coach, will be far more likely to remain with the organization for an extended period, compared with those who are not supported during the transition.

The selection of the coach is critical. A lot of people have coaches and still fail. Pick a coach who brings to the table not only stellar coaching skills but also knowledge of the industry and familiarity with the type of situation the executive will be facing, and then clearly specify what the coach's role will be.

Shaping the Executive Team

Whether you are an incoming CEO or a tenured CEO, it is important to continually evaluate your team to ensure that you have people with the right capabilities in the right jobs, moving the company in the right direction. In the midst of a transformation, this analysis takes on much more significance because you need a really strong top team to go on the journey. CEOs leading transformations need people on their team who want to shape the future and who want to create something together. Different phases require different skill sets.

New CEOs, either from outside or through internal promotions, are most likely to exit executives when they step into the role. "Outsider" CEOs tend to exit the chief human resources officer (CHRO), chief legal officer, and chief marketing officer (CMO) first. By contrast, insider CEOs are more likely to exit the legal counsel, the CMO, the head of sales, or the chief operating officer (COO) but retain the CHRO. In any case, a very common theme among CEOs is that they wish they had made the decision to exit certain individuals sooner than they did. As Sarah Green Carmichael puts it, when CEOs look back, they almost always say, "I knew in my gut that was not going to work with that individual, and I wish I had trusted that gut feeling and made that decision faster." Delaying the decision can put them behind on the transformation.[1]

First-time CEOs may hesitate because they don't feel like they know enough about what's going on and want to give people the benefit of the doubt. Experienced CEOs who are taking on a new role tend to act more quickly.

Outside CEOs face particular conditions that can make the decisions easier. Outsiders are normally brought in for one of two reasons: The company couldn't develop an insider, or the external environment has shifted considerably. Either way, outsiders must drive change, and they need new people with new skill sets.

Keeping executives with negative energy does more harm than good. But even letting disruptive leaders go is not an easy decision. These are talented individuals, and finding good talent is hard. Yet, you have to let them go anyway, especially if you are leading a transformation. The longer you wait, the more damage these individuals do and the greater the drag on the organization.

The drag effect of the negative energy of these seven archetypes is clear:

1. **The Troublemaker**. These are not the nonconformists who push boundaries, question assumptions, and, when working well, help the organization think outside of the box. Some individuals simply like to create chaos around them. The ones who consistently create chaos and push the boundaries in negative ways are the ones to look out for.
2. **The Overpromiser/Underdeliverer**. People with inflated self-images can make boastful promises. That is totally fine if they deliver. But when their egos consistently write checks their capabilities can't cash, that's a problem.
3. **The "Customer Schmustomer."** Customers are hard to gain and easy to lose. The one thing you don't need is a senior leader who somehow doesn't understand that business is all about winning and keeping them.
4. **The Incapable**. You hire and pay people to do a job. *Your* job is to be clear about what that entails and to give them the tools and training they need to get the job done. *Their* job is to do it. If they either can't or won't after a few chances, then you've probably given them one chance too many.

5. **The Flake.** Some people look the part but, when push comes to shove, can't be counted on to get the job done or even show up on a regular basis. You simply can't trust them, and life is too short to have employees you can't trust.

6. **The Entitled.** Some people are more thin-skinned and entitled than they have any right to be. Half their mind is on the job and the other half is waiting for someone to slip up so they can whine and complain, or even threaten litigation. Don't give in to that kind of behavior. Cut them loose.

7. **The Insubordinate Subordinate.** Whatever your rules of conduct are, you must uphold them fairly and consistently across the board. Whether an employee is insubordinate to her boss, or a top executive lies about something material on his resume, if it happens and it breaks the rules, you should see the person out the door.

These archetypes are extreme cases. In most situations, CEOs need to replace executives because they were hired for the wrong job to begin with, because the company outgrew them, or because the company is pivoting in a way that plays against their strengths. These people can be the most challenging to let go, particularly if they fit well with the company's culture and have performed well historically.

Facing the Ugly Task

Once you realize you must let an executive go, what do you do?

It turns out that, because executives have experience being on the other side of the conversation, they tend to be quite professional about it. Still, there is a four-step process that will treat the executive fairly and help your organization to accelerate.

Step 1: Analyze the Root Cause

Rather than treat a termination as an executive's failure, you need to figure out why you hired the wrong person for your company in the first place. You may have blown it for a variety of reasons.

Perhaps you did a poor job defining the position. If you don't know what you want, you will be very unlikely to get it. Far too often, CEOs hire executives based on an abstract notion of what they think the executive should look and act like. For example, we worked with a $16 billion company where the CEO leading a transformation brought in a head of sales for the enterprise but at the same time brought a new head for the largest business unit, who thought he also owned sales. Lack of clarity on roles made the sales position fail because the other executive thought he owned more than he did. The company learned and did not refill the position.

Another common mistake is to hire for apparent lack of weakness rather than evidence of strength. This is especially common when you run a consensus-based hiring process. The group will often find the candidate's weaknesses but won't place a high enough value on the areas where the executive needs to be world class. As a result, you hire an executive with no significant weaknesses but who is mediocre where you need her to be great. If you don't have world-class strengths where you need them, you won't be a world-class company.

Maybe you hired for scale too soon. The most consistently wrong advice CEOs are given is to hire someone "bigger" than required. "Think about the next three to five years and how you will be a large company" is how the (extremely bad) advice usually sounds. It's great to hire people who can run a large organization—if you have one. It's also great to hire people who know how to grow an organization very fast if you are ready to grow your organization very fast. However, if you do not or you are not, then you need someone who can do the job for the next 18 months. If you hire someone who will be great 18 months from now but will be poor for the immediate future, the company will reject that person before she ever gets a chance to show her stuff.

Perhaps you hired for the generic position. There is no such thing as a great CEO, a great head of marketing, or a great head of sales. There is only a great head of sales for your company for the next 12 to 24 months. And that position is not the same at Microsoft as it is for Facebook. Don't look for the candidate out of "central casting." This is not a movie.

Sometimes, the executive has the wrong kind of ambition. Despite her skills, the company may reject her. For example, in a large technology company that was executing a turnaround, the CEO hired a strong, highly regarded executive, who could have been CEO at a smaller company. Having been a CEO at one time and aspiring to be one again, this new executive created walls around his turnaround plan—he felt he didn't need to be managed but should just deliver results. He felt he was the CEO of the business unit rather than the president of a large business unit inside an integrated enterprise. The mismatch ultimately led to his replacement, and an executive was hired whose ambition was aligned with the role.

Often, you may have failed to integrate the executive. Bringing a new person into your company in an important role is difficult. Be sure to review and improve your integration plan after you let an executive go. Don't make the same mistake twice.

Step 2: Inform the Board

Informing the board is tricky, and many issues can further complicate the task. This may be the fifth or sixth executive overall whom you've had to exit, or maybe this is the third executive in this role. Maybe the executive was referred by a board member who thinks she is a star, or the executive is part of the succession plan.

Your choices are to (1) alarm the board or (2) enable an ineffective executive to remain in her position. While the first choice is not great, it's a heck of a lot better than the second. Leaving a failing leader in place will cause an entire department in your company to rot slowly. Let that happen, and the board will soon be much more than merely alarmed.

You should have three goals in mind with the board. First, you must get their support and understanding for the difficult task at hand. You should start by making sure they understand the root causes and your plan to remedy them. This will give them confidence in your ability to hire and manage executives in the future. Second, get their input and approval for the separation package. Executive packages are larger than regular severance packages. Finally, you must preserve the reputation of the executive being let go—the failure was very likely a team effort, and it's best to portray it that way. You don't make yourself look good by trashing someone who worked for you. A mature approach will help keep the board confident in your ability to be CEO. It's also the fair and decent thing to do.

The news is handled better with individual phone calls rather than in dramatic fashion during a board meeting. Calling takes a bit longer but is well worth the effort. Individual calls are particularly important if one of the board members introduced the executive to the company. Once everyone agrees individually, you can finalize the details in a board meeting or group call.

Step 3: Prepare for the Conversation

After you know what went wrong and have informed the board, you should tell the executive as quickly as possible. We recommend scripting or at least rehearsing what you plan to say so that you do not accidentally misspeak. The executive will remember the conversation for a very long time, so you need to get it right.

You should review any performance reviews or written performance conversations to understand any inconsistencies in your prior communication. Then focus on these three keys to getting it right: First, be clear on the reasons. You have thought about this long and hard; don't equivocate or sugarcoat it. You owe it to the executive to be clear about what you think happened. Second, use decisive language. Do not leave this open. This is not a performance review; it's a termination. Use phrases such as "I have decided" rather than "I think." Third, have the severance package approved and ready. Once the executive hears the news, she will stop caring about the company and its issues and instead will be highly focused on herself and her family. Be ready for this by being prepared to talk about the package.

The executive will be keenly interested in how the news will be communicated to the company and the outside world. It is best to let him or her decide. Steve Ballmer, for instance, got to communicate his decision to step down as CEO of Microsoft on his own terms in 2013, paving the way for the transition to the thus far extremely successful tenure of his successor that we described at the beginning of Chapter 9.

Step 4: Prepare the Company Communication

After you have informed the executive, you must quickly update the company about the change. The correct order for informing the company is (1) members of the executive staff—because they will need to be prepared to answer questions both internally and externally; (2) the executive's direct reports—because they will be the most impacted; and (3) the rest of the company and any relevant external constituents. All of these communications should happen in the same day, preferably within a couple of hours. When disclosing the exit to the direct reports, make sure that you have a plan for whom they will report to in the meantime and what's next (executive search, reorganization, internal promotion, or something else). Generally, it's smart for the CEO to take over the role of the departing executive in the meantime—this is what IMI CEO Mark Selway did, running one of the company's three divisions for a year before appointing the current divisional director, Massimo Grassi. If the CEO steps in, he has to act in the role, meaning he will attend staff and one-on-one meetings, set objectives, and so on. Doing so will provide excellent continuity for the team and greatly inform the thinking on whom to hire next.

When you update the company, you might worry about employees misinterpreting the news and thinking the company is in trouble. Anticipate this, but do not try to engineer around such a reaction. When you expect your employees to act like adults, they generally do.

In the end, every CEO likes to say that she runs a great company. It's hard to tell whether the claim is true until the company or the CEO has to do something really difficult. Terminating an executive is a good test.

How to Ensure That You Don't Have to Exit Executives (As Often)

To ensure that you have the right team, especially if you are bringing people in from outside, the following three points are imperative:

■ **Take the responsibility seriously.**

Strategic needs should dictate selection criteria for new executive. That's not always easy to do because of market and peer pressure. The CEO may be too concerned about the company's perception in the market and may favor a star who is not strategically aligned with the organization; the top team may be concerned by internal morale and prefer a quick fix to a more sustainable replacement. Both may be tempted to think that getting somebody from outside the organization is a better option, simply because this person represents an influx of new blood, trusting that his charisma or experience will trump his lack of knowledge about the company or the industry. To circumvent these problems, it is important that whoever is making the decisions understands the criteria involved in finding the best replacement, either internally or externally. When you do, it'll be easier to identify the skills and experiences that your new executive will need.

One of our superaccelerators, Tata Consultancy Services, shows how important this sort of discipline can be in selecting executives. It made a strategic choice to build people from within the company, with long-term grooming for succession. It chose to do so despite huge and fast growth that could have led to short-term thinking and compromising on capabilities and values. This discipline means that the company's teams are exceptionally aligned and can make quick decisions, for instance, when there are changes in the marketplace.

Even when a company decides to hire an executive search firm to find candidates, there's no escaping the need to identify your competitive challenges and industry context as well as the skills a replacement executive will need. Doing so will allow you to guide (rather than be guided by) the recruiters. And it will ensure that recruiters look for a specific set of skills and experiences rather than simply running through their Rolodexes of available executives and the usual suspects.

Remember that, as American writer Elbert Hubbard said, "One machine can do the work of 50 ordinary men. No machine can do the work of one extraordinary man."[2]

■ **Set realistic performance expectations.**

Establish clear and realistic performance expectations. Allow the new executive time to adjust—even if he or she hails from inside the organization. Joining a new company, even as a seasoned executive, is always daunting, and when that executive is joining an organization that is going through a transformation, it makes things more challenging still. The CEO and the team must be ready to withstand the inevitable setbacks and should not rely on the new executive to be the "savior" who will drive performance up in one quarter. Don't set targets to please the capital markets. Do it to support your company's acceleration agenda.

New executives are often tempted to promise unrealistic turnaround numbers, but that's precisely the wrong thing to do. Instead, they need to be reminded to restart the clock by deflating unrealistic expectations and avoiding the acceleration trap.

- **Remain vigilant and provide support.**

    Once the new executive is on board, the job of the CEO or the top team is far from over. Indeed, it's only starting. Resist the temptation to leave the new executive well enough alone for a while, and remember that, because most replacement executives perform no better than their predecessors, you must be more vigilant than ever. Remember that if the replacement came from outside, not only will the organization be new but so will the journey that the organization is undertaking. Boards and top teams must provide strong strategic oversight following a dismissal, because turnarounds aren't easy. They take subtlety, sophistication, and staying power.

■ ■ ■

Hiring and letting go CEOs and executives are often critical parts of the acceleration process for a company. These decisions should not be taken lightly but will need to be taken quickly, as soon as the issues become apparent.

Next, we'll look more broadly at the role that boards should play in helping companies accelerate.

Notes

1. Sarah Green Carmichael, "Who new CEOs fire first," *Harvard Business Review*, July 8, 2013, hbr.org.
2. Erik Brynjolfsson and Andrew McAfee, *The Second Machine Age: Work, Progress, and Prosperity in a Time of Brilliant Technologies*, New York: W. W. Norton & Company, 2014.

CHAPTER 13

The Board as Catalyst

The board of a high-profile U.S. company contained a Who's Who of distinguished leaders, including former secretaries of state, senators, generals, admirals, and a defense secretary. But the board became the subject of the sort of nightmare story in *Forbes* magazine that no director ever wants to see. The headline on April 27, 2016, decreed a "crisis," followed by the question: "Where was the board?"[1]

The company is Theranos, which promised to revolutionize blood testing by requiring only a few drops of blood from patients rather than a full vial and which raised capital at a valuation as high as $9 billion—but which never actually got its technology to work.

Fitting with tradition in Silicon Valley, the company had a great "creation myth": The founder, Elizabeth Holmes, had a fear of having her blood taken in the doctor's office and found a solution, so she dropped out of Stanford at age 19 to start Theranos. As the company's valuation in private markets soared, her 50 percent ownership stake made her the richest self-made woman in the world. She heightened the mythmaking by adopting a sort of uniform, always wearing black turtlenecks and deliberately drawing comparisons to Steve Jobs and his closetful of black mock turtlenecks. She declined to describe in any detail how the Theranos technology worked, saying that she didn't want to tip off competitors about her breakthrough. But she assured the world that great progress was being made on commercializing the technology, and there were so many investors that believed her that Theranos helped popularize the term "unicorn," used for privately held companies with at least a $1 billion valuation.

Then the *Wall Street Journal* reported that Theranos wasn't using its own machines for the vast majority of the blood tests it was conducting at health clinics inside Walgreens pharmacies.[2] Theranos was actually using competitors' machines, built on traditional technology. The reason: Theranos's machines weren't reliable, because it's really hard to get enough of a sample from just a few drops of blood. The Theranos story unraveled. Walgreens canceled its partnership with Theranos.[3] Under pressure, Theranos invalidated two years of test results it had provided patients.[4] Investigations began, including a criminal probe into whether Theranos had deliberately misled investors.[5] The U.S. government said Medicare and Medicaid funds couldn't be used to pay for Theranos tests after checking 81 patient results and finding all of them inaccurate. The government also fined Theranos and banned Holmes from owning or operating a medical lab for two years.[6] *Forbes*, which tracks the fortunes of the world's wealthiest, not only took Holmes's name off its list but also marked her net worth down to zero.[7]

Theranos's blowup, and the fact that many of its problems are being laid at the feet of the board, underscores two key points about the evolving role of boards. First, directors need to be more active than they have been in the past. The days are long gone when a director was chosen essentially as a reward for past successes and when the work consisted of a quarterly trip to a meeting to rubber-stamp what management was doing. Increased regulation of boards, including through the Sarbanes-Oxley Act in the United States, and shareholder activism ensure that demands on directors will stay intense and perhaps become even more severe.[8] Second, the composition of a board needs to be carefully managed, based on developing research. The Theranos board, for instance, may have included very impressive and accomplished people, but none had experience with a biotechnology start-up, so they didn't know the right questions to ask to hold a high-profile CEO accountable as she pursued a breakthrough with some bewilderingly complex science.

The Emerging Research

In the face of new demands on boards and board members, the latest research suggests that boards are evolving, but the transformation feels gradual compared with the speed of business and the growing need for acceleration. Too many are still too passive, such as the board of the Susan G. Komen for the Cure foundation, which could have avoided the scandal that resulted from the decision to stop funding Planned Parenthood if directors had simply engaged in a discussion rather than accepting management's plan as fact.[9]

If a board is to be a catalyst for acceleration—and it must be—the board must focus on the issue. A board that is not looking at acceleration will neither inspire nor require a top team to do so. And a management team that is being held back by a board that doesn't appreciate the speed, scope, and significance of a shift will fail.

When we looked at the boards of directors of the superaccelerator companies versus those of nonaccelerators (see the Research Appendix for details) we were struck by some common characteristics (Table 13.1):

- Superaccelerators have fewer board members than do nonaccelerators. This suggests that having "too many cooks in the kitchen" may hurt boards' ability to make decisions quickly and well.

TABLE 13.1 Characteristics of superaccelerating and nonaccelerating boards

Superaccelerating boards	Nonaccelerating boards
Average board size: 10.69 members	Average board size: 12.97 members
Average percentage of outside-industry board members: ~46.6%	Average percentage of outside-industry board members: ~59.5%
Median tenure for board members: 9.10 years	Median tenure for board members: 6.76 years
Average percentage of board members younger than 60 years old: 37.2%	Average percentage of board members younger than 60 years old: 30.9%

- Superaccelerators have less outside-industry representation than do nonaccelerators. This suggests that industry diversity should be encouraged "only in moderation," as too much industry diversity can actually inhibit board decision quality and timing.
- Superaccelerators have longer-tenured board members than do nonaccelerators. This suggests that board continuity can lead to better decisions and performance and perhaps that better company performance can lead to more stable boards.
- Boards of superaccelerators have more directors under the age of 60 than do boards of nonaccelerators. This suggests that business wisdom may come not only with age but also with experience that is relevant to current issues.

High-performance boards also appear to share a clear vision, including about the criteria for membership on the board, and have a strong "ownership mind-set." A culture of clarity and ownership seems to help these boards become better at having awkward conversations with management when needed, while otherwise providing breathing room for them. Such cultures help the top team anticipate and adapt without having to ask the board's permission at each step.

Four Types of Boards That Drive Acceleration

We've identified four variations of boards that can help a management team drive an acceleration agenda. It is entirely possible that one company can reflect more than one type of board at the same time.

Working Board

A Working Board is often associated with companies that are following the Portfolio Investor recipe for acceleration (see Chapter 10 for the recipes).

A Working Board helps the management team stay ruthlessly objective about the opportunities and resources in hand and available elsewhere. This board's eye is always on the horizon.

An Asian health care company shows a Working Board in action. With $1.6 billion in profit in 2015, the company has achieved significant growth through the years by pursuing highly focused acquisitions in related products and expanding from a products business into services, starting with its intra-company servicing contracts.

There are four principles to note from this company's board.

First, the relationship between the CEO and nonexecutive chair is highly symbiotic. The two, who are 15 years apart in age, show strong respect, ruthless transparency, and a high degree of personal accountability. Each publishes a letter to the board prior to every meeting, noting the focus points and actions and decisions expected to surface in the meeting. At the end of each meeting, the CEO and nonexecutive chair stay over and hold a one-on-one "roundup" to clarify actions and reactions. They hold monthly in-person meetings with board members, which result in synergy among the full board and a shared understanding of the state of the business.

Second, members invest a significant amount of time with the business. They spend, on average, 300 hours a year on their duties. Board meetings are at company locations around the world. Local management presents a business review the day before the formal board and committee meetings. Board meetings always include dinners just for independent directors. Once a year, there is a dinner for board members and their spouses, to increase connections and maintain the relational aspect of business.

Third, 100 percent engagement is demanded, and it is self-monitored by the group. A new board member who agreed to the 100 percent commitment before joining but did not demonstrate it was asked to leave the board after the third meeting.

Fourth, members are as diverse as the customer base and represent all regions in which the business operates (the board includes citizens of six different countries).

Thinking Board

A Thinking Board is typically found in those companies following the Customer Intimate recipe. This type of board brings the client's perspective into every conversation, decision, and conflict. Members ask, "If your best customer were in the room right now, what would he or she add to this debate?" These types of boards are singularly focused on the factors that will most accelerate growth and are ahead of the CEO and management team in that regard. They are not looking to be educated by management. They are masters in their own right and many times are extending their industry legacy through their role on a board. They can credibly represent the informed view of key external stakeholders in any conversation—role-modeling the behavior that keeps the top team thinking externally and longer term.

A national real estate firm shows what a Thinking Board looks like. It acts like a brain trust for this hypergrowth business, which has grabbed more than 30 percent market share. It has done this through rapid expansion of its current business into new geographies—basically scaling exponentially what it does better than any competitor. There are four principles to note from this board.

First, members are an all-star team who know more than the CEO does. In an industry where relationships and personality matter, they are better connected than the management team could ever be. They source deals and talent through personal calls. They call out competitors' bluffs in ways that management never could. They sometimes caution Zen patience and sometimes suggest risky, sudden turns—with uncanny accuracy.

Second, each director has made his mark (and money) in the world and is operating from a "mission first" role on the board. The directors don't need to be on the board—they want to be. The work is beyond money and prestige for them, so they have the freedom to act without a need for wealth or status. Leaving the board would be a huge deal for management but nothing for them.

Third, each director works one-on-one with the CEO to challenge his blind spots directly and hard. This requires the CEO to spend a lot of time with each director; meetings of the whole board are short, sometimes perfunctory. The real work is being done between board meetings, and no one is threatened by that approach.

Fourth, more than half of the directors are "CEO ready" should they need to step in on an interim basis, but they have zero interest in doing so. They are not competing with the CEO to be the smartest person in the room.

Responsive Board

A Responsive Board is typically found in companies following the Execution Engine recipe. A Responsive Board challenges management to keep things simple and fast. The board asks, "How does that work when you are 100 times bigger? How does that work with every customer, every day, everywhere? How does that investment support your top three priorities?" This type of board forces the company to focus, focus, focus. It makes sure there are no pet projects that don't serve the core. It helps the company keep the weight off and get more oxygen into the system.

A global IT services company shows how a Responsive Board contained a "kitchen fire" that could have taken down the house. While revenue growth was steady—partially due to long-term contracts with the federal government—profitability was falling. Competitors were "stockpiling arms" and preparing to come fast from multiple directions while the management team was staring straight ahead. One lost contract—which the management team had assured the board was an easy win and would have covered a huge revenue shortfall—started the spiral. The board brought in a new CEO within six weeks. He turned over 80 percent of the management team within 90 days. The business was split into two distinct growth engines—with different paces—within two years. The CEO then turned to the board and said, "What about you? You were here when the kitchen fire happened. How are you going to change?" When the board looked at itself, it realized, belatedly, that it had violated a few key principles.

First, directors were not in the game. The board had nine directors, but most had been out of the business world for at least five years. There were no sitting CEOs.

Second, directors were not relevant. The directors were selected based on relationships with the former chair—who was good friends with the former CEO—and not on industry experience or business relevance. The director with experience closest to the current strategy was in an academic role at an Ivy League school.

Third, the chair had focused too much on compliance. An accounting violation had surfaced that threatened to require a full financial restatement, and directors wisely hired a new audit chair to sort out the matter—but allowed discussions about the accounting issues to dominate the boardroom, losing focus on the business and its competitive threats.

Inspiring Board

An Inspiring Board is often found in companies following the Talent Magnet recipe, where people really are the greatest asset and competitive advantage. This type of board spends a significant amount of time understanding the "who" behind the "how." Members know the management team—in fact, they help to select and develop them. Directors talk with clients. They review talent, succession, and retention risks at every meeting. This type of board attracts great talent and keeps the CEO in constant check.

A global professional services firm provides a great example of a board that is obsessed with talent and sensing market trends early and often. This board's success is based on a few key principles.

First, it takes a data-driven approach to talent. This board works with the CEO to get the information necessary to make talent decisions. Members have direct and open access to management and use those avenues to gather their own data and perspective. This data-driven approach is also applied to other topics that the board considers.

Second, members bring the outside in. Because the board has the pulse of the business and has multiple real-time perspectives, board meetings are centered on decisions and external factors that could affect the company's risks, not internal performance updates. All internal updates are posted and digested before meetings, with questions asked and answered ahead of time.

Third, the board drives accountability, but not with the CEO: It presses each of the CEO's direct reports. Accountability for personal performance is real for the entire management team.

How to Accelerate Board Performance

Boards come in many shapes and sizes. They are odd and, in many ways, unnatural. They are "meter readers," who turn the pressure up or down or, unfortunately, sometimes do nothing at all until it is almost too late. Even if board members are all of high quality—and they must be—boards are subject to interpersonal dynamics that can hamper effectiveness.

They also face a number of structural challenges to their daily work. They are physically distributed teams who meet only occasionally and mostly in formal settings. They work for the company part-time and receive almost all their information secondhand. They need to balance pursuing an agenda of performance when their mandate is focused on assurance. They have a difficult role as they interface between the shareholders, who may see management as too detached, and management, who may see shareholders as people they have to give information to but not as the real owners of the corporation.

Even if these structural challenges are addressed, this does not necessarily ensure accelerating board performance. Our research on foundations and building blocks for high-performing boards identified four best-practice capabilities that boards need to develop to be truly effective.[10]

First, boards must be great about people, continually reviewing top talent and engaging in succession planning. Second, boards must have a clarity of vision and strategy that is shared and understood. Third, boards must promote team dynamics through the leadership of the board. Fourth, boards must maximize their capacity to consider and adapt to risk and innovation.

According to Heidrick & Struggles' board effectiveness and high-performance leadership surveys—undertaken across Europe, Asia Pacific, and North America—the key areas where boards consistently struggle or underperform relate to having (1) a comprehensive review of top talent performance and engagement in succession planning; (2) a clear strategy that is understood by each board member; and (3) the right balance of skills, knowledge, and experience to constructively challenge senior management.

One way to think about increasing a board's effectiveness is to review where it spends its time. We think about a board's role as three main focus areas: governance, performance, and learning. The governance role is about stopping bad things from happening; it's the foot on the brake. The performance role is about making good things happen; it's the foot on the gas. The learning role is one where the board is self-critical. It is the view from the internal camera. Table 13.2 further illustrates these three focus areas and the board's responsibilities within each.

TABLE 13.2 Three focus areas for boards

Focus (approximate share of director time)	Primary perspective	Objective	Approximate frequency	Primary discussion forum
Governance: 40%	Backward and internal	Risk management and compliance	6 times per year and as required by governance laws or company situation	Committee with findings, exceptions, and decisions elevated to board level

Examples:
- Audit committee: audit of financials and performance against budget; capital investments; internal risk review
- Compensation committee: executive performance and compensation; critical talent and high-potential talent succession risk; retention and development
- Nominating and corporate governance: board succession and recruitment; committee membership and chair roles
- Board chair: board dynamics and alignment; annual general meeting

Performance: 50%	Forward and external	Accelerated growth	2–3 times a year	Full board or key subset of directors

Examples:
- Company vision; top priorities/key initiatives; key performance indicators for relevant drag and drive factors
- Director's firsthand experience visiting customers, attending user conferences, visiting R&D sites, greeting new businesses, mentoring leaders, and inspecting production facilities
- Competitive analysis
- Organic and inorganic growth options; innovation progress
- Review of CEO, executive team, and top talent; check on resource fluidity and liquid leadership (succession, retention, and outside market perspective)

Learning: 10%	Introspective	Personal improvement	1–2 times a year	Full board

Examples:
- Director education on topic unique to company
- 360-degree review of board, committee, and individual director performance (including management perspectives)
- Performance review of full board, committee, and individual directors, conducted every 3 years using outside experts for additional objective perspective, market best practices, and disciplined implementation plan

This balance of brake, gas, and personal accountability is the tricky thing the board has to do in order to judge the degree of acceleration the company needs. And having your foot on both the gas and the brake simultaneously without looking out the windshield or in the rearview mirror can be particularly dangerous.

In addition to time allocation, our experience with extraordinary boards shows you also must focus on the four capabilities that we identify and explore at length in Chapters 14 through 17: ripple intelligence, resource fluidity, dissolving paradox, and liquid leadership. With those capabilities, boards will be able to make connections about the future that may not be visible to management, while encouraging management to make quick entries into markets and quick exits; help match talent and other resources to the right opportunities; role-model how to manage the business through a lighter use of hierarchy; and bring perspectives that could turn roadblocks into opportunities.

If You Do Nothing Else, Do These Five Things

Regardless of the kind of board you choose to have, you should emulate these five things that the very best boards do:

1. **Hire one or two "utility player" directors.** Every accelerating board needs a few wise, battle-worn business leaders who have lived through multiple business transformations and cycles from the front seat and come with the commensurate respect and sophistication to ask the exact right question at the right moment—they coax out of management the real issues at heart. In a crisis, you need such leaders in the foxhole with you.
2. **Demand a strong CEO.** The board, no matter who is on it, how often it meets, or what it may collectively know, is not running the company. The board's most important daily requirement is to oversee the performance of the CEO, and it must insist on strength for this role.
3. **Focus on the relationship between the CEO and the chair/lead independent director.** If we were to measure only one aspect of performance of a board to determine the projected level of success, we would look at the relationship between these two individuals. Do they know each other? Do they respect each other? Are their perspectives and experiences complementary? Can they honestly debate, disagree, and then move on?
4. **Overindex on industry experience.** Businesses need to make "shortcut" decisions rapidly. Boards need to be the headlights that can see further ahead and wider peripherally than management can. They can't be in the car learning to drive or in the passenger seat enjoying

the ride. There is no time to learn on the job. Financial acumen is the number one request and requirement. Industry-specific financial acumen is the difference between a good board member and a great board member. In the past year, five out of six industries in the *Fortune* 500 drew most often from within their own industry when appointing directors.[11]

5. **Be willing to fire yourself.** Boards that don't constantly monitor their own performance will fail. The days of "professional directors" are over. This is not a retirement role; being a director is an active career choice. If you are not "all in" and relevant to where the business is going, you should be fired or should fire yourself—or you will be known for being on a board of a company that missed the obvious and failed, which is even worse.

The Williams Companies board showed how this approach should work when 6 of 13 directors resigned in the aftermath of Energy Transfer Equity's decision to back out of a merger agreement with Williams because falling oil and gas prices had cut Williams's value. The directors disagreed with the CEO's strategy for Williams as a stand-alone business, so they fired themselves. "Ironically, given the current CEO and board leadership, I believe I will be more effective from outside the company than within, and will seek to protect our interests and the interest of other shareholders from outside this diminished boardroom," hedge fund investor Keith Meister wrote as he resigned from the board.[12]

Honda took matters into its own hands in 2011, reducing its board from 20 members to 12 to speed up decision making, not long after Toyota had made a similar move.[13]

■ ■ ■

Every board should function as smoothly as the board that Jeffrey A. Sonnenfeld describes at UPS. He says the board developed through a virtuous circle, where good chemistry led to trust and to sharing of difficult information, which led to openness and give-and-take, which led to more trust, and so on. In the mid-1980s, the company had made a bold move and set up partnerships with delivery businesses around the world, and achieved great success, but then decided to go global itself and built a much broader footprint. Sonnenfeld writes: "This strategic reversal is generally considered a brilliant move, one that might never have happened had board members not respected and trusted one another enough to consider that a smart move could be trumped by an even smarter one."[14]

Many managers and board members complain about the short-term focus that markets force on them—we call it "quarteritis"—but the capital markets act as a superb disciplinarian. They will weed out the slow from the fast. So boards must help organizations pursue an acceleration agenda. Boards that embrace this role are evolving much faster than their peers. Disruptive boards and board members will redefine the relationship between the board and the management team and will play a pivotal role in accelerating strategy, creating role models that will redefine corporate governance for the benefit of all.

Notes

1. Pamela Wasley, "The Theranos crisis: Where was the board?" *Fortune*, April 27, 2016, fortune.com.
2. John Carreyrou, "Hot startup Theranos has struggled with its blood-test technology," *Wall Street Journal*, October 16, 2015, wsj.com.
3. "Walgreens terminates relationship with Theranos," press release, June 12, 2016, news.walgreens.com.
4. John Carreyrou, "Theranos voids two years of Edison blood-test results," *Wall Street Journal*, May 18, 2016, wsj.com.
5. Christopher Weaver, John Carreyrou, and Michael Siconolfi, "Theranos is subject of criminal probe by U.S.," *Wall Street Journal*, April 18, 2016, wsj.com.
6. Andrew Pollack, "Elizabeth Holmes of Theranos is barred from running lab for 2 years," *New York Times*, July 8, 2016, nytimes.com.
7. Matthew Herper, "From $4.5 billion to nothing: Forbes revises estimated net worth of Theranos founder Elizabeth Holmes," *Forbes*, June 21, 2016, forbes.com.
8. Matthew Heller, "Investor activism expected to substantially increase," *CFO*, November 3, 2014, cfo.com.
9. Jeffrey Goldberg, "Top Susan G. Komen official resigned over Planned Parenthood cave-in," *The Atlantic*, February 2, 2012, theatlantic.com.
10. Heidrick & Struggles, *Foundations and Building Blocks for High-Performing Boards: Asia Pacific Corporate Governance Report 2014*, June 6, 2014, heidrick.com.
11. Heidrick & Struggles, *2016 Board Monitor: Mapping Incoming Boardroom Talent*, May 4, 2016, heidrick.com.
12. David Benoit, Alison Sider, and Liz Hoffman, "Board resignations set up potential proxy fight at Williams," *Wall Street Journal*, July 1, 2016, wsj.com.
13. Jeff Glucker, "Report: Honda slashes board size to speed decision making," *Autoblog*, February 23, 2011, autoblog.com.
14. Jeffrey A. Sonnenfeld, "What makes great boards great," *Harvard Business Review*, September 2002, hbr.org.

The Four Key Skills

This final section gets into an area that is rarely covered in management books. Most will offer a prescription on what is to be done and perhaps lay out a plan of attack for reaching that goal. But, in our experience, businesses need to take one final step: They need to develop capabilities that allow the planned changes to really take hold and that will undergird a new way of approaching business. While these capabilities aren't completely new, the four covered in this section do require a new way of looking at old issues.

In Chapter 14, on what we call ripple intelligence, we describe a more powerful way of making sense of what's going on in the outside world. Historically, companies have taken a very mechanistic approach—the knee bone is connected to the thigh bone, the thigh bone is connected to the hip bone, and so on. Companies look at a rise in the cost of supply and think about the effects, or they see a competitor's action and think about that. But the world is too complex to think about events in isolation. In fact, your market is like a pond that people keep throwing rocks into. Each rock—some big, some small—splashes and creates ripples that interact as they spread through the pond. Your job as the manager is to understand how those ripples will play into each other and to spot the opportunities and the dangers. One surprise that comes out of our research is that it's possible to train people and vastly improve their ability to make predictions. People routinely overestimate their abilities, but you can demonstrate to them their deficiencies and coach them to remove biases that cloud their judgment. As little as an hour of training improved individuals' ability to predict by 14 percent, and the gains lasted more than a year. Even better, if you bring together the right capabilities and establish the right dynamics, you can build teams that are far stronger than individuals.

Chapter 15, on resource fluidity, builds on research that shows that companies that reallocate capital rapidly do much better than those that take the traditional approach, where budgets are slight variants of what they were the year before. Our research found that the same holds true for human resources: Quickly moving them to the best opportunities creates big wins.

This is hard, of course. Anyone who has hold of corporate resources wants to keep them. This chapter explains how to break the stranglehold on resources by, for instance, establishing a centralized repository of resources that are merely loaned to business units for a time. You also need to plan continuously, get away from the three- or five-year budgets that freeze resources in place, and take out layers of management, which can get in the way of fluid sharing of resources. Increasingly, you even need to think about sharing that goes beyond the corporate boundaries. Some 20 percent to 40 percent of a workforce these days consists of people employed by someone else, so you need to figure out how to integrate quickly and deeply while also being ready to let them go at a moment's notice when they are no longer needed.

Chapter 16, on dissolving paradox, describes how to get to a higher level of thinking than most companies achieve today. Level 1 thinking is about binary decisions: Either you get all the resources, or I do. Level 2 is about operating on a scale: You get 80 percent, and I get 20 percent. Level 3 is about coordinating to stretch the power of the resources: You feel as though you get 80 percent, and I feel that I get 50 percent, because we're sharing 30 percent. Level 4—where companies need to get to whenever possible— is about what we call the "strategic unlock." If, say, customer service and product development are competing for funds, you find ways to funnel customer feedback directly to development teams to improve their products and reduce development costs. Everybody wins.

In Chapter 17, on liquid leadership, we address an issue that many businesses are facing: Confronted by increasingly demanding customers, do you get rid of corporate hierarchy so those close to the customer can make decisions rapidly and compassionately, or do you maintain the hierarchy to keep control and provide consistency to customers? Our answer: Neither. And both. You keep the hierarchy but increasingly manage outside it, marshalling resources in mostly informal ways to go after problems and opportunities.

CHAPTER 14

Ripple Intelligence
Join the Dots

Chaos theory tells us that the flapping of a butterfly's wings in Tokyo can lead to a tornado in Kansas. Or that roads with cars moving at 35 mph or less can suddenly form massive traffic jams when someone merely taps his brakes and the effects cascade to other drivers. Drivers get to the end of the congestion, look around for an accident or some other cause and find nothing—because the cause was almost nothing. They drive off, confused.

The sort of system thinking that stems from chaos theory has shown up in some limited uses in the world of business, such as in manufacturing polymers and detecting leaks in coal mines, but the analysis in the executive suite still mostly compartmentalizes causes and effects rather than understanding their complex interactions in large systems. Our competitor did X, so we will do Y. A foreign government did Z, so let's think about the implications for our business in that country. The fact is that X, Y, and Z all interact, along with A, B, C, and potentially a host of other variables. Once we do Y, competitors, customers, suppliers, and so forth will all react. That foreign government's action will affect all the actors in that country, not just us, and will ripple through the region and perhaps the world. That ripple will intersect with the ripples caused by the actions that our competitors took and by our response, by our customers' reactions, by our competitors' reactions to those reactions, and on and on.

Although companies won't be able to evaluate all those ripples with the precision that the mathematics of chaos theory now allows when someone is, say, predicting traffic, executives can take a major step toward dealing with complexity by building what we call "ripple intelligence." Think of the effect of a rock dropped in a pond. Now imagine the effect of multiple rocks (of different sizes) thrown into those same waters. Add the effects of wind and weather. Ripple intelligence gives you a vantage point from above. This enables you to look down and see how all the forces combine so you can predict how trends and contexts may intersect, interact, and change directions.

Ripple intelligence allows companies to accelerate in the following ways:

- Anticipating how and when the business may be disrupted.
- Rising above the clutter and connecting disparate events, discovering patterns, and anticipating distant threats and opportunities.
- Evaluating emerging trends to determine if they are game-changing, transient, significant, or slow-burn.
- Keeping up to date as decisions create new ripples that interact with existing ones to create more opportunities and more threats.

Ripple intelligence provides CEOs with an early warning system so they have time to plan a range of responses and then choose and execute as appropriate.

In interviews with 150 CEOs worldwide for *The CEO Report*, developed through a partnership between Heidrick & Struggles and Saïd Business School at the University of Oxford and published in early 2015, the CEOs said that there was a great need for such an early warning system. One noted: "No one really [imagined] Russian tanks in Eastern Ukraine, Crimea, what's going on in the South China Sea . . . plus the slowest, shallowest [economic] recovery we've ever had." Another noted "the rise of 2.2 billion new middle-class consumers, technology going three times faster than management, geopolitics." The first CEO wondered: "What if this is just the new normal?"

Consider someone trying to understand what will happen with oil prices. As initial causes, you have, among many others, the technology breakthroughs that have led to the fracking boom in the United States and a surge in supply that has sent prices tumbling. You also have environmentalists who oppose fracking and who have achieved more influence because of the U.S. presidential campaign. There are nascent fracking developments in other countries, and federal legislation in the United States has allowed American companies to export oil for the first time, which could depress prices in world markets. Meanwhile, Russia is having economic problems that may affect its oil production, and you have some European countries that have talked about shunning Russia because of its aggression in Crimea (though they don't generally seem to be following through on their threat of reducing oil purchases). Saudi Arabia, for its part, has announced that it won't cut production despite low oil prices—perhaps to punish Russia and Iran for supporting Syria's government. The Saudi decision makes many fields uneconomic for fracking, but the resources the fields represent still loom over the market because fracking rigs can go back into production quickly. Saudi Arabia's thinking about oil production added another dimension when it announced that it would sell some 5 percent of the state oil company, Aramco, so the kingdom can pile up assets that the country will carry into a world where its oil either runs out or is supplanted by other energy sources.

In the short run, some of the effects are clear enough: Lower prices will likely hurt shale producers and will slow the development of renewable energy. In the intermediate and longer terms, though, the interactions of forces become much more complicated. How will political tensions in the Middle East change if prices stay low? What if the United States continues increasing its oil independence and plays less of a military role in the region because the Middle East has become less strategic? Will Russia continue its aggressive foreign policy, and what might the implications be for the Middle East and for oil?

To develop the kind of ripple intelligence that will allow companies to sort through such complex issues and map out their response, they need to do five things:

1. Develop a 35,000-foot view.
2. Embrace the power of doubt.
3. Train, train, train.
4. Form the right teams.
5. Test and learn.

We will discuss each of these capabilities in detail.

Develop a 35,000-Foot View

One of the CEOs we interviewed said: "Trying to forecast the future has become an impossible task." Another said: "Michael Porter used to talk about sustainable competitive advantage. . . . There is no 'sustainable' anymore, but you still have to find competitive advantage."

While ripple intelligence allows leaders to cope with such a high-pressure environment, our research suggests that, for most leaders, thinking in this way doesn't come naturally.

Many CEOs talked about the need to reset priorities and even let go of the operational focus that had helped them reach their positions. One said that his executive team handles the day to day so he can concentrate fully on the 35,000-foot level, looking for ripples outside the company. He spoke of "hovering" above the business, his customers, consumers, competitors, and other market players, continuously searching the environment for emerging connections. "I get a bird's-eye view," he observes, "scanning the horizon and context without clutter." He evaluates events individually, and then takes a second pass that combines events and ideas, to look for patterns and trends. He seeks trends and risks that might hurt the business as well as those that could provide opportunities for the company.

The keys to this sort of environmental scanning are contextual thinking and a long-term perspective. As another CEO puts it, "It's like when you ride a bicycle: You always have to look a little bit further—if you look just in front of your wheel, you lose your balance." In practice, this requires examining how ripples from one event might interact with ripples from other events in the short, medium, and long terms.

Of course, ripples that appear isolated and unimportant may remain so. Managers need to keep an eye on emerging trends through their peripheral vision but avoid acting prematurely. The trick is to recognize when it is necessary to expand the problem-solving space and "make the problem bigger," as one CEO suggests, and when to move to a decision.

A tool that can help—used by the CEO who delegates day-to-day responsibility so he can focus on the ripples in his market—looks at trends based on speed, scope, and significance.

At the moment, everyone knows the importance of speed. In one CEO's words: "You have to separate the noise and the normal stuff from fundamental shifts that are taking place and then be able to determine how quickly those shifts are going to manifest or disrupt what you're doing, versus those things that you have more time to adjust to."

But focusing only on speed may misdirect energy and attention to events that seem urgent but in fact are of limited scope or significance. To manage energy effectively, leaders need to be equally attuned to all three aspects of each challenge they face.

To gauge the size of any response to a combination of ripples, executives must understand the scope—how far-reaching the effects will be. Does something affect just one part of the company, one type of customer, or one geographic market, or will the effects have a wider influence?

Leaders must also gauge significance, which refers to how deeply any change affects the organization. Predicting and assessing significance mean asking "how, how fast, and how much" a particular event or trend will affect the business. As another CEO notes, "You have to begin to sort out the results you're getting. Are they a result of a broader macroeconomic or industry shift taking place, or are they more enterprise-specific?"

Some changes will influence the business model, strategy, or operations of the business. We call these technical changes—important but not deeply disruptive. But other changes are more profound and foundational, challenging the organization's mission and core values. What looks like a purely technical decision can also have value-based implications that make it foundational. Cyber threats, for example, are likely to represent technical changes for most businesses but will be foundational for a smaller group, such as computer companies.

Remembering that fast doesn't necessarily mean urgent or important is a critical first step in determining where to focus attention.

Embrace the Power of Doubt

Doubt is a capability to be cultivated rather than a weakness to be cured. Doubts are to leaders what nerves are to elite athletes: a source of focus and insight when harnessed constructively, a threat to peak performance when not.

"If you don't doubt yourself in a constructive, positive way, you are borderline dangerous for your company," one CEO said. In a world of intersecting trends, clarity can be a dangerous illusion. As another CEO said, "If you're that clear, you've probably missed something."

Many CEOs, in fact, start from unflinching certainty. In the interviews for *The CEO Report*, only 71 percent initially acknowledged doubt. A further 10 percent admitted doubt, too, when asked to reconsider, but 19 percent said they had none. A more recent study that Heidrick & Struggles conducted with David K. Rehr, a professor at George Mason University, surveyed roughly 500 U.S. CEOs of professional and trade associations and found a similar result: Only 74 percent acknowledged doubt.

But reimagining doubt as a positive allows leaders to accelerate their organizations by sharpening their ripple intelligence, enhancing their ability to make decisions, and mitigating business and decision-making risks in times of complexity and uncertainty.

Our understanding hinges on two insights: First, harnessing doubt allows senior executives to balance themselves within an "uncomfortable" comfort zone in which they feel able to act decisively, even in times of uncertainty. Second, the type of doubt and the size of this comfort zone are defined by dimensions of both knowing and feeling—all of which can be mapped on a stylized two-by-two matrix (Figure 14.1).

If you don't have enough information and are worried about that fact, you are in danger of paralysis. If you don't have enough information but intend to plunge ahead anyway, you may be guilty of hubris. If you have the information you need but are still worried, you are wrestling with angst. If you have the information you need and are confident—which would seem to be the magic quadrant—you still need to guard against myopia.

Once leaders understand which quadrant they find themselves in for any given decision, they can think about tailoring strategies to turn doubt into a powerful tool and thereby expand their comfort zones while protecting against the various risks of decision making.

FIGURE 14.1 The power of doubt

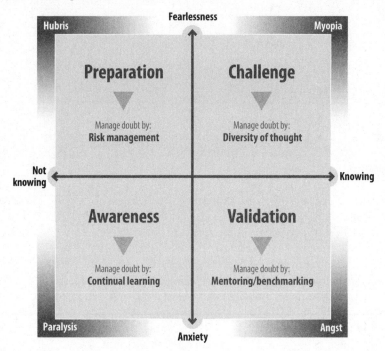

One of the most important things is having people around you who will challenge you when you are wrong. For some CEOs, doubt expressed itself as an "honest humility about what you're capable of knowing and an insatiable sense of curiosity." Several CEOs focused on data collection and analysis. Still others approached it on a more personal level—for example, by traveling, seeking out diverse conversations, and gathering information from a broad selection of sources. As one CEO pointed out, "The customized news feeds we all enjoy can generate blinkers on the sides of our heads and constrain our views." Therefore, he makes a point of reading outside his typical areas of interest to remove the blinkers and broaden his horizons.

In circumstances where CEOs report feeling residual anxiety despite good information, they can "outsource doubt" by turning to peer mentoring or benchmarking for validation or to "safer" environments such as family, friends, or CEO associations. Validation is critical for tempering doubt and channeling its productive power. Moreover, it mitigates the risk of doubt spiraling into angst, wasteful information searches, or unhealthy self-challenge.

Those more fearless leaders who feel well informed tend to "value the friction and the debate that goes on around even the small stuff" so they don't get too comfortable and risk overconfidence. In fact, such leaders often go out of their way to create environments where honest and constructive debate is not only welcome but expected. Among the CEOs we interviewed, the most common sources of debate were the board and board chair, although some CEOs have established designated panels to serve as devil's advocates. One CEO says, "[I] always have someone bringing me an angle, a vision that I clearly didn't see."

However, as one CEO laments, "One of the 'aha [moments]' about being CEO is you stop hearing the truth." So leaders need to expressly invite dissent. "One of the biggest lessons to me," one interviewee said, "is the deliberate effort to listen to the organization; it's really easy to pretend to listen."

The key to embracing the power of doubt is getting comfortable making decisions in the gray area in between, or, in the words of one CEO, to "get comfortable with discomfort." It helps to acknowledge that doubt is both a feeling and an information issue—numbers just illuminate an issue; they don't make the decisions for you.

CEOs who are comfortable making decisions with limited information often rely on experience or gut instinct. However, they acknowledge that, in new situations where their gut may be wrong, "it's also important to marry that gut feeling with the ability to be humble enough to ask." Leaders in this category rely on traditional risk-management approaches to protect against the possible negative consequences of their decisions. This helps give them a sense of preparation while protecting against the hubris that the "CEO knows best." "Because if you are not careful and you think that you are indestructible," notes one respondent, "then that's where the dangers lurk."

Processing doubt takes time. Judiciously assessing the speed, scope, and significance of change is paramount so that CEOs can identify the decisions to delegate, determine the decisions to make, and then dedicate sufficient time for productive doubt.

One CEO neatly summarized the challenges that leaders face as they try to accelerate and the reason to inject doubt. Being a CEO, he said, requires "an almost insane combination of extreme confidence, bordering on arrogance, combined with complete humility."

Train, Train, Train

People tend to think they're much better at things, including making decisions, than they actually are. Findings from social scientists indicate that 70 percent of high school seniors say they are above average at leadership, and 25 percent put themselves in the top percentile; only 2 percent say they are below average. Among college professors, 94 percent say they are doing above-average work. At one company, 32 percent of the engineers said they were among the top 5 percent of performers; at another, 42 percent put themselves in that top category.[1] That's the bad news.

The good news is that people can get better through training. The even better news is that teams can be constructed that are better than individuals and that testing can produce a feedback loop that allows individuals and teams to keep improving.

We say this based on a host of research, including work that colleagues of ours did with the Good Judgment Project, which they helped launch in 2011. The team competed in a tournament funded by the Intelligence Advanced Research Projects Activity (IARPA) that had more than 25,000 forecasters answer questions that U.S. intelligence agencies posed to their analysts. The forecasters made more than one million predictions about issues such as the chance of financial panic in China and the chance that Greece would leave the eurozone. The team that included our colleagues won decisively. They even bested the intelligence agencies' analysts.[2]

Left to their own devices, people make all sorts of errors. They bring with them personal biases, sometimes reinforced by economic incentives—nobody wants to acknowledge a problem that would hurt their bonus or end the need for their job. Groupthink often rears its head, especially once the CEO has indicated a preference for a course of action. We think in straight lines, while technology changes on an exponential curve. According to physics professor Albert A. Bartlett, "The greatest shortcoming of the human race is our inability to understand the exponential function."[3] People are also far too confident. They simply aren't as good at forecasting as they think they are.

But the Good Judgment Project showed that as little as one hour of training improved the accuracy of forecasts by roughly 14 percent over a year. Training can disabuse people of basic errors in reasoning, such as the belief that having a coin come up heads several times in a row means that it's more likely to come up tails the next time. Training can also introduce concepts such as Bayesian revision—how to adjust estimates as new information comes in. The Good Judgment Project trained people to keep an open mind about that new information, rather than falling for what is known as confirmation bias—the tendency to look for data that confirms what you believe and to ignore data that contradicts your thesis.

The project underscored the sort of approach that guided Charles Darwin, who wrote: "I had, also, during many years, followed a golden rule, namely, that whenever a published fact, a new observation or thought came across me, which was opposed to my general results, to make a memorandum of it without fail and at once; for I had found by experience that such facts and thoughts were far more apt to escape from the memory than favourable ones."[4]

The Good Judgment Project heightened people's awareness of their weaknesses by giving them "confidence quizzes." People were asked a question and told to give an answer in a range that they were 90 percent confident contained the right answer. For instance, people might be asked how old Martin Luther King, Jr., was when he was assassinated and say they were 90 percent sure he was 40 to 55 years old. (He was 39.) Typically, at least half of the correct answers fell outside the range that a participant had said was 90 percent likely to contain the answer.

Our colleagues note that bridge players tend to be very good predictors and say some companies have employees play poker to learn to avoid cognitive biases. For example, Susquehanna International Group, a quantitative trading firm, requires that new hires play poker on company time. The idea is partly to have the hires learn about cognitive traps, such as wishful thinking, and to sensitize them to the value of thinking based on probability— "focusing on information asymmetry (what the opponent might know that I don't), learning when to fold a bad hand, and defining success not as winning each round but as making the most of the hand you are dealt."[5]

Form the Right Teams

Teams consistently outperform individuals on predictions—but they have to be the right kinds of teams. The Good Judgment Project built teams partly by continually evaluating forecasters and culling the lesser performers. It found that the best were, not surprisingly, "cautious, humble, open-minded, analytical—and good with numbers." They were aware of the possibilities of bias, demonstrated sound reasoning, and believed in the power of data.[6] Teams need to be diverse, too, with a mix of those who know the subject area and nonexperts who have license to challenge the presumed experts.

NASA learned the value of diversity when it decided to open to the public its data on solar flares after 35 years of research failed to predict when they would occur or how intense they would be. It turns out that a retired radio frequency engineer in a small town in New Hampshire had been contemplating a theory that related to the problem and, armed with NASA's data, was able to predict flares 8 hours ahead with 85 percent accuracy and 24 hours ahead with 75 percent accuracy. Allstate, Carlsberg breweries, and others have also had breakthroughs with so-called open innovation, combining internal expertise with views from outside experts and nonexperts.[7]

Natarajan Chandrasekaran, CEO and managing director of Tata Consultancy Services (one of the superaccelerators), is a fan of diverse views when it comes to anticipating the technological changes that might affect his business. "We gather information from our research and innovation group, from our strong industry partnerships, and from our TCS co-innovation network

[COIN]. We have about 1,400 start-up companies on our radar right now. And yet, while we are respectful of all the knowledge we get from these various listening posts, our contact with customers is key. Our leadership team meets with at least 500 companies a year; we look closely at what our customers are thinking, saying, and what business model changes they're considering. We can't just follow the 'hype cycle.'"

Perhaps the most important example of the value of the generalist comes from the Kennedy administration. President Kennedy had assembled a group of advisers that came to be known as "the best and the brightest," yet they made a series of mistakes that led to the Bay of Pigs fiasco, a failed invasion of Cuba, in April 1961. The same group of advisers then confronted the Cuban Missile Crisis just a year and a half later—but with one key change. President Kennedy had appointed his brother Bobby, the attorney general, to play the role of devil's advocate and challenge the experts. When the top general in the U.S. Air Force urged bombing the Soviet missile sites in Cuba, confident that the Soviets wouldn't have the stomach to retaliate, Bobby Kennedy didn't let the expert stand unchallenged, as had been the case during the run-up to the Bay of Pigs. Bobby got the group to debate, and they decided that the Soviets would have to retaliate or lose face forever. The United States didn't bomb—and historical documents show that the Soviets would surely have retaliated, starting an escalation that might well have ended in nuclear war. Instead, the United States and the Soviet Union found a way for all to back down.[8]

Test and Learn

Testing first requires that predictions be precise. It's not enough to say that a product will do fairly well or that someone joining the company will get up to speed quickly. There needs to be a number associated with that product's sales; there must be a metric and a time frame associated with the performance of that new hire.

Economists have learned that they're always right as long as they don't attach a date. There will be a recession . . . sometime. But companies can't allow any of that fuzziness if they are to improve their ability to make predictions.

Once you have people making precise predictions—in terms of the percentage likelihood that a result will fall within a certain range—you can use statistical tests to see who is doing well at predicting and who is not. But you have to go beyond that. You also have to understand the process that has been used to generate the predictions, so you can see what's working, what isn't, and how you can improve. Understanding the process means looking not just at participants and their data but also at group dynamics.

To track how decisions are made, companies should systematically collect records of the decision making, including videos or transcripts from meetings. Leaders should review those records and match them with the outcomes that resulted from those decisions, to see which approaches worked and which didn't. The leaders should then train the decision makers both on what to do and on what not to do. Lather, rinse, repeat—this review needs to be continual so that decision making keeps improving.

Be careful, though, not to let reviews turn into scolding based on hindsight. Daniel Kahneman, winner of the Nobel Prize in Economics, has written: "Decision makers who expect to have their decisions scrutinized with hindsight are driven to bureaucratic solutions—and to an extreme reluctance to take risks."[9]

The world will still be a fast changing and confusing place, but leaders will be able to make much better sense of it and accelerate if they build ripple intelligence. Getting a 35,000-foot view, embracing the power of doubt, training, forming the right teams, and testing and learning will help you see all the complex interactions that are created as people and events keep tossing big economic, geopolitical, and other types of rocks into your pond.

Notes

1. Adam Grant, *Originals: How Non-Conformists Move the World*, New York: Viking, 2016.
2. Paul J. H. Schoemaker and Philip E. Tetlock, "Superforecasting: How to upgrade your company's judgment," *Harvard Business Review*, May 2016, hbr.org.
3. Albert A. Bartlett, "Arithmetic, population and energy," lecture, University of Colorado Boulder, September 19, 1969.
4. Charles Darwin, *Life and Letters of Charles Darwin: Volume 1*, Hamburg: Tredition Classics, 2013.
5. Paul J. H. Schoemaker and Philip E. Tetlock, "Superforecasting: How to upgrade your company's judgment," *Harvard Business Review*, May 2016, hbr.org.
6. Paul J. H. Schoemaker and Philip E. Tetlock, "Superforecasting: How to upgrade your company's judgment," *Harvard Business Review*, May 2016, hbr.org.
7. Erik Brynjolfsson and Andrew McAfee, *The Second Machine Age: Work, Progress, and Prosperity in a Time of Brilliant Technology*, New York: W. W. Norton, 2014.
8. Irving L. Janis, *Psychological Studies of Policy Decision and Fiascoes*, Second Edition, Boston: Cengage Learning, 1982.
9. Daniel Kahneman, *Thinking, Fast and Slow*, New York: Farrar, Straus, and Giroux, 2013.

CHAPTER 15

Resource Fluidity

Match Resources to Opportunities

Perhaps the most famous example of the platitude that generals always fight the last war is the Maginot Line. Influenced by the success of defensive tactics in World War I, French Minister of War André Maginot had a line of impressive fortifications and gun installations built along the country's eastern border during the 1930s. Military experts hailed the work as genius. But, during World War II, with so much of France's military power locked in place, the Nazis just sent tanks around the edge of the line and the Luftwaffe over it and reached Paris in no time.

Generals have learned the lessons from the Maginot Line and have developed ever more mobile capabilities, but businesses are still mostly fighting the same old battle because too many of their resources are locked in place.

One reason for the lack of flexibility is that businesses assign resources to business units, and it's hard to ever get them back (possession being nine-tenths of the law). That control in the business units would be fine if the external environment would just stay as it is. But it doesn't. In fact, the outside world is changing faster than ever, so whatever assignment of resources is made today soon will be out of phase with the market. Companies try to coordinate across business units to adapt to the changing environment, but the effort is complex and time-consuming and often doesn't even work because the units guard their resources so jealously.

In most businesses, resources can't move fluidly across silos in organizations. (When Howard Stringer became CEO of Sony, he stumped a translator when he said the company had too many silos. Grain silos are rare in Japan, which grows rice. But the translator came up with a good approximation: "octopus pot." The pots are designed to make it easy for an octopus to get in but never to get out—very much like business silos.[1]) Resources also can't move across time because of budget cycles; we've all seen managers rush to spend money right at the end of a fiscal year because they know they can't carry it over into the next cycle.

Resources don't move well across corporate boundaries, either, even though they increasingly must. Companies have outsourced, for many years now, noncore functions: the cafeteria, the mail room, even the IT center. But companies today must become far better able to draw in part-timers, contract employees, and resources from partners. This ability has moved from being a peripheral skill to being a core necessity.

Let's step back and think about why we even have organizations in the first place. Why do we need them? Why can't we each simply do stuff and sell the output? The answer is that we need to combine labor, capital, and ideas to create more collectively than any individual can do alone. No individual can build a Boeing Dreamliner. So the organization is a vehicle by which we match labor, capital, and intellectual property to opportunities. We call these opportunities products, markets, and customers. An organization is a clearinghouse, a central channel coordinating the matching process.

When an organization is working well, this process is achieved seamlessly, with almost zero transaction cost. When an organization functions badly, high transaction costs show up in what we call bureaucracy, silos, and structural rigidity.

To accelerate and succeed, businesses need to consciously develop what we call resource fluidity, which is the ease with which organizations match capabilities to opportunities.

At some level, business leaders know that their resources need to be more fluid, or fungible, but human and organizational issues get in the way. Look at the example of a "universal bank," so called because it offers retail and commercial banking, investment banking, asset management, and wealth management. The idea is that this is a balanced set of assets that plays well together. For instance, when times are tough and market headwinds are strong, the investment bank faces problems, but capital flows to safe havens, so the organization has the steady support of the retail bank. The well-off entrepreneurs looked after by the wealth management division can also be sold investment banking products for the companies they own. Fair enough. But the leaders of the divisions all want the CEO job, and none wants to see his or her operation lose resources, not only because it's tough to justify your run for the top job if your division is shrinking but also because the resources are going to an internal competitor. At this universal bank, it was clear that the economic returns from wealth management were, in the long run, twice those of the investment bank, but the leader of the investment bank pleaded with the CEO to keep pouring resources into that division so that it wouldn't fall below critical mass and compromise the natural balance of the group.

Similarly, a supplier of financial services technology identified a major opportunity but didn't pursue it for five years. When asked why, an executive said, "The capabilities we need to pursue this are spread across three or four different business units. Each would get credit for only a small portion of the revenue, so they have little incentive to go after the opportunity."[2]

To counteract the natural tendencies of people and organizations, you have to build the skill of resource fluidity by continually focusing on the three enablers: (1) fluid reallocation of capital resources; (2) people mobility; and (3) resource sharing and reuse. All three are essential. Having one or two won't get you to where you need to be to support the acceleration of your business.

Fluid Reallocation of Capital Resources

Research has shown that companies that are more fluid about how they allocate capital do better than those that take the traditional approach, which can look like a sort of corporate socialism, working off the previous year's budget and just adjusting a bit up or down rather than greatly rewarding the best opportunities and withdrawing funds from the worst. Cigna, for instance, is willing to reallocate capital sharply as its corporate priorities shift (for example, in the wake of a periodic review of business units). David Cordani, the president and CEO, told us: "If we determine that a business can provide substantially more value for customers, we will absolutely allocate more money—and talent—to it. But a big increase in resources comes with a big increase in accountability. The goals and targets go up along with the resources we allocate."

What research hasn't addressed is the next level: Once you've developed a freer mind-set, what steps do you take to make sure you're allocating your capital as effectively as possible?

Our research into acceleration has found three necessary steps. You must be able to make decisions on strategic direction without regard to the organizational structure, you must remove strategic resource ownership from business units, and you must plan continuously.

Free Strategic Direction from the Organizational Structure

The maxim says that structure follows strategy—as it should. What often happens, though, is that, once a structure is in place, subsequent strategic decisions are made with the structure in mind. Now, strategy follows structure rather than the other way around. The structure of the organization creates a mind-set that constrains the kinds of opportunities that the company considers.

Let's say you are a consumer goods organization that has a typical structure for a family of products (bakery, candy, dried pasta, coffee, and the like). It is very easy to use the filter of the structure to make sense of new opportunities and miss ones that cross business units. Perhaps there is an opportunity to develop a new retail concept—for instance a company-owned coffee shop where candy and baked goods are also offered—to create a special customer experience. That concept wouldn't make sense for just coffee, just candy, or just baked goods, which are focused on their existing, individual sales channels, so the units would likely miss the chance. If, however, strategic decisions are made without the constraints of the existing structure, this opportunity would be evaluated on its merits as a market-defining opportunity for the organization as a whole.

Your organization needs to enable the scanning, identifying, and prioritizing of valuable opportunities—internal as well as external—irrespective of the organizational structure. As you quickly assess the value of possible opportunities, you need to become comfortable making decisions without 100 percent of the information required. And you must be able to quickly abandon an opportunity when it is no longer valuable.

Dissociate Resource Ownership from Business Units

In a fluid world, resource ownership cannot be associated with particular businesses. Resources—whether financial, human, or intellectual—need to be owned by the corporation and then loaned to a business unit for the pursuit of an opportunity. Once the opportunity is over (because it has been exhausted or abandoned or needs different resources), the allocated resources go back to the pool they are a part of so that they can be provided to the next opportunity that would make the best use of them. Budgets, staff, technology, and ideas are not the property of any organizational unit; they belong in a pool of corporate resources that can freely float from opportunity to opportunity.

A well-known investment bank takes this sort of approach, which employees call "Indonesia." Under tightening global standards, the bank has to maintain 6 percent common equity as a percentage of risk-weighted assets, and jurisdictions are each demanding that the bank meet that standing in their area—so 6 percent in the United Kingdom, 6 percent in Switzerland, 6 percent in the United States, and even 6 percent in each U.S. state. Rather than just lament that so much capital has to be locked into specific areas and can't be shared, the bank uses the requirement as a forcing function to make sure it moves *other* pots of capital around outside the regulatory environment. Employees refer to the capital-management approach as Indonesia because, just as the island nation must integrate its diverse constituents spread across the world's largest archipelago into a single state, the bank must operate centrally despite its many "islands" of capital. (Some wags, who dislike the regulatory regime, say it should be called Maldives because it will soon be under water.)

Cisco takes a similarly aggressive approach to allocating resources. It looked at its 150 most important clients and worked backward to make sure that all the resources that might be needed to support them would always be available on short notice, no matter where in the organization those resources resided. General Electric and L'Oréal are also great examples of companies with corporate resources pools.

Tata Consultancy Services, likewise, has designated a single point of contact, no more than two levels down from the CEO, for all its strategic relationships and goes to great lengths to marshal resources for that person, says Natarajan Chandrasekaran, the company's CEO. He says a main focus is on coordinating efforts at pace: "Structures create boundaries. When you have, say, 10 business units, each business unit by itself will usually be very agile, but the problem comes in the interface. When a business unit has to work with some other business unit, things always slow down. So we say that the speed of the company is in the interface."

Plan Continuously

If your organization does strategic planning the traditional way, with a strategy function and once-a-year input from the business that leads to a five-year plan, it won't achieve resource fluidity. Resource fluidity requires that organizations be able to spot and develop opportunities constantly, not once a year during the annual planning cycle.

Although you can certainly have highly trained individuals focused on spotting opportunities, you also need to be sure that everyone in the organization has their antennae up. You need as broad an early warning system as you can get and then need to feed the input continually into the planning process and go after any new opportunities right away.

You also need to continually *stop* doing things. Professional poker players will tell you that the biggest mistake amateurs make is to stick around in hands too long. In Texas hold 'em, for instance, less-experienced players look at their two initial down cards, realize that there is only a remote chance of winning, and yet decide to kick in what seems to be a modest amount of money in the hopes that a winning hand will materialize when the rest of the cards are turned over. They lose a lot of money that way, and a lot of businesses do the same because they haven't instilled the discipline to stop projects or products as soon as they start looking like a bad bet—or when a better bet becomes available.

Vijay Govindarajan, a professor at the Tuck School of Business at Dartmouth, tells a story about how showing the willingness to kill a product can liberate the thinking of a senior team. He says he witnessed a planning process at a technology company that first decided to provide the normal level of financing for the main product and then moved to the topic of how to nurture the successor product. As the team tried to find enough resources, someone delicately asked why they wouldn't just kill funding for the existing product (tightly identified with the CEO) right away and redirect the resources to the successor. The CEO paused but then agreed, and Govindarajan says the team's thinking has been more fluid ever since.[3]

For its part, Huawei, a large Chinese maker of networking equipment, has a permanent office of restructuring and is always looking for how it needs to adapt to change in the market.

People Mobility

To match human resources to opportunities, you must know your people very well. You need a central view of where your human resources reside, how good they are, how utilized they are, and how expensive they are. This does not mean creating a bloated corporate center that owns every resource. What it means is that you have to develop an approach to centrally knowing your resources so you can quickly deploy them to the best opportunities.

Even once you have a very good overview of the human resources that you have available at any given time, you still need to bring opportunities and people together. This is where the secret to successful implementation of resource fluidity lies.

Developing the process that will match individuals or groups to the opportunities is not a small task. If you make it extremely complicated, it will not work. If you make it too simple, it will be inefficient.

You need to establish new ways in which the company manages its people and opportunities and also change the way people think about themselves as a resource. Implementing process changes will yield only partial results unless you address the underlying mind-set that employees are someone's "property" and cannot be mobilized to support initiatives happening somewhere else in the organization.

To understand your human resources, match them with the opportunities, and change the mind-set about ownership, you need to do the following: Establish a corporate resources pool, rotate people through jobs and roles, operate with transparency and fairness, and take out layers.

Establish a Corporate Resources Pool

Having a corporate resources pool does not mean that you have to create a central HR function that owns everybody. What it does mean is that you need to let the business units know that human resources are central and that people are being lent to them because of a specific opportunity. The units also need to know that, as opportunities arise, people with the requisite skills will be pulled together to pursue them—no matter what units those people are working in at the time.

Using a corporate human resources pool requires considerable care and coordination—you can't just pull a talented person out of a unit if that person is making a core contribution to an important effort and can't be replaced. But people need to be a central, fluid resource. Think less about shifting people wholesale from one division to another, and think more about creating "task and finish" teams of your most talented people across the business to tackle value-creating projects that are under-resourced. Apply your most talented staff to your most pressing opportunities, regardless of divisional ownership for the staff or for the opportunities. Companies that excel at this resource fluidity approach constantly create temporary teams that attack an issue and then move back to business as usual. In some spheres, this approach is known as CTC (Change the Company) and RTC (Run the Company). CTC activities are time bound, and they move to RTC as soon as processes can be streamlined and clear accountabilities can be established.

Rotate Roles and Jobs

Establishing a mechanism for rotating jobs and roles serves two main purposes. It exposes people to the talent sitting elsewhere in the organization. It also cross-trains people, which facilitates the sharing of human resources across units; people then don't have as much of a learning curve when required to do a task that is not a normal part of their activities.

The rotating needs to be managed carefully, however, because a learning curve still exists, even if it isn't as steep as it might have been.

Require Transparency and Fairness

For human resources to be shared fluidly, there must be transparency. Opportunities need to be shared openly so that everyone has a chance to contribute. Then resources have to be shared to explore the opportunities as effectively as possible. Decisions have to be transparent, too, so everyone can see they are made fairly. Every party involved in a decision has to be consulted—for instance, if an individual is being moved from one project to another, the owners of both projects and the individual in question need to be consulted. We do not want to allocate human resources to an exciting opportunity if it is going to damage another equally exciting one.

For an example of resource fluidity, let's look at professional services firms. Most operate with a model that focuses both on serving their customers to the best of their capabilities and on developing their people. Consultants know what opportunities are available not only in their regional market or preferred functional practice but across the world, as well. They can volunteer to be staffed on any project anywhere, but the teams that are put together need to be designed to provide maximum impact for clients. That dictum applies both to existing projects and to new ones, so a consultant won't get his or her wish if he or she either isn't the right fit for the team being assembled or is not replaceable on his or her current team. The fluid environment of a professional services firm requires transparency and fairness or clients would lose out and employees would become disgruntled quickly.

Take Out Layers to Align Incentives

Turkeys didn't vote for the U.S. holiday of Thanksgiving. If they had, they wouldn't have wound up displayed as the meal in the middle of our dining room tables. Similarly, we shouldn't let people "vote" on their preferred organizational structures, because that leads to lots of titles, lots of organizational layers, and lots of inefficiency.

If a few of us in a group report to Sally, a few to Johnny, and a few to Billy, each manager has incentive to have his or her people work well together—but not to get the entire group to do so. Take out the layers of the three managers, though, and the group leader will make sure that everyone in the group is cross-trained, has aligned incentives, and so on. When you take out layers, you reduce the number of people who can get in the way of optimization and let the resources flow where they need to go.

Most organizations underestimate the number of layers they have. The neat clarity of an "organigram" will often suggest that there are only five or so layers in place. However, this picture is often deceiving. One global telecommunications company did a forensic analysis of its spans and layers and found that in some corners of the business there were nine actual layers of decision making and an average span of control of 1 leader to 3.2 subordinates. The company implemented an approach called "Space to Lead" and took out a couple of layers, widening the spans considerably. Of course, there was some pain, as the lower number of managers had to accommodate the same amount of work, but this pain quickly translated into urgency in eradicating unnecessary work and complexity.

Resource Sharing and Reuse

To accelerate, it's not enough just to make human and capital assets easier to redeploy within a company. You also have to develop processes that make it easier for the people to plug in when they land in a new situation—giving them a common language, familiar responsibilities, and a standard approach to the problem. In addition, you have to break through corporate walls to include talent that belongs to other companies. It's useful to recall the now-famous quote attributed to Bill Joy, a cofounder of Sun Microsystems: "Not all the smart people work for you." You need to go to wherever the rest of the smart people are and incorporate them as best you can.

Make Processes "Plug and Play"

Have common underlying processes that can easily be adapted for each business unit rather than having to be reinvented every time. If all the business units have a common approach to product introductions, for example, you can shift product introduction employees between units without them having to learn a whole new approach to doing the same thing.

OpenText, a Canadian company that develops and sells enterprise information management software, has acquired a number of software vendors over the past several years. Each company had its own project management process, which made sharing resources across these organizations arduous. In 2013, the company began to integrate the different processes into a plug-and-play approach that could be used throughout the whole organization. Ten senior project managers shared their best project management tools and practices and jointly selected the ones to keep. They built a standardized tool kit that is now used by all project teams. The new methodology instantly saved time because project teams no longer had to reinvent every document for every project. The methodology also allows for human resources to flow more freely across projects because they all use the same tools. In addition, OpenText customers now enjoy a consistent project management experience, whether they are launching a new web site or rolling out business process management software.

Break Through the Corporate Walls

By various estimates, 20 to 40 percent of a corporation's workforce these days consists of workers employed by someone else, and about one-fourth of the entire workforce is made up of people who work solely on a project basis rather than hang their hats somewhere full-time.[4] Many banks now have just as many contract employees providing their technology support as traditional employees. Many oil companies have more contract employees drilling and servicing their wells than they do full-time staffers. Google has roughly 30,000 employees on its main campus in Mountain View, California, but has about a further 100,000 contracted people who are employed by other companies but who wear Google badges and work on the campus.

Many do routine tasks such as walking employees' dogs, running the large health club, keeping the cafeteria operating at full speed around the clock, or operating the dormitory where employees can spend the night or just catch a nap, but many play crucial roles as core members of coding, sales, or marketing teams.

Company walls are becoming porous. Organizations are functioning more as parts of an ecosystem rather than as stand-alone entities. Facebook isn't just a social media company. It represents an ecosystem. More than nine million external web sites connect to Facebook, including Pinterest, OpenTable, and Amazon. More than four million companies, including Sony, Starbucks, and Skype, use Facebook to interact with customers. Some 20 million apps hook into Facebook, including Candy Crush and BuzzFeed. And more than one million developers use Facebook's platform, paying 30 percent of revenue to the company for any revenue they generate.[5] That sort of ecosystem approach to competition means much more cooperation than has ever existed before, and the increasingly digital nature of work has made it easier to move work—and workers—back and forth across corporate boundaries.

The move toward merging outside and inside resources will continue, so companies need to find different ways to manage the more fluid workforce. At the moment, purchasing departments decide what vendor to bring in on a project, but then the operating manager has to coordinate the actual work with the vendor's people. Competition between outsiders and full-time employees can arise, administration issues can be a problem, and so on. Companies using outsiders need to make sure that everyone is aligned on strategy, performance, administration, and relationships.

Some may see this breaking through corporate walls as leading to a transactional approach to human resources, where extreme outsourcing would be adopted and people would just be hired as needed. This approach has some merit, but acquiring resources can take more time than if you own the resources directly. Additionally, you can never be 100 percent certain of the quality of the outsourced resources that you are getting, regardless of the reputation of the organization providing them.

■ ■ ■

If people see leaders fighting for or hoarding resources, or attempting to co-opt resources from one another, it is highly unlikely that they will embrace the idea of resource fluidity. Instead, senior teams need to role-model resource fluidity and ensure that they create interdependency, where the success of one member cannot be achieved unless others share in it. This means that the teams must have shared incentives and that they are rewarded by how much the organization as a whole grows or by how they collaborate to achieve common goals. Unless senior teams share an agenda and purpose, it would be impossible to float resources freely in the organization. A common agenda unifies the teams and avoids situations that cause one part of the organization to conflict with another. If you are in the top team, all these points are exponentially important because you ultimately control all the resources and because you are role-modeling for all the teams underneath you.

Resource fluidity is about constantly optimizing the fit between opportunities and resources. You need to be infinitely adaptable at moving the right people, the right capital, the right intellectual property, and the right equipment and technology to the right opportunity at the right time—and then on to the next opportunity at the right time, too.

Notes

1. Gillian Tett, *The Silo Effect: The Peril of Expertise and the Promise of Breaking Down Barriers,* New York: Simon & Schuster, 2015.
2. Amanda Setili, *The Agility Advantage: How to Identify and Act on Opportunities in a Fast-Changing World*, San Francisco: Jossey-Bass, 2014.
3. Vijay Govindarajan, *The Three-Box Solution: A Strategy for Leading Innovation*, Boston: Harvard Business Review Press, 2016.
4. Jon Younger and Norm Smallwood, "Aligning your organization with an agile workforce," *Harvard Business Review*, February 11, 2016, hbr.org.
5. Martin Reeves, Knut Haanaes, and Janmejaya Sinha, *Your Strategy Needs a Strategy: How to Choose and Execute the Right Approach*, Boston: Harvard Business Review Press, 2015.

CHAPTER 16

Dissolving Paradox
Reframe the Issue

Paradoxes can be fun brainteasers. The ancient Greeks had Zeno's paradoxes, one of which says you can never get from Point A to Point B. You go halfway to Point B, then half of the rest of the way, then half again, and half again . . . but you never get all the way there. Mathematics gave us Russell's paradox: Does the set of all sets that don't contain themselves contain itself? (And led to variants such as the so-called barber paradox: Does a barber (a man) who shaves all and only men who don't shave themselves shave himself?)

But paradoxes in the world of business are rarely fun, and you have to master them if you are to lead a healthy, accelerating organization. To create and lead healthy teams and a healthy organization in a world that is volatile, uncertain, complex, and ambiguous (VUCA), you must cultivate the ability not to shrink or hide from apparent tensions. You can exploit tensions and learn from them, and, critically, you can help others to do the same.

Being a leader throws up many apparent (and we should stress the word "apparent" here) tensions. There are apparent contradictions that are narrow and technical (the desire both for clear, single-point accountabilities and for natural, easy collaboration) and apparent tensions that are big and wide (we want to have both performance and health). CEOs face the simultaneous need for authenticity, which means holding fast to values, and adaptability, which means changing. Leaders need a degree of narcissism to believe that they can do things that others cannot, but they also need to be humble so they can learn and course-correct.

Wendy Smith, Marianne Lewis, and Michael Tushman write that there exist three major paradoxes for leaders to resolve:

1. *Are we managing for today or for tomorrow?* The need for quarterly earnings reports for publicly traded companies—and the punishment that comes in the stock market from even a small disappointment—focuses

attention on the short term. But Amazon, for one, has been wildly successful by taking the long view, based on CEO Jeff Bezos's conception of the company as "the everything store" and his hyperaggressive view that "your margin is my opportunity."

2. *Do we adhere to boundaries or cross them?* These boundaries can be geographic, cultural, or functional. The paradox occurs, for instance, when a company knows that its global supply chain can be efficient yet lack flexibility.

3. *Do we focus on creating value for our shareholders and investors or for a broader set of stakeholders?* Unilever CEO Paul Polman aimed at both goals in 2010 when he launched the Unilever Sustainable Living Plan. The plan is to double the size of Unilever by 2020 while also contributing to better health for more than one billion people and decreasing the company's environmental impact by 50 percent. Polman says the investments in social and environmental goals will increase profits in the long term. Still, senior team leaders feel a high level of anxiety about the short-term effects and are fighting about resource allocation.[1]

There are many things for leaders to reconcile, many contradictions to wrestle with—and many ways to go wrong.

The solution is less about "solving" the apparent paradoxes than about making sure that the leader, his or her top team, and the organization can handle the ambiguity of trying to achieve apparently contradictory objectives. We believe, therefore, that one fundamental skill for the accelerating leader is to master the paradox.

To describe what we mean by mastering the paradox, we will describe four levels of thinking, of which unlocking the paradox is level 4. This is not a new idea. The concept of thinking beyond simple binary positions is ancient—the Hegelian dialectic of thesis and antithesis being resolved into a synthesis is probably the best-known example but is only one example of how this has been expressed. Still, the idea of mastering paradox is powerful and needs to be applied to businesses.

The Four Levels of Thinking

Level 1 thinking sees problems as binary. Decision making is about choosing between two options, and one option must lose. Combine that with the fact that often the two options each has its group of supporters, and this sort of thinking can quite often become a battle of wills. If people lose, they often sabotage the chosen option just because they lost.

In the literature around game theory, there is a demonstration of this called the ultimatum game. Take two people—let's call them Jack and Jill.

You give Jack $10, and ask him to suggest to Jill how they will share the $10. Jill then can either accept the proposal—in which case they both get to keep their proposed shares—or reject it, in which case neither of them gets any money. If Jack offers a split where he keeps $9 and Jill gets $1, Jill will often reject the proposed split because it is unfair, even though she would be better off (by $1) if she accepted.

In a business, this way of thinking can be very damaging. Imagine a manager undermining an initiative that is working because she thinks her rejected initiative should have been funded as well. Reducing decisions to a few stark options and then choosing one can exclude better options and risks alienating your leadership team.

Level 2 thinking recognizes that there are shades of gray. When asked to choose between two options, the level 2 thinker will probably try to find a compromise. If you can give both sides something, exercising some give-and-take, there will be a deal to be struck somehow. In the ultimatum game above, you'd propose a 50-50 split.

While that approach might help win a theoretical game in an economics classroom, it again doesn't work universally in the ambiguous world of business. By constantly splitting the difference or giving people some of what they ask for, you encourage people to ask for two moons so they will get one. You encourage extreme arguments and brinksmanship because decisions are made not so much on the merits of the arguments but rather on the strength with which they are stated. This style of decision making encourages cynicism.

Level 3 thinking looks for a mutually beneficial arrangement that is not just about splitting the difference. If there are two projects fighting for limited resources, the level 3 thinker will try to find creative synergies so that, for instance, the projects share costs. Faced with a challenge around serving customers economically, the level 3 thinker may start segmenting the customer base into ever more detailed categories to attract and retain them.

The level 3 thinker is smart and, when successful, creates solutions that are intellectually impressive. However, level 3 also creates complexity. The brilliant solutions introduce exceptions, caveats, and nuance, which over time accrete and can collapse under their own weight. For instance, the overhead associated with smaller customer segments could become far too complex and costly.

Milton Friedman said, "Most economic fallacies derive . . . from the tendency to assume that there is a fixed pie, that one party can gain only at the expense of another,"[2] but level 4 thinking redefines the game. It can produce a major advantage: Unexpected ideas have few competitors. Faced with an apparent paradox, level 4 thinking doesn't pretend that the paradox isn't there or think that a nimble bit of problem-solving can leave it behind. Rather, level 4 thinking embraces the paradox. It finds ways of making two objectives—apparently at odds—not only mutually compatible but also mutually reinforcing. It doesn't try to optimize the current reality; it looks forward to building a new one. It broadens the aperture of problem-solving and reframes the issue.

Take the common desire in business to have both speed and stability. These can seem at odds, but, in the right circumstances, they can reinforce each other. One example is plate spinning. The plate needs to be spinning at speed to be stable on the stick; only when the plate slows does it lose stability. And when the plate is stable, the plate spinner can more easily give it an extra spin to increase the speed. Speed begets stability; stability begets speed.

For those who think in numbers, there's an imperfect but easy way to think of the four levels. You can think of level 1 as a zero-sum game, with winners and losers. You can think of level 2 as a search for the lowest common denominator. Level 3 could perhaps be described as double counting. And level 4 is the creation of positive synergy—that is, making one plus one equal three.

If you like colors rather than numbers, think of level 1 as black and white and level 2 as shades of gray in between. Level 3 is a rainbow, and level 4 looks at the light in a whole new way, through a prism.

An Application

Let's imagine a single business problem being tackled using the four different levels of thinking. Imagine a consumer-facing business with the twin strategic imperatives of cutting costs and improving customer service—not an unusual situation by any stretch. The CEO is leading the annual planning cycle, and it is time to decide between the investment in customer service that the head of sales thinks is necessary and mandated by the strategy and the cuts in spending on customer service that the CFO has insisted are necessary and mandated by the strategy.

For the level 1 thinker, one of the two is right and gets the CEO's full backing, and the other is wrong and doesn't. We don't know a better way of creating a divided, political team.

The level 2 thinker tries to solve the puzzle. The head of sales can have half the requested investment, and the CFO can claim half the savings. Honor is, superficially, shared. Of course, the risk is that, in trying to deliver both (separate) halves of the strategy, you end up delivering neither.

The level 3 thinker tries to resolve the polarities with clever tactics. There are a couple of ways this could go. One we've seen is to focus on particularly lucrative customer segments (the easier, cheaper ones to serve) as a way of delivering both objectives. In the short term, this is smart.

However, you have ended up relying on a customer base that your competitors will do everything they possibly can to take away from you.

The level 4 thinker tries to dissolve the paradox. Here, the CEO recognizes that she has to both cut costs and improve customer service. The key is that she realizes that doing one can actually make the other easier. Better customer service means fewer problems to fix, fewer replacements, and fewer costly interventions (i.e., costs being cut). Similarly, cutting costs allows us to deliver better customer service, partly in the sense of lower prices but also because the organization will be nimbler, closer to the front line of customer service, and more focused on delivering a great experience.

If we aspire to excellence, we need to do both and create a positive flywheel effect. We call this the "strategic unlock"—a mind-set change that allows the organization to replace tension with mutually supporting objectives. Here, the unlock is the following: "A superior operating system will allow us to get things right the first time, saving costs."

Note that the strategic unlock never comes for free. Unfortunately, it is not a simple case of looking at the problem from a different angle and everything is hunky-dory. A superior operating system is no easy thing to develop. It takes thought, energy, and investment.

Five Actions

There are five big things leaders need to do to master paradox and accelerate their organizations.

1. Know How You Are Thinking

We are very capable, as humans, of thinking about the same issue in different ways, depending on a whole host of factors—stress, level of distraction, habit, preferences, and even time of day. We are similarly capable of thinking about the same problem in a level 1, 2, 3, or 4 way—and often without being conscious of the shift.

Our observation of teams making collective decisions over the years is that the variation in how individuals think at different times is greater than the variation among peers. Or, put another way, the difference between a good day and a bad day for even a mature member of your team is likely to be bigger than the difference between your most mature and immature team members on average days. This means that the leader needs to be aware of what level of thinking he or she is using when tackling a particular problem or issue.

By realizing either what thinking style you are using or the way you are seeing a problem, you will be better able to at least make sure that you are consciously selecting an approach, rather than defaulting to a more comfortable, lower level of thinking than might be appropriate.

Flags that you might be thinking in a level 1 way are when you find yourself thinking the following:

- My idea must win.
- The only thing that matters is X.
- If I set my team against each other, they will compete and demonstrate superior performance.
- Why won't people do what I tell them?
- We agreed we were going to do one thing; why are we now revisiting that decision?

For David Marquet, the commander of the USS *Santa Fe*, a U.S. nuclear submarine whose staff had low morale, performance, and retention, his epiphany about why his leadership style was not working (he was stuck in a level 1 paradigm) came when he gave an impossible order, and his crew tried to carry it out.

Possible flags that you are operating at level 2 include thinking the following:

- She got her way last time; it's my turn now.
- Let's do a little bit of each.
- I need to keep everyone happy.
- Where's the compromise?
- I won't challenge what my colleague is saying, in the hope that he won't challenge me.

In one petrochemical company, we saw a group of product managers collectively trapped in level 2 thinking. Each of them submitted plans for how much feedstock the particular product he or she managed would need—that is, what mix of products should be refined from, in this case, crude oil. Each product manager submitted inflated plans, to maximize his or her share of production and minimize the chance of not having product to sell. They all did this, they all knew that the others did this, and they all knew that the result was suboptimal. But none of them could break the cycle and submit honest plans.

Thinking at level 3 will mean thoughts such as the following:

- There must be a clever solution here if we just think about it harder.
- We'll figure out a way to have the best of both worlds.

- It's okay if we have lots of exceptions—I can keep track of them all.
- I need more detail to find the solution.
- This solution will last for a few months, when I will find another one.

And how can you tell whether you are thinking at level 4? Possible flags include the following thinking:

- We are focusing on the wrong objectives. We are really trying to achieve something else.
- We are considering broader interests, not just narrow or sectional ones.
- Our traditional way of thinking is out-of-date. We need to think about this differently.
- If we do this right, we will build the next generation of leaders.
- Good! I have found a problem that I don't have an answer to—there's some value hidden here.

Any decision-making process rests on a whole host of unspoken assumptions, and the way to increase your level of thinking is to question those assumptions, broaden your outlook, and consider a wider range of possibilities. If you find yourself stuck thinking at level 1, question whether X and Y have to be mutually exclusive and explore the possibility of a mixture of the two. To advance on from level 2, challenge the notion that you have to sacrifice one to achieve the other. Is there a way to accomplish the best of both? In level 3, think through scenarios that relax additional constraints about trade-offs, use of resources, and time to potentially uncover an entirely new way of looking at the situation. By challenging these innate assumptions, you free yourself of preconceived biases and open up your thinking to a far broader variety of possibilities, which may include the strategic unlock that will allow for an ideal solution to your paradox.

Mars, which makes candies and other food products, faced a major problem in 1998 when Russia defaulted on its foreign debt and the ruble crashed. As Paul S. Michaels, then-president of Mars, tells the story: "Overnight, the entire economy came to a grinding halt. Our whole customer base stopped ordering. . . . They had no money." Rather than pull out of the country, though, Mars provided its products to stores and said they didn't have to pay until they sold the goods. Michaels says many stores that carried Mars products avoided bankruptcy as a result and "were in a position to thrive following the crisis while many others had closed their doors." Mars thrived, too.[3]

This is level 4 thinking. Faced with a crisis, many organizations focus on value extraction—getting as big a slice of the pie as possible. Mars realized that this was the wrong objective. The executives' belief in mutuality allowed them to understand that the objective was actually value creation—you need to have a pie to share—and so they did something that seemed counterintuitive but that actually built the foundation for longer-term success.

The other idea that is important here is that the level 4 thinker relishes the paradoxes rather than avoids them. Look at how John F. Kennedy talked in 1962 about the American space effort: "We choose to go to the moon in this decade and do the other things, not because they are easy, but because they are hard, because that goal will serve to organize and measure the best of our energies and skills."[4]

The right tough problem, unlocked in the right way, can unleash energy and ingenuity by giving an organization focus—and purpose.

Table 16.1 summarizes the different levels of thinking and the underlying assumptions that their adherents bring to problem-solving.

Figure 16.1 shows how the style of collaboration relates to the type of problem being addressed.

2. Know What Sort of Problem You Are Facing

The second thing the leader must do is figure out the right sort of thinking for the context. Not every choice is a paradox that can be mastered—sometimes you have to decide whether to bid on a contract or not. And not every moment is the right moment to reframe the problem—if you spot a safety issue on an oil rig, you fix the issue. You can think later about why the problem occurred and use higher-level thinking to prevent a recurrence.

TABLE 16.1 Four types of problem-solving

Level	What we wrestle with	Keyword	How we cooperate	How we see others	Leadership stance	Follower response to leadership stance	What we value when we problem-solve	Source of identity
4	Paradox	And	Win-win	Amplifiers	Dissolve	Ambitious	Cohesion	Together we are better.
3	Polarity	Both	Balance	Accelerants	Resolve	Acknowledged	Creativity	I can find a solution.
2	Puzzle	Degree	Trade-off	At odds	Solve	Anxious	Compromise	We can do a deal.
1	Problem	Or	Win-lose	Adversaries	Absolve	Apathetic	Clarity	I am better than you.

FIGURE 16.1 Four levels of thinking

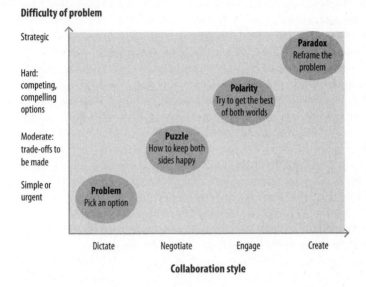

So how do you know whether the situation calls for level 4 thinking? There are three simple tests to determine this:

1. Are both ends of the spectrum, or both options, valid and authentic? Am I, or are we, genuinely grappling with how to do two important but apparently mutually exclusive things?
2. Are we getting in our own way? Without intervention, are we likely to end up sabotaging ourselves and suboptimizing?
3. Is there an opportunity to develop the team by enhancing the quality of the thinking? Is solving the issue collectively going to be an opportunity for the team to learn how to perform better collectively? Is the old way of thinking not going to be good enough?

If the answer to all of these questions is yes, there is a genuine opportunity to use level 4 thinking to solve the problem.

There are a number of reasons why a decision might not actually be suited to a level 4 solution. Some choices are just too small—it's often not worth investing the time and effort required to come up with a level 4 solution if the potential value gained by doing so is marginal. You wouldn't bother investing in an ingenious solution to the problem of what to have for breakfast, so why do so with an equally minor business decision? In other cases, a level 4 solution may be out there, but it might take you too long to come up with it. If you can't produce the level 4 "unlock" quickly enough, it can be damaging to spend additional time and resources pursuing it instead of focusing on other things.

Zeno's paradox seems to suggest that you can never move from Point A to Point B because this would require an infinite number of steps, and in his time this represented a real philosophical problem. The modern mathematics of infinite sums and calculus allows the paradox to be resolved and understood, but these techniques were not invented until long after the death of Zeno, who was not equipped with the tools to master his own paradox. It would have been fruitless for him to push for a mathematical solution to the problem, and it can be similarly unproductive for leaders to strive for level 4 solutions to their own paradoxes that are simply too far out of reach.

It is also possible that a level 4 solution to a problem may present itself, yet it may not be the best course of action to take. For example, the level 4 "unlock" may require an initial investment that is just too large for your company to handle, or it might take too long to put into place, leaving you at a loss for too long before you start to reap the rewards of your efforts. A small chain of toy shops, for example, might be able to reduce buying costs and improve the quality of its products by building its own manufacturing facility, but the up-front costs and time required for such a project would be too great for the business to embark on. However, a much larger business in the same industry could afford to accept the short-term losses to gain the longer-term benefits of such a development.

It is also possible that competition might come into play. If a rival that is better suited to implement your level 4 solution will be able to copy what you are doing and rapidly overtake you, it might be better to hold back and consider a different approach. Under these kinds of circumstances, it can sometimes be beneficial to settle for an option that may seem at first to be less brilliant but that is better suited to your current situation.

A useful tool in deciding which approach to take is the kind of scenario planning mentioned in Chapter 6, which can help in envisaging how various choices taken now will play out in the future. What will the likely outcomes of each course of action be in the short, medium, and long terms, and which of these possible futures is the most desirable for your company?

3. In the Right Situation, Embrace the Paradox

The simultaneous presence of competing tensions is an important driver of change and adaptation and therefore progress. So what managers need to do is smile, not frown, when they find a tension. When Muhammad Ali was asked how many sit-ups he could do, he said he didn't count them. "I only start counting when it starts hurting," he said. "When I feel pain, that's when I start counting, because that's when it really counts."

Don't wish away the tension, but welcome it as a source of insight. Explore it rather than suppress it. Jesse Sostrin, author of *The Manager's Dilemma*, suggests "following the contradictions." He says: "An employee sees something alarming, but doesn't talk about it. A board member starts to tell you something informally, but suddenly stops. Moments like this provide opportunities to guide you through potentially troubled situations if you take the time to learn from them."[5]

Your ability to embrace the paradox, and to encourage your team to embrace the paradox, can become a source of competitive advantage. Embracing and mastering paradoxes is what allows organizations to accelerate and thrive.

Take, as an illustration, planning. There are benefits to a plan or strategy, just as there are advantages to being nimble and deviating from a plan if the situation demands it. The level 4 thinker embraces this apparent paradox. He or she is not tempted by the thinking of level 1 (either we stick to the plan whatever happens, or there is no point in having a plan), level 2 (let's have half a plan!), or level 3 (we'll have a plan for every eventuality). The level 4 thinker recognizes that the best strategic plan can be changed. This is not a call for anarchy. Rather, it recognizes the paradox and embraces it.

The planning process is necessary, but the point of planning is not the plan. The point is the planning.

It is in the planning process that scenarios are talked about, insights derived, preferences revealed, and tensions explored. It is because of the work done planning (and not the plan itself) that, when the unpredictable future comes to pass, we know better how to react.

4. Find the Strategic Unlock

A major goal for leaders looking to improve an organization's acceleration is to reconcile apparently contradictory objectives by finding what we call the "strategic unlock." Sometimes the "unlock" can be as straightforward as just explaining how objectives are actually reinforcing rather than in tension with one another. On other occasions it may mean appealing to a higher-level objective. With Mars, for example, it was powerful to frame the objective as making a bigger cake and not getting caught up in a level 1 or 2 argument about how to divide up a smaller cake.

Smith, Lewis, and Tushman suggest switching our thinking from "a well-intentioned consistency to consistent inconsistency." Don't, as a senior leader, get locked into an idea. Don't assume that resources are limited; viewed in a new light, they may be abundant. Don't take a traditional, military-style approach to management that demands control and stability. Instead, manage a dynamic equilibrium by first pulling apart all the aspects of the paradox and then finding creative new ways to connect them.[6]

A national telecommunications company we worked with needed a strategic unlock for a challenge it faced: to find a way to provide broadband connectivity to residents in affordable housing in an inexpensive way. Initially, the company thought in a very level 1 way: "We will stick with our current model and only take on creditworthy customers, or not do business at all." The prospect of an additional 2.4 million customers was attractive, though, so the company tried to think in a level 2 way. The company tried to find a compromise by serving some tenants, asking, "Can we find those with better risk profiles and avoid the worst risks while not damaging our brand reputation?" But not offering broadband at all to a particular type of customer would damage the company's reputation as a national telecom provider, as would turning down too many potential customers. So the company tried to come up with a clever fix in a level 3 way. The company thought about treating the housing associations as virtual internet service providers (ISPs). The company could supply them with broadband at wholesale prices and remove the requirement for individual credit checks. This was not a bad solution—far from it—and it was a lot more constructive than the level 1 or 2 thinking that we saw. However, it would still take a lot of effort to manage what would effectively be a small revenue pool with very tight margins, and the potential for management to lose focus on the virtual ISP model was a big concern. The company instead needed a level 4 solution.

The strategic unlock was not to think of individual, marginal customers for broadband (albeit 2.4 million of them) but rather to think of them as a group of potential customers for telecommunications. This meant not only that the telecom provider had a duty to try and serve them, as part of its purpose is to provide telecommunications to all citizens, but also that the company should think about revenue differently. Instead of just focusing on broadband revenue when a customer was added, the company should seek follow-on sales of extra products, including multimedia packages. Traditionally, these follow-ons accrued to a separate part of the business to aid accountability, but, in this case, this split was unhelpful. Once the company switched its thinking, the opportunity became large enough to get the attention it needed within the organization.

There is a risk that the strategic unlock can seem trivial, especially in retrospect. A bit like the punch line to a joke or the answer to a brainteaser, a business problem can be infuriating and impossible to solve and then, once you have the answer, seem obvious and trivial. This can be especially true if you are just informed about the solution and weren't part of the team that had the full experience of discovering it. There is also a risk that we think there are a small number of unlocks, and it is easy to figure out which one of, say, five to use. This is clearly not the case, as otherwise we would all be thinking at level 4 for much more of the time and mankind would be facing dramatically fewer tough, irresolvable problems.

Finding the right unlock for the problem you are working on is tough and requires both effort and vigilance. But the reward can be huge.

5. Build an Enduring Organization

Part of what the leader must do is to help explain how the organization's multiple objectives can not only be reconciled but also actually complement each other. However, this is often done badly. For example, saying that both safety and controlling costs are of paramount importance and just leaving it at that doesn't help people make difficult decisions. It sets them up to behave in a level 1 or, at best, a level 2 way. Worse than that, it can breed cynicism, as employees will easily start to believe that the focus on costs is more important than that on safety, particularly as safety failures can be large, public, and very noticeable.

The leader must go beyond explaining a new mind-set and inculcate in team members the ability to unlock the paradox for themselves. As David Rock and Jeffrey Schwartz write: "For insights to be useful, they need to be generated from within, not given to individuals as conclusions."[7] Like an egg, if it's broken from the outside by others, life doesn't survive, but if it's broken from within, life starts. This is true for several reasons. First, people will experience the adrenaline-like rush of insight only if they go through the process of making connections themselves. The moment of insight is well known to be a positive and energizing experience. Second, neural networks are influenced moment to moment by genes, experiences, and varying patterns of attention. Although all people have some broad functions in common, in truth everyone has a unique brain architecture. Human brains are so complex and individual that there is little point in trying to work out how another person ought to reorganize his or her thinking. It is far more effective and efficient to help others come to their own insights.

The broader organization needs to understand the multiple objectives it has and how it should react when they appear in tension with one another. This means explaining that both cost and safety are important but also how they interact. It means explaining the strategic unlock—and not only explaining it but reinforcing it repeatedly so that the organization understands it both intellectually and instinctively. The leader needs to create an organization that is not surprised when it is confronted with decisions where both safety and costs are issues.

These are bound to occur. Hundreds, probably thousands, of people in the organization need to understand that they will occur, be able to spot the tensions, and be able to act appropriately. They need to "get the gray"; in other words, they need to recognize that they will have to make decisions that reconcile apparently contradictory objectives, they need to not be paralyzed by this, and they must be able to act in the optimum way.

■ ■ ■

All organizations face competing objectives. There are a range of possible responses to this, with the most difficult but often the most value-adding being to "master the paradox," often with a strategic unlock. The leader of a healthy organization must make sure not only that he or she is able to do this at the right times but also that he or she is building the capability to do so across the organization as a whole.

Nobel Prize–winning physicist Niels Bohr once said, "How wonderful that we have met with a paradox. Now we have some hope of making progress."[8]

Notes

1. Wendy K. Smith, Marianne W. Lewis, and Michael L. Tushman, "'Both/and' leadership," *Harvard Business Review*, May 2016, hbr.org.
2. Milton Friedman and Rose Friedman, *Free to Choose: A Personal Statement*, New York: Harcourt, 1979.
3. Paul S. Michaels, "The Mars mutuality journey," *The Brewery*, January 2014, freuds.com/the-brewery.
4. John F. Kennedy, "Rice Stadium Moon Speech," Rice University, September 12, 1962, er.jsc.nasa.gov.
5. Jesse Sostrin, "Follow the contradictions," *strategy+business*, June 6, 2016, strategy-business.com.
6. Wendy K. Smith, Marianne W. Lewis, and Michael L. Tushman, "'Both/and' leadership," *Harvard Business Review*, May 2016, hbr.org.
7. David Rock and Jeffrey Schwartz, "The neuroscience of leadership," *strategy+business*, May 30, 2006, strategy-business.com.
8. Ruth Moore, *Niels Bohr: The Man, His Science, and the World They Changed*, New York: Alfred A. Knopf, 1966.

CHAPTER 17

Liquid Leadership
Connect Beyond Hierarchy

In the 1850s, the head physician in a ward of a hospital in Budapest conducted extensive research on how hygiene might limit infections and began a program that required the medical personnel to wash their hands frequently. The program virtually eliminated a fever that was rampant, and science has since proved his theory decisively. But the medical community at the time criticized the physician, Ignaz Semmelweis, and blocked his program. (He later died in an insane asylum—of an infection he contracted there.) In 2005, Blockbuster CEO John Antioco saw the grave threat that Netflix posed to the Blockbuster movie-rental chain. He instituted an aggressive plan to end Blockbuster's hated late fees and to invest in an online platform, to counter Netflix's DVD-by-mail service and its plan for video streaming. But Antioco couldn't get the rest of the company to move along with him and was fired. Blockbuster filed for bankruptcy protection in 2010 and liquidated the vast majority of its assets.[1]

Both Semmelweis and Antioco had the authority to institute their changes. So what went wrong?

The answer is that they, like so many senior executives, didn't have all the power they thought they had or that their titles seemed to invest in them. Even top executives have to bring the organization along with them rather than merely ordering change. Leaders cannot be content with simply getting people to do what they want; leaders have to make people want what they want. Leaders often believe they can succeed by using the disciplines of change management, but that's really the same thing as telling people to do what you want, albeit in a slightly more artful way. To make change really happen, it shouldn't be managed; it should be empowered. That distinction is the difference between authority and leadership.

Bob Nardelli was so well regarded that he was approached about the CEO job at Home Depot just minutes after he was passed over for the top job at General Electric in 2000, when Jack Welch retired and Jeff Immelt was named his successor. But Nardelli merely ordered change at Home Depot, to make it more efficient in the GE style, and the organization didn't come along with him. In his six years as CEO, Home Depot's stock dropped 6 percent while arch rival Lowe's stock doubled.[2] Condé Nast's *Portfolio* magazine later listed Nardelli as one of the worst American CEOs of all time.

With a market composed of fickle consumers and workplaces brimming with employee identity crises, the requirements to compete are evolving so quickly that leadership is struggling to stay ahead; unsuccessful efforts to sustain organizational readiness will come at an extremely high cost. Successful business leaders must shape their organizations to be nimbler and more flexible.

Working through a traditional hierarchy just takes too much time. Have you ever had to ask for permission to make a decision in a hierarchical organization? If you have, then you know what we are referring to. Hierarchy's ugly relative, bureaucracy, takes over the process and makes it extremely long and energy-draining. Rigid leaders exercise control and power at every step, sometimes stalling decisions. Control mechanisms, put in place to filter out bad decisions, add time.

Communications in hierarchical organizations can also be problematic; messages get diluted, modified, or aggrandized as they make their way up and down the hierarchy. Communication from the top is always important, but the tone from the top needs to be met by an echo from the bottom.

In addition, a hierarchical structure is not prepared to deal with what does not fall neatly within the structure it supports, and, in the current business environment, a lot of attractive opportunities may not sit squarely in one unit or another. Selling solutions to customers, for example, may require pulling in products and services from disparate units. Several functions might likewise have to collaborate to build a common platform to be sold to customers. With a hierarchy, projects can wind up in no-man's-land because collaboration is hard. Hierarchies are not conducive to lateral relationships.

Finally, by definition, hierarchies put decision making in the hands of those who are far from the customer. Instead of allowing people on the front line to make decisions that will directly affect the customer, hierarchical organizations have frontline workers bring a situation to the attention of a supervisor, who may consult his or her supervisor, who may then turn to his or her supervisor, and so on, until someone who is five or six levels removed from the customer makes a decision that affects the customer directly. Organizations try to address the remoteness issue with ideas on empowerment or distributed decision making, and there are famous examples of success, including Nordstrom, Ritz-Carlton, and Zappos. But most companies pay lip service to these ideas. They act based on the belief that those higher up in the hierarchy are better qualified to make decisions.

Some have tried to get nimbler by eliminating hierarchy in organizations, through movements such as holacracy or self-managing teams. There are some examples of large organizations that function very well in a completely flat and free structure, such as Morningstar, W. L. Gore, and Semco Partners. But most companies of a certain size have difficulty implementing a leaderless approach, and, in our experience, there are benefits to hierarchy. It brings operational benefits by providing a clear way to assign tasks and responsibilities. Hierarchy also provides psychological benefits for those who are attracted by environments defined by control and upward mobility. Many aspiring junior executives dream of climbing the ladder to gain more authority.

Imagine you are a banking executive in a conversation with one of your many regulators and you suggest that you are abandoning hierarchy in favor of holacracy. It would be a short conversation.

So we are not advocating the elimination of hierarchy. Instead, we propose that people acknowledge its defects and work around its boundaries to drive acceleration. Stop thinking about a corporate ladder, and start thinking about a corporate lattice. Matt Brittin, Google's president of EMEA business and operations, told us, "Personally, I try to ignore structure completely," though he acknowledges that he may receive some dispensation because of his seniority.

Resorting to power and authority is responding to what employees valued 30 years ago. Instead, what is needed to allow organizations to accelerate is what we call liquid leadership.

This begins by developing the following specific set of skills:

- *Become a techie.* You may not be technologically savvy, but you must get to know the role that technology plays in the evolution of your business—beyond IT, social media, web sites, apps, and so on. Don't simply depend on your chief technology officer (CTO) to lead the way. As a leader in your business, change your mind-set about technology and educate yourself and those around you. If you plan on being in a leadership role for the rest of your career, the 21st century demands that you be knowledgeable enough about technology to test it, engage with it, and use it to harness the profitable evolution of your business.
- *Be entrepreneurial.* The fiercely competitive marketplace has made it mandatory for leaders to be more entrepreneurial, connect the dots of opportunity, and find nontraditional ways for their business to grow and prosper. Beyond creativity within the existing business, leaders must be prepared to get involved in new ventures that may require them to open up new markets, launch new products, and be involved in mergers and acquisitions. Because the market is changing so quickly, an entrepreneurial attitude has become an unwritten requirement in a

leader's job description. At Comcast (one of our superaccelerators), this attitude is viewed in highly practical terms: "We value an entrepreneurial mind-set wedded hard to a respect for operational excellence," said William Strahan, executive vice president of human resources at Comcast Cable. "To spot opportunities you've got to know how the business runs; you've got to know how to do the math."

- *Be a thought leader.* Today's leaders must be bold, articulate, and courageous visionaries who are not afraid to speak up and change the conversation or introduce new ideas and ideals. Being a constructively disruptive leader is important, and if you are not pushing your organization, its employees, and the industry at large to think differently, you will not only grow complacent but also forget how to think like a leader. As a consequence, your organization will become more vulnerable to its competitors. Thought leadership is about thinking differently and not being afraid to express those differences, to keep people honest and enable fresh thinking and thought-provoking dialogue that challenges people to perform better and more creatively. Unfortunately, most leaders use the thinking and ideas of others rather than challenging themselves to create an original leadership identity that has sustainable impact and influence. In fact, leaders who don't express original thought will soon find themselves losing their competitive edge, power, and decision-making authority—and the doors their job title once opened for them will begin to close.

- *Allow the right autonomy in your workforce.* To avoid getting bogged down in bureaucracy, it is vital to allow your employees to make certain judgments for themselves. This leads to employees feeling valued and allows decisions to be made faster and often more appropriately because the person on the front lines can be the one making the choices that directly affect the customer. Working like this shifts the leader's responsibility from decision making to the preparation of employees to enable them to make the right calls themselves. For guidance on how to achieve this, refer to Chapter 11 for techniques and practices for driving behavioral change throughout your organization.

- *Evolve with your business.* Changes in the natural evolution of a company's business model now demand that its leaders serve as change agents to lift and lead the entire company. As a change agent, you must know how to sell change. This requires a set of skills that you may not have been asked to have when you first took the job. You must learn to be a change agent and assume the responsibilities that go along with that.

- *Touch the business as much as you lead it.* Leaders can never forget about the customers and must never grow complacent about understanding their changing needs and demands. Consumers have become much more demanding, and it's more difficult than ever to earn their loyalty and trust. Leaders, regardless of hierarchy or rank, are affected by consumer behavior; therefore, they must be more mindful and educate themselves (and their teams) about consumer demands. Leaders must know enough about how each part of the business affects customers directly and indirectly so they can think, plan, and execute with customers firmly in mind.

■ *Prepare to manage crises.* Don't let your corporate challenges become headlines. Leaders must be prepared to handle any crisis with agility and elegant transparency. The advent of social media—and a national media hungry to sensationalize any misstep—requires leaders to have the necessary preparation, resources, and technologies to respond to a crisis in a timely and responsible fashion.

Once you have developed these skills, you will be able to accomplish the core requirement for a liquid leader: the ability to lead across boundaries. This means that leaders need to pull toward them people who may not work directly for them but whom they influence by the quality of their ideas and leadership.

Leading Across Boundaries

Liquid leadership addresses all of the challenges of hierarchy by working with it to make things happen. The liquid leader thinks about hierarchy in a more expansive way, paying attention to the informal links that allow working across boundaries. A liquid leader leverages social networks, of which he or she is probably a significant node, to facilitate the flow of information or expertise across the organization. The liquid leader may also be a broker, mediating between those who need something and those who have it, making connections that would not happen otherwise.

Liquid leaders are also adept at forming and leveraging informal relationships that are not necessarily directed by the company's hierarchy. The leader may volunteer to informally mentor somebody in another division or may maintain relationships with fellow students and former professors and colleagues as they move to different positions across an organization or outside of it. The relationships not only serve to maintain a healthy level of curiosity and freshness but also can help solve actual business challenges.

Just like water, liquid leaders seep through the crevices created by hierarchy and help create a more connected and dynamic working environment. They do not act alone and use their large influence and wide network of relationships to generate a culture of liquid leadership throughout the organization, helping other managers at all levels to embody the traits of the liquid leader. Teaching and mentoring others, they lead by example and exemplify the change they look to bring about.

The liquid leader also extends the idea about fluid use of resources and people to the way that teams work together, removing bottlenecks and allowing the team to make decisions effectively. Collective decisions can be made quickly and don't have to move through management levels, making organizations nimbler and better able to respond to changing market conditions. The liquid structure allows decision makers to leverage knowledge across the whole enterprise, leading to faster and better decisions. If the liquid leader is a member of the top team, the benefits of focus, effective decision making, and a fast rhythm become apparent to the whole organization and role-model what is expected of other teams.

In a hierarchy, a team cannot go faster than its boss. With team-based, informal relationships, the team makes changes and catches up with the leader later.

A Focus on the New Workforce

Liquid leadership addresses the needs of the workforce of today and tomorrow, not of 10, 20, or 30 years ago. A liquid leader exemplifies the following behaviors:

- *Manage individuals.* When you're under pressure, it's easy to forget that employees are unique individuals, with varying interests, abilities, goals, and styles of learning. But it's important to customize your interactions with them. Ensure that you understand what makes them tick. Be available and accessible for one-on-one conversations. Deliver lessons cued to individual developmental needs. And when it comes to promotions, look past rigid competency models and career ladders to growth opportunities tailored to the ambitions, talents, and capacities of each person.
- *Structure through teams.* The relentless focus on leading individuals needs to be paired with an approach to organizing tasks and work that focuses on teams. Teams are proven to achieve better results than individual contributors can deliver on their own in most tasks. Your approach to getting things done can help teams, regardless of your level of involvement in their everyday activities. Structuring the organization through teams will also allow you to expand your networks and informal relationships (by increasing your span of influence), which will also, in the end, help drive acceleration and better performance.

- *Go big on meaning.* Most employees value jobs that enable them to make a difference, and many organizations now emphasize meaning and purpose in the hopes of fostering engagement. But you can't rely on incentives such as bonuses, stock options, or raises. You've got to inspire people with a vision, set challenging goals, and pump up their confidence so that they believe they can actually win. Articulate a clear purpose that fires up your team, set expectations high, and convey to the group that you think they're capable of virtually anything.
- *Focus on feedback.* The vast majority of companies limit themselves to the dreaded annual performance review and often mingle developmental feedback with discussions about compensation and promotion, rendering the developmental feedback much less effective. Some organizations are changing their ways, but even if yours sticks with traditional reviews, you can still supplement that with the kind of continuous, personalized feedback that the best leaders employ. Use regular—at least weekly—one-on-one conversations to provide lots of coaching. Make the feedback clear, honest, and constructive, and frame it so that it promotes independence and initiative.
- *Don't just talk . . . listen.* The best leaders spend a great deal of time listening. They pose problems and challenges, and then ask questions to enlist the entire team in generating solutions. They reward innovation and initiative and encourage everyone in the group to do the same.
- *Be consistent.* Who could be happy with a boss who does one thing one day and another thing the next? It's hard to feel motivated when the bar is always shifting in unpredictable ways and you never know what to expect or how to get ahead. So be consistent in your management style, vision, expectations, feedback, and openness to new ideas. If change becomes necessary, acknowledge it openly and quickly.
- *Embrace all generations.* Don't gravitate to the generation to which you belong. Connect the dots of all the talent, unique perspectives, and experiences. You will need to change your attitude and approach to accommodate the needs of a multigenerational group and seize all the opportunities.

Just getting these issues right will likely go a long way toward making your leadership style more fluid and effective.

How Liquid Leadership Looks in Practice

In November 1999, Sony CEO Nobuyuki Idei introduced to a gathering of company executives Sony's plans to become "a broadband entertainment company." The company had been very successful with the Walkman, and there was great interest about what the next Walkman-like block-buster would be. Among the products introduced was one called the "Memory Stick Walkman," a digital music player and recording device the size of a pack of chewing gum. "The heir to the Walkman," everybody thought.

However, immediately after the introduction of the Memory Stick Walkman, Idei showed a second device: the Vaio Music Clip. This was also a digital player and recorder. The audience was confused. Why two devices that served the same purpose?

What had happened was that different departments within Sony had developed their own digital music devices using proprietary technology. The departments not only didn't agree on a single product approach; they didn't even communicate with each other. As a consequence, in a couple of years Sony dropped completely out of digital music, leaving Apple to dominate with the iPod. Similarly, Sony started work on an e-book reader two years before Amazon launched Kindle but couldn't get different parts of the organization to cooperate and dropped the project.[3]

Sony was a very hierarchical organization, with incredibly creative people who preferred to remain in their silos and not build connections with the rest of their equally creative colleagues in other areas. A liquid approach to leadership would have encouraged connectivity, information sharing, and experimentation across divisions. At a minimum, the liquid approach would have controlled duplication of efforts and waste of resources. More likely, the approach would have improved the quality and market relevance of the products being developed. It would have also placed a focus on creating a much more engaged workforce because of the expanding horizons.

Sony is not the only company suffering from this hierarchical, silo-focused approach to leadership. We all see the problems of such a structure when we buy a ticket online and find that an agent on the phone can't change it; when we buy something online but can't return it in a store; when we have to involve a higher-up in simple decisions simply because he or she is "the boss"; or when there is unnecessary duplication of efforts in different parts of an organization.

By contrast, look at the Cleveland Clinic, one of the biggest medical centers in the United States, with a more than $7 billion operating revenue and 49,000 employees in 2015. The hospital has always had somewhat of an unconventional spirit, being one of the few hospitals in the country where doctors share in profits as opposed to being individual practitioners. The hospital experienced ups and downs because of economic conditions in Cleveland, but smart decision making turned it into the second-largest employer in the state behind Walmart. Expansion to other states started in the 1970s, and discussion of international expansion is common these days.

The hospital had very sophisticated technology and logistics processes that kept things operating very smoothly, facilitating the transfer of resources from one hospital to the other. However, the more complex the technology and the bureaucracy grew, the more siloed the organization became. Specialist silos, recognized for their excellence with multiple awards, became entrenched.

Toby Cosgrove, who became CEO of Cleveland Clinic in 2004, changed all that. Cosgrove had a very successful career and was running a strong team in the thoracic and cardiovascular surgery unit, responsible for a third of the hospital's revenues, before becoming CEO. A couple of years after his appointment, Cosgrove announced two big changes to break down internal silos: First, staff would no longer be classified according to the usual doctor/nurse distinction; everybody would be known as "caregivers" and responsible not only for treating physical ailments but also for attending to the patients' spirit and emotions. Second, he wanted to reorganize the hospital in order to move away from specialist areas into multidisciplinary institutes that treated diseases or particular areas of the body, thereby encouraging surgeons, physicians, and other staff to collaborate in the treatment of patients.

He shocked the system. Operations had been divided by department, with a quasi-caste system that put cardiac surgeons above everybody else, but in January 2008 the clinic unveiled 27 new institutes with labels such as "digestive disease," "dermatology," or "plastic surgery."

In late 2013, the Cleveland Clinic was the top-ranked hospital in the United States in terms of patient satisfaction. Clearly, Cosgrove is a liquid leader, but such a transformation would have not been achieved had he not instilled a similar approach to leadership in all of his caregivers.[4]

■ ■ ■

The strategic revolution in today's rapidly changing business environment clearly mandates a new type of leadership, and research suggests that the right leadership can account for more than one-fifth of the equity value of a business.[5]

To capitalize on developing trends and drive future success, organizations must begin building leadership strength now. The winners of tomorrow will be those organizations with strong leaders who demonstrate agility, authenticity, connections to their talent, and sustainability. The winners will use their skills to remain at the ready, anticipate opportunities, harness the power of change, and stay ahead of the shifting business environment. In other words, they will embrace liquid leadership.

Notes

1. Greg Satell, "To create change, leadership is more important than authority," *Harvard Business Review*, April 21, 2014, hbr.org.
2. Chunka Mui and Paul B. Carroll, *The New Killer Apps: How Large Companies Can Out-Innovate Start-Ups*, Shelburne, VT: Cornerloft Press, 2013.
3. Gillian Tett, *The Silo Effect: The Peril of Expertise and the Promise of Breaking Down Barriers*, New York: Simon & Schuster, 2015.
4. Gillian Tett, *The Silo Effect: The Peril of Expertise and the Promise of Breaking Down Barriers*, New York: Simon & Schuster, 2015.
5. Deloitte, *The Leadership Premium: How Companies Win the Confidence of Investors*, March 2012, deloitte.com.

CHAPTER 18

Conclusion
It's More than a Program

When we once worked in a mining organization, we made a point about the need for follow-through on a change initiative and offered a bit of evidence: Studies show that, when a doctor writes a prescription, only about a quarter of patients fill it and take the drugs as prescribed, all the way to the end of the regimen. An engineer bristled and said, "My cardiologist says he gets 65 percent compliance"—which made our point perfectly. A prescription from a cardiologist is more serious than just about any corporate effort, yet a third of patients still don't comply.

Following through on the prescription for changes that will lead to acceleration will require a formal, disciplined approach, so in this final chapter we'll describe the five steps needed to get from the starting line to success—exploration, aspiration, creation, implementation, and transition. We'll go through each, explaining what needs to happen at each stage.

More important, though, we will describe the roles leaders need to play. We've split this description into two—what the business leaders need to do as business leaders and what change leaders need to do. In almost every successful transformation we have seen, there is some specialist expertise in change leadership. Often, the center of gravity is in HR, but it can just as easily be in risk or strategy. The split between the two roles of business leader and change leader is, in some senses, artificial, not only because the actions of both need to be carefully integrated in service of a common goal, but also because it is rare to see either a successful business leader without change leadership skills or a successful change leader without some business leadership skills. However, we do deliberately make the split. In any organization embarking on large-scale change, the requirement for the dedicated, technical change leadership skills that we lay out here is large, and it is real. An organization embarking on a change program needs to take a clear view of whether it has sufficient change skills within its organization and, if not, move to bolster them.

We'll also point out where, based on our experience, you're most likely to run into problems and will go into the seven most important lessons about how to stay on the right road.

The Five Steps to Acceleration

Table 18.1 provides a brief description of the five steps to acceleration.

Table 18.2 presents a summary of the outcomes, actions, roles, and skills necessary at each step on the road to acceleration, which we will unpack in the rest of this chapter.

1. Exploration

The first step to acceleration is all about taking a hard look in the mirror and assessing the current state of the organization. This includes using a mixture of quantitative tools—including the SAQ, OAQ, TAQ, and LAQ as well as targeted analysis, such as deep dives into key operational areas. You will also use more qualitative approaches, such as focus groups and exercises, to understand underlying mind-sets. The outcome needs to be an empirically sound, factual analysis of how able the organization is to accelerate and of how performance can improve.

During exploration, the analysis and synthesis need to be done as much as possible *with* the organization rather than *to* the organization. Otherwise, people may resist the conclusions.

Business leaders must be courageous. The process will throw up uncomfortable truths, create conflicts, and trigger negative emotions. Leaders must be ready with solutions. Change leaders must be confronting during

TABLE 18.1 The five steps to acceleration

Exploration	Aspiration	Creation	Implementation	Transition
Taking a hard look in the mirror and assessing the current ability to accelerate	Aligning behind a clear idea of where acceleration is needed to confer competitive advantage	Designing a powerful set of interventions that will deliver high and sustained levels of acceleration	Experimenting, piloting, and embedding tangible actions, processes, and programs to deliver acceleration	Driving acceleration into business as usual

TABLE 18.2 Necessary actions and skills for each acceleration step

	Exploration	Aspiration	Creation	Implementation	Transition
Outcomes	**Analysis:** An empirically sound, factual analysis of the current ability to accelerate and its impact on performance **Understanding:** A deeper interpretation of the facts into a synthesis that gets to the heart of acceleration	**Organization:** A specification of the pattern of acceleration that would confer the most advantage to the organization; hard choices made **Individual:** A personal commitment to lead differently and be different	**Behaviors:** An immediate shift in the expectations as to appropriate behavior in the organization **Processes:** The design of new and different processes that will produce new and different behavior	**Experiments:** The careful piloting and testing of new approaches prior to rollout **Scale:** Creating change at large; moving new processes and approaches from the testing stage to full implementation	**Measurement:** Assessing payoff for new approaches and adjusting **Embedding:** Baking the new processes into business as usual and reflecting the benefits into budgeting and financial planning
Actions	Surveys on the organization's ability to accelerate Focus groups Desktop analysis of current data Performance impact analysis Mirror workshop Limiting and liberating mind-sets	Top team aspirations Unlocking strategic paradoxes Immunity to change Understanding individual imprints Building development agendas (organizational and individual)	Identification of core behaviors Strengths and gap analysis ABC model Change-architecture development New customer processes Redesign of core metrics	Hothouses Incubators Pilots Large-scale interventions Reviews and measurement Applications at scale Deciding rollout strategy Analysis of impact of levers	Focusing on key dials Measuring/remeasuring Deep dives Translation into financial planning Energy management

(Continued)

275

TABLE 18.2 (*Continued*)

	Exploration	Aspiration	Creation	Implementation	Transition
	Broader engagement of senior leaders Deep-dive analysis into critical areas Imprint of the top team	Purpose	Identification of change agents Leadership challenge program		
The business leader must be . . .	Courageous. The acceptance that organizations do not change without effort and conflict, and the resolution to personally commit to challenging and changing themselves and others	Ambitious. The optimism and determination required for forging a new way of working	Innovative. The desire to look for new ideas, approaches, and ways of working that will stretch and enhance current delivery and boundaries	Focused. A single-minded focus on those core initiatives and actions that will deliver the largest shifts in accelerated performance; ensuring follow-through and delivery	Determined. The fortitude required to maintain effort and energy on ensuring interventions are embedded into business as usual
The change leader must be . . .	Confronting. Seeking ways to build a clear and aligned view within the organization of what is working	Inspiring. Inspiring others to coalesce around a vision of accelerating performance, what the benefits would be, and	Designing. Creating and integrating a set of symbolic and substantial behavioral and process changes to deliver	Teaching. Sharing knowledge, experience, and best practices needed to test, evaluate, and roll out an	Supporting. Energizing, cajoling, and championing leaders to embed tried-and-tested new processes

Change skills	Connections and causality: The ability to forensically demonstrate the relationship between acceleration and performance and to highlight issues offering the most promise	Storytelling: Fluency with best-practice examples that can serve as encouragement and learning	Weaving: The ability to not only identify the appropriate interventions but also combine them in a way that changes the fabric of the organization	Positive appreciation: The personal resilience and optimism that enables the spotting of progress and the highlighting of successes	Systems thinking: The capability to take an overview perspective and see the connections and linkages between the established organization and the new interventions
	well and what changes are required; holding ground in the face of denial, anger, and other strong emotions that change engenders	a belief that it is possible to achieve	maximum impact for energy expended	acceleration-improvement process	and role-model new behaviors into business as usual

the exploration step. That doesn't necessarily mean being confrontational, though it could. The goal is to help the organization understand the true nature of its challenge.

The skill that most organizations will need here is the ability to understand the connections within all the research to get to the true underlying pathology.

2. Aspiration

The second step, aspiration, is about aligning behind a clear idea of the form of acceleration that will confer the most competitive advantage. This isn't easy. The aspiration step will involve saying no to some apparently worthwhile ambitions, only because one can't be great at everything. At other times, aspiration will require hard work to create innovative models and ways of operating—a key place where you will need to find the "strategic unlock" that we described in Chapter 16 when discussing how to dissolve paradoxes.

Business leaders must be able to take competing claims for where the business should excel and either choose among them or find the unlock that combines them into a new model. For example, a distribution company that was facing an apparent choice between being exceptional at customer service and trying to be a low-cost operator realized that great customer service would reduce error rates and bring down operational costs.

Business leaders must also be ambitious here. They must figure out how the organization should work—in particular, where it needs to be extremely agile. That is tough intellectually. But it is not purely an intellectual challenge; the leader must also carry the organization with him or her.

Change leaders must be inspiring and create supportive coalitions across the organization. A helpful skill is the ability to craft a compelling story that weaves together the need for change, the desired end state, and some examples of the sorts of changes that are needed and that have worked for others.

To know how they are doing, leaders need to use acid tests—a small set of quite tangible, objective measures of how well the organization is implementing a recipe. As we said in Chapter 10, where we listed possible acid tests for each of the four acceleration recipes, they won't be the same in every company but need to have enough bite to clarify a slightly abstract term like "Execution Engine."

3. Creation

Creation, the third step, is about designing a set of interventions that will deliver sustained, powerful change. In the memorable words of Laurence J. Peter, author of *The Peter Principle*: "Bureaucracy defends the status quo long past the time when the quo has lost its status."[1] So leaders need to carefully define the new behaviors that will be required—as we've shown, nothing changes unless behavior changes. People can find changing their behavior difficult, so leaders need to help by using an approach like the ABC (Any Behavior Change) model outlined in Chapter 11.

Processes need to change, too, to support the new behaviors—today, many processes are more rubber band than broadband. If the organization decides, for instance, that it wants to be highly agile in its response to customer complaints, processes for handling complaints will probably need to be thoroughly redesigned. Little saps morale and precious willpower to bring about change more than being asked to change behaviors but then not being given the necessary processes and tools to do so.

Business leaders must make sure that genuinely new ways of working are being created where they are needed. Change leaders must make sure that the changes being designed reflect best practices, are consistent and coherent, and are sequenced in such a way that they reinforce each other as they are implemented and are inspirational. The skill that is particularly helpful is the ability to weave a set of changes together into a single, more powerful whole.

4. Implementation

This step of the process is all about experimenting, piloting, and embedding tangible actions, processes, and programs. By this fourth step, there should be a clear understanding of the problems the organization is facing. There should also be a widespread view of what the organization needs to become and of what behavioral and process changes will be tried to bring about that change. This is the step where everything comes to life.

In this step, the organization experiments with some changes to see whether and how they work. Results need to be measured, partly so that the changes can be tweaked before they are rolled out but also to keep building the case for change—for example, "With the new order fulfillment process, we cut costs by 15 percent and increased customer satisfaction from the low 40 percents to over 80 percent."

Rollout mechanisms for the changes need to be part of the experiments. In some organizations, the experiments will be simple. A retail bank, for example, could test in some branches and then roll out changes branch by branch and region by region. In other organizations, testing how to roll out changes can be a lot more complicated because there are not clear delineations by geography, function, or customer. In these cases, there is likely to be an initially complicated set of experiments and rollouts that may cut across different parts of the organization at different speeds or in different combinations. The key is to keep the architecture as simple as you can.

The business leaders need focus. A lot of change will be going on, often in a complicated architecture, and it needs to be done carefully and methodically. To add to the difficulty, a lot of the leaders' efforts—particularly at the top of the organization—will be more like trout tickling than dynamite fishing. Reshaping and refocusing a top team, for example, requires an almost constant flow of careful, subtle actions, only rarely interrupted by big, dramatic gestures. Leaders need to ensure that difficulty is not used as an excuse not to change and that follow-through and delivery occur and are celebrated.

Crucially, change leaders must make sure that learning happens during the rollouts. Even in our "simple" example of the retail bank, rolling out a new model to all branches is a massive effort. The bank likely doesn't possess the internal capability to effect a quick and easy rollout, so leadership teams will need to ensure that the rollout program is simple and efficient, with learning occurring and being used at every step of the process.

The key skill for change leaders during this step is appreciation. A large majority of the organization will be asked to change how they work and the beliefs they have built up about how to act. Almost every instinct will be to halt the change program. So appreciating and celebrating success along the way will be vital.

5. Transition

Transition is the final step in the acceleration process and is all about turning acceleration into business as usual. The impact of the changes that have been tried to this point should be measured. Successes should get embedded into the business and taken out of the change program. Changes that are not successful—or not as successful as they could be—will likely stay on the list of change initiatives and be reworked until they succeed.

Business leaders will need to be determined at this stage. There is a natural temptation to bank the successful changes and just celebrate them. But this is the moment to make sure that the new ways of working are quickly embedded into business as usual, subject to all the usual monitoring and performance management of the business. This frees the resources and bandwidth in the change program to focus on new challenges.

Change leaders need to be supportive here, making sure that the spirit behind the changes is remembered, that the successes are celebrated, and that the new behaviors are firmly in place. The skill that can be particularly helpful is systems thinking—making sure that the new ways of working dovetail with the rest of the business and that, even as new behaviors and new processes are embedded into the existing organization, the whole is still coherent.

Table 18.3 demonstrates how change can occur. It shows three successive annual surveys asking employees in a large, multinational bank to pick the words that best describe the organization's culture. At first blush, the changes might seem superficial—indeed, three of the top five words or

TABLE 18.3 Top 15 phrases describing one organization's culture

	Year 1	Year 2	Year 3
1.	Collaborative	Collaborative	Pace
2.	Consensus-driven	Pace	Customer intimacy
3.	Contributing to the greater good	Trust	Collaborative
4.	Trust	Contributing to the greater good	Autonomy
5.	Pace	Values-driven	Trust
6.	Efficient	Innovation	Contributing to the greater good
7.	Values-driven	Consensus-driven	Values-driven
8.	Autonomy	Customer intimacy	Openness
9.	Innovation	Autonomy	Innovation
10.	Aligned	Aligned	Competitive
11.	Purpose-driven	Competitive	Consensus-driven
12.	Customer intimacy	Openness	Teamwork
13.	Fulfilling work	Fulfilling work	Thoughtful
14.	Competitive	Respect	Fulfilling work
15.	Openness	Efficient	Respect

phrases are the same, just slightly rearranged—but dig even a little deeper, and you can see the change occurring. The second-most descriptive phrase in year one, "consensus-driven," has dropped to number 11 by year three, and numbers 6 and 11 in year one, "efficient" and "purpose-driven," have disappeared entirely by year three. "Customer intimacy" climbed 10 places in two years, and "teamwork," which didn't appear in the top 15 in year one, was up to number 12 by year three.

A few lessons emerge for leaders driving change and embedding it in their organizations:

- Not everything has to change. Almost every organization has strengths to keep and build on. Identify and highlight them, so that they don't inadvertently disappear.
- Changing an organization may take time. It may take several years before the full benefits are felt. Of course, we advocate accelerating as much as possible—and, indeed, the rate-limiting factors should be identified and addressed—but instant change is not a realistic goal.
- Make sure that the changes can be easily measured and communicated. Table 18.3 shows a subjective measure, of course, but this can be bolstered with more objective acid tests, like the ones we described earlier.

Lessons Learned

Many organizations have committed themselves to developing distinctive levels of organizational acceleration that confer competitive advantage.

Most have failed.

In the process, however, they contributed to some hard-won lessons that have great relevance to all companies on the journey. If you embrace these lessons, learned both from the winners and from those that fell by the wayside, you will have a great chance of pursuing your plans all the way to the end and seeing your organization accelerate well past the competition.

The seven main lessons include the following:

1. You have to keep going.
2. You must change the people or change the people.
3. You have to intervene.
4. Leadership is key.
5. Teams are the building blocks of acceleration.
6. If it's not evident to the customer, it's not real.
7. It's more than a program.

1. You Have to Keep Going

Research into companies that have achieved high and sustained levels of acceleration shows that resilience defines the winners. That resilience has to come in two time frames: years and generations.

YEARS Organization acceleration does not improve in a straight line. Later gains are won with more difficulty than are earlier gains, and the rate of improvement varies widely. The companies we studied typically saw improvements in two out of three years but experienced a decline in the other year. If that single year of decline knocks your commitment, investment, and consistency, you are likely to join the ranks of the also-rans.

An automotive company we studied had achieved a high level of acceleration but hit a budget challenge when the Asian economy slowed in the wake of the global financial crisis. This coincided with the appointment of a new CEO. The top team, naturally enough, focused on its operational problems and took its eye off the ball of organization acceleration. In one year, the company's acceleration declined by more than it had gained in the previous three years.

All organizations will face this kind of situation at some point. Resilience separates the winners from the losers. Accelerating companies must commit to the journey for many years, even though this is often much longer than the typical life span of the senior leadership team.

GENERATIONS It is sobering that the most agile organizations have been consistently working at acceleration for generations of management. These companies, while not always categorizing their efforts under the label of "acceleration," have demonstrated a continued commitment to building superior institutions.

Imagine a 50-year-old manager who has been in your company for 20 years. She has seen many CEOs, many change efforts, and many leadership styles. She has learned to adapt to the company's way of doing things but finds the company too slow, too bureaucratic, and too complex. Then the organization acceleration program arrives. She is inclined to agree with the messages, but it is one program of many she has seen, and it is competing with her 20 years of learning in the company that tell her not to take the program too seriously.

Now take a 50-year-old manager at an oil and gas company who also has a 20-year tenure. Every leader he has encountered, while not perfect, has demonstrated a consistent set of leadership behaviors that value diversity of thought, inclusion, and integrity in pursuit of high agility. There have been some shocks in his 20 years, such as a profit warning, but the company has always righted itself and has returned to demonstrating real commitment to acceleration.

Assume both of these managers are of similar intelligence, diligence, and intent. The first will wonder if acceleration is "for real," and the other will regard acceleration as the "default option."

How long does it take to build this default? It depends on the velocity of circulation: the rate at which leaders enter and leave the company. By far the easiest time to set expectations is at the beginning of someone's tenure. Someone either new to the company or new to a role is at his or her most malleable.

For some organizations, achieving resilience at the generations level will be tough. Patterns of behavior are sticky. It will take powerful, repeated, and consistent interventions to change behaviors—not necessarily because they are resistant but because they are human.

2. You Must Change the People or Change the People

Nothing changes unless behavior changes, as we demonstrated in Chapter 12. Everything that happens in an organization has its roots in the behavior of an individual, a team, or a network. A new strategy, a product design, a customer interaction, or a system error all stem from human behavior. For an organization to accelerate, it must make substantial and sustained changes in the behavior of its people.

There are two main mechanisms for changing people: development and replacement.

DEVELOPMENT Formal training is important for development, but the job is crucial. Many leaders can cite some training program that was influential, but the job itself provides the vast bulk of the training through challenges, feedback, successes, and failures.

Or not.

Jobs with compressed grades above and below, with little or no connection to an end-point deliverable, or with no scope for learning and growth produce predictably little development and are a breeding ground for bureaucracy.

A pensions and investment company provides a good example of on-the-job development. Like many private equity and activist investors, the company has a well-honed approach to identifying, buying, improving, and selling portfolio companies. Typically within the first three months of ownership of a company, it will have measured acceleration, replaced the chair and half the board, reduced layers as part of a decrease in management costs of around 30 percent, and designed a simple but powerful scheme of incentives for individual and team effort. In other words, it designs big jobs and not only fills them with big people but also gives those people the right environment in which to continue to grow.

This is not to deny the importance of structured leadership development. A well-designed and comprehensive training strategy can enable acceleration. But it is secondary to the design of the job itself.

REPLACEMENT Those individuals, particularly leaders, who cannot or will not operate in a manner consistent with an accelerating organization should be removed and replaced.[2] This is obvious, yet this best practice is often ignored. Organizations typically tolerate poor leaders for far longer than they should. This not only directly impedes performance, but also acceleration as it provides a powerful signal to the organization that it is not taken seriously.

A bank we studied was forced into an aggressive stance on replacing people in the wake of the series of scandals that rocked the financial services industry, including rogue traders, Libor manipulation, misselling, Ponzi schemes, and an investigation into the foreign exchange market. Regulators, governments, and clients pressed for a clean sweep, and in addition to those found guilty of wrongdoing, the company replaced its chair, CEO, seven of the nine top team members, and around 150 of the top 250 managers. The replacement process was not easy, but it worked. Performance improved both in absolute terms and compared with peers that took longer to grasp the situation.

3. You Have to Intervene

A technology company we studied showed the need to intervene. It is a great company, highly agile and producing high performance right at the heart of the digital revolution. It has consistent leadership, the pick of talent, and a strong first-mover advantage.

But as a result of the global crash, the company hit the most challenging set of business circumstances it had ever faced. Leaders were confident about their organizational behavior. They reasoned that they had been so agile so consistently for so long that they could afford to shift their attention to other priorities when revenue was falling and margins were shrinking. They were wrong.

Just when this company needed to be at its best to cope with turbulent times, it saw its biggest-ever fall in agility. Leaders found out the hard way that agility declines rapidly if ignored. This is rather like personal fitness, where it takes a distressingly short period of excess eating and skipping the gym to get out of shape. In fact, the evidence suggests that agility declines approximately twice as quickly as it rises.

As the technology company learned, it isn't enough to coast. Leaders need to continually intervene to stay agile. Gym membership alone does not produce agility. Hard work is required.

If part of an organization receives no intervention, it is most unlikely that its agility will spontaneously improve. Simply targeting senior management and assuming that an improvement will trickle down is an erroneous strategy.

The correct approach is more analogous to a sniper shot than a blunderbuss. A degree of forensic precision is required to identify the parts of the organization where the most value will be achieved through interventions in acceleration.

But how many interventions and how much investment? The evidence is rather counterintuitive here. You should actually start with the issues that have the least direct impact on behavior and more generally set the context: articulating the story, clarifying values, and crafting leadership expectations. Only once these are addressed should you move to those initiatives that more directly affect the four paramount objectives for any company—that is, revenue up, costs down, cash in, and risk out. In essence, you need to first remove the possibility for excuses, such as, "I would do something about the cost structure of my unit if only the company strategy was clear."

However, do not be tempted to stay only with these more general initiatives. They will move the organization from poor to adequate in terms of acceleration, but they certainly do not get you to great. Agile companies move beyond the general to very specific interventions designed to build competitive advantage: changing commercial mind-sets as part of a pricing program, building manufacturing competency as an enabler of cost reduction, addressing team performance as an element of a customer service strategy, and so on.

4. Leadership Is Key

Although intervention is required at all levels of an organization to produce a distinctive level of acceleration, the most critical level, by far, is leadership. The tone is set from the top. Leadership behavior casts a long dark shadow when inappropriate but can also be a primary source of illumination.

A technology company provides a live case study. This company was a rare case where authoritative leadership worked. The personal knowledge and influence of its leaders meant that a command-and-control model of leadership met the needs of the rapidly growing business. But as the company grew in scale and diversity and as its first-mover advantage receded, the fracture lines in this model of leadership began to appear. The new diversity of the market showed up internally as complexity and bureaucracy. The rapid pace of technological evolution was met with a sluggish corporate metabolic rate. Results suffered.

The case for change was clear. The company's board gambled and appointed a new CEO, who quickly shifted the leadership style from authoritative to challenging. The CEO achieved the change partly through constant repetition. He spent much of his first six months making it completely clear that the company had to change fundamentally if it hoped to be relevant for the future. Analysts concluded after the first 100 days that the CEO was being seen as a change agent rather than a caretaker. Financial results have been stellar.

5.   Teams Are the Building Blocks of Acceleration

People perceive their world of work through the lens of their immediate team. The number of individuals who experience their team as derailing (measured through the TAQ) but their organizations as accelerating (measured through the OAQ) is less than 10 percent. Those individuals who rate their team as accelerating have a whopping 80 percent chance of rating their organization similarly. Without accelerating teams, there are no (or very few) accelerating organizations.

The problem is scale. In any reasonably sized organization, there are thousands of teams—thousands of individual units that require tailored and targeted action. The challenge is how to fight on so many fronts. An oil and gas company we studied took this challenge seriously. Servicing many hundreds of oil and gas platforms worldwide, the company's basic operating unit is the team. The company achieves repeat business, essential in such a capital-intensive industry, largely on the basis of team performance.

The company's approach to team improvement focused on four major components and, our research shows, can serve as a good template for others. These components include the following:

- **Size of the team.** Many teams are simply too big, because leaders focus too much on inclusiveness. Our exemplar pruned every team to eight or fewer. (The approach mirrors the one Jeff Bezos takes at Amazon, where he has instituted a "two pizza rule": any meeting whose participants can't be served by two pizzas is too big.)

- **Clarity of objectives.** In a complex operating environment, many metrics are required, including those essential for safety. However, metrics are not targets and should not be confused with targets. The company maintained its battery of metrics but reduced its targets per team to four or fewer and stated them simply.
- **Capabilities.** We all know of teams with star players but poor performance. It is the combination of capabilities that determines the pay-off. This company developed a simple set of capability maps relevant for each type of team and then worked with determination toward that mix.
- **Leadership and behavior.** The best team will founder without leadership and team spirit, so the company measured these soft factors with characteristic rigor and held team leaders to account for improvement.

6. If It's Not Evident to the Customer, It's Not Real

For years in the early 2000s, a friend of ours who was a senior executive at a major car company told us that the company was changing as fast as it could. But the changes were focused internally, not on customers, so they ultimately didn't matter. The company filed for bankruptcy.

By contrast, another carmaker we've studied shows the acceleration that can occur when the customer is the starting point for change. Rarely has a corporate transformation been so all-encompassing.

In 2009, the senior team of this automotive company oversaw many processes: strategy creation, budget setting, investment monitoring, and the like. But the senior leaders did not drive and personally endorse new models before their release on the market. This most critical of all processes went on below the radar of the top team. And the malaise went deeper. Customer complaints (and praise) weren't handled directly by senior leaders but by a separate department buried very deep in the hierarchy. When an audit of the top 200 managers was made, fewer than 50 had contact with customers once a month.

This was not a customer-focused company.

Then, different owners came on the scene and completely changed the model range and the manufacturing footprint, made a massive investment in quality, introduced new production technology, and vastly improved customer service. This company launched one of the most comprehensive organization acceleration programs seen to date, with customer focus as the central idea: Hundreds of leaders spent thousands of days revamping their organization. Everything from recruitment to development to organization structure was revisited.

The strategy is working. Customers can see the change, so the change is real. *CAR* magazine now identifies this company as being the closest to challenging the premium manufacturers.

7.   It's More than a Program

A house without plumbing does not make a good home. But the plumbing is just the plumbing.

Organizations that have sustained a distinctive level of acceleration invariably have a tightly defined program architecture and appropriate control processes that manage the soft stuff with the same rigor as is applied to the hard stuff. The program allows the company to sort through the plethora of priorities, select targets for interventions, monitor progress, revise plans, and so on.

However, a program is not enough. It is merely the plumbing. The program will contain the major interventions specifically designed to improve acceleration, but there is life outside the program. How the organization responds to performance challenges, how it celebrates results, how it communicates new products, how it designs its real estate—every single action the organization takes carries an implication for the state of acceleration. If the acceleration program is managed perfectly but other actions lack coherence or conflict with the program, acceleration will suffer.

Organizations that accelerate the most all pursue the programmatic element of the effort. But it is merely in the background.

■ ■ ■

We'll leave you with those seven lessons because they serve as a reasonable summary for this book.

As we've shown, the principles of META work. So you need to assess where you stand in terms of mobility, execution, transformation, and agility at all four levels: strategy, the organization, teams, and leaders. Then consider how you can accelerate at each of those levels. You need to learn or make sure you possess the four core capabilities: ripple intelligence, resource fluidity, dissolving paradox, and liquid leadership. Then you must pick a recipe, design a program that will let you drive change throughout your organization, and follow through and follow through and follow through.

Then you have to revisit the acceleration issue again. And again. And again.

Remember, the jungle always grows back.

Notes

1. Laurence J. Peter, *Peter's Quotations: Ideas for Our Time*, New York: William Morrow, 1977.
2. Of course, any replacement of individuals should be legal, respectful, carefully considered, and consistent with any contractual or negotiated agreements.

Research Appendix

This appendix describes the range of tools and surveys used to support our findings. Wherever possible, we have referenced reliability and validity scores.

1. Strategy Acceleration

The Strategy Accelerator Questionnaire (SAQ)

The SAQ is a diagnostic tool that provides an accurate "acceleration profile" based on an assessment of the 13 drive factors of adaptive strategy:

- **Mobilize**: embrace uncertainty, pressure-tested decision making, and shared vision
- **Execute**: future core competencies, execution feasibility, and adaptive playbook
- **Transform**: balanced portfolio, fail fast, and rapid response
- **Agility**: foresight, learning, adaptability, and resilience

The SAQ evaluates the extent to which the process of defining strategy in an organization enables acceleration and examines how it positions the organization to outperform competitors in terms of profit and growth, no matter what the future brings.

The tool allows us to identify blind spots in the organization's ability to realize growth aspirations and readiness to respond to the changing external environment (see Figure A.1).

HOW THE SAQ WAS DEVELOPED   Our underlying hypothesis was that in today's constantly evolving world, organizations that accelerate are capable of sensing and acting in a timely manner. A study of 1,200 leaders from a variety of industries, conducted by faculty at Wharton Executive Education affiliated with DSI (now a Heidrick & Struggles company), found that 60 percent of

FIGURE A.1 The SAQ model

senior executives admitted their organization had been blindsided by three
or more high-impact events within a five-year period, and that this impeded
their ability to accelerate performance. Of those executives, 97 percent said
their organization lacked an adequate early-warning system, leading to unforeseen impacts to the core business or product lines.

This information, combined with our consulting work and research in
strategy and decision making, formed the basis for developing a conceptual
adaptation of what it takes to accelerate strategy. This conceptual model
was informed by a draft survey with more than 20,000 global leaders in
companies representing diverse geographies and functions.

We examined the extent to which the activities outlined aided understanding, measuring, and developing skills to think and act strategically.

RELIABILITY: INTERNAL CONSISTENCY   Internal consistency is measured by
Cronbach's alpha, a statistic that represents the degree to which items on
a scale consistently measure the same underlying construct. The maximum
value that can be attained is 1.0, so the closer the coefficient is to 1.0, the
more reliable the scale. As a rule of thumb, statisticians and academics use
0.7 as a cut-off for a reliable scale.

The Cronbach's alpha levels for the SAQ elements show that all elements have strong alpha levels (in the range of 0.7 to 0.8). This means that each of the elements consistently and reliably measures the underlying construct that it is intended to represent.

CRITERION-RELATED VALIDITY   Criterion-related validity measures how well one set of variables (for example, the SAQ elements) predicts results on an important outcome (say, top-performing firms in terms of their ability to accelerate performance). If scores on the SAQ elements are shown to be correlated with overall effectiveness in accelerating strategy, then making improvements on the elements is likely to lead to greater effectiveness in thinking and acting strategically.

Multiple regression analysis shows that frequent use of the elements is strongly correlated with perceived overall effectiveness in terms of thinking and acting strategically. This finding supports the criterion-related validity of the SAQ as a predictor. By building competence on the SAQ elements—and using these behaviors more frequently and consistently—organizations are likely to improve their perceived effectiveness in thinking and acting strategically.

OTHER KEY FINDINGS

- The elements are strongly correlated, which confirms that strategic thinking is a complex cognitive process. Only when an organization uses all of the elements as an integrated whole will it achieve the greatest results with regard to strategic competence.
- For most of the elements, the ability to accelerate strategy does not necessarily improve with increased time on the job (or age). Focused development effort is needed to see meaningful improvement.
- The degree to which accelerating strategy is imperative depends on the complexity of the environment (multiple interactions from unexpected sources), dynamism of the environment (highly unpredictable speed and direction of change), and hostility of the environment (organizational initiatives count for very little against tremendous competitive, political, or technological forces).

2. Organizational Acceleration

The Organization Accelerator Questionnaire (OAQ)

The OAQ is a diagnostic tool that provides an accurate "acceleration profile" based on an assessment of the 13 drive factors of organizational performance:

- **Mobilize:** customer first, energizing leadership, and clarity
- **Execute:** simplicity, ownership, and winning capabilities
- **Transform:** innovation, challenge, and collaboration
- **Agility:** foresight, learning, adaptability, and resilience

Each of the drive factors has three energizers that define each factor. There are, therefore, 39 energizers measured in this tool (see Figure A.2).

The OAQ measures both an individual's perception of the organization and his or her personal experience within it. It can be completed by the entire organization, by senior leaders, or by a representative sample of the organization.

The tool allows us to compare different teams within the same organization. The results provide insights into what aspects within the organization are working well (drive) and what is preventing the organization from achieving acceleration (drag).

HOW THE OAQ WAS DEVELOPED

Heidrick & Struggles Acceleration Survey   In early 2016, Heidrick & Struggles conducted a survey of 237 global senior executives to better understand how companies deal with issues pertaining to accelerating performance.

FIGURE A.2 The OAQ model

The survey was built both to uncover practices that accelerating companies have in place and to start testing hypotheses emerging from our extensive experience helping companies around the globe improve their performance. The survey was organized around the idea of META. We were also interested in learning how companies, teams, and individuals experienced drive or drag. Additionally, we were looking for correlations between levels of acceleration and financial performance.

RELIABILITY: INTERNAL CONSISTENCY   We developed 39 drive factors at the organization (13 factors), team (16 factors), and individual (10 factors) levels. To test how well the drive factor scales worked from an internal consistency point of view, we undertook a reliability analysis. For the analysis to work, we require at least three items or measures for each scale.

To test the reliability of the scales, we used Cronbach's alpha to measure internal consistency. The maximum value that can be attained is 1, so the closer the coefficient is to 1, the more reliable the scale.

We developed 13 organization drive factors. To obtain the reliability of the 13 drive factors we developed at the organization level, 9 were first analyzed to calculate a reliability coefficient. These 9 drive factors all obtained a coefficient greater than 0.7, which means that the three items within each drive factor are measuring the same construct; the remaining 4 factors could not have a coefficient calculated because they only had one corresponding item (see Table A.1).

TABLE A.1 Cronbach's alpha reliability coefficient for the Organization Accelerator Questionnaire drive factors

Drive factors: Organization	Cronbach's alpha
Customer first	0.78
Energizing leadership	0.89
Clarity	0.85
Simplicity	0.77
Ownership	0.75
Winning capabilities	0.84
Challenge	0.82
Collaboration	0.88
Innovation	0.79
Resilience*	-
Learning*	-
Adaptability*	-
Foresight*	-

*Single-item factors

CORRELATION ANALYSIS This section focuses on the association between each of our drive factor scales at different levels. R-correlation coefficients are calculated between two factors. Coefficients range from −1 to +1. The higher the coefficient, the greater is the correlation.

All of the correlations were positive. That means that, if respondents scored high on one factor, then they are likely to have scored high on the other factor, and vice versa. All the coefficients were statistically significant.

For example: At the organization level, there is a highly significant positive correlation ($r = 0.835$) between challenge (support, straight talking, tackling difficult issues) and collaboration (trust, open communication, one organization), indicating that tackling different issues is associated with open communication and trust.

MEASURING ACCELERATION We calculated acceleration based on how respondents rated their organization on Mobilize, Execute, Transform, and Agility ranging from 1 (Appalling) through to 7 (Outstanding), as shown in Figure A.3.

To calculate the META score we used the following formula:

$$\text{Acceleration} = (M + E + T + A)$$

Scores within our sample would range from a minimum of 4 to a maximum of 28. We then divided our sample into 5 quintiles, and labeled the categories derailing, lagging, steady, advancing, and accelerating.

FIGURE A.3 Measuring acceleration

	Appalling 1	2	3	4	5	6	Outstanding 7
Inspiring aligned action based on a compelling ambition and purpose with a simple set of strategic priorities	○	○	○	○	○	○	○
Harnessing and streamlining resources to consistently deliver excellence in execution and continuous operational improvement	○	○	○	○	○	○	○
Experimenting and innovating to create new growth engines and to reinvent existing businesses ahead of the market	○	○	○	○	○	○	○
Adapting and pivoting at a faster pace than competitors to create competitive advantage	○	○	○	○	○	○	○

FIGURE A.4 Revenue trend

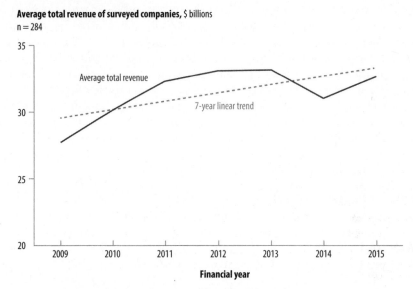

Average total revenue of surveyed companies, $ billions
n = 284

Source: Heidrick & Struggles analysis of FT 500 data

LINKING ACCELERATION TO PERFORMANCE This section focuses on the association between acceleration and organization performance. To begin with, we plotted average total revenue for the organizations in our sample, where it was publicly available, over a seven-year period (see Figure A.4).

Next, to measure organizational performance at the company level, we used the compound annual growth rate measure (CAGR) and calculated the mean annual growth rate over a three-year and seven-year period using the following formula:

$$\text{CAGR} = \left(\frac{\text{Ending Value}}{\text{Beginning Value}} \right)^{\left(\frac{1}{\text{\# of years}} \right)} - 1$$

Within our survey, we also collected other measures that could potentially have an impact on organization performance, such as the five stages of business growth: start-up phase, early-growth phase, stable-to-mature phase, mature phase, and decline phase. We also captured information relating to the size of the organization (number of employees globally) and respondent's role within the organization.

It would not be surprising that views differed at different levels within the organization; for example, CEOs and members of the board may paint a more positive picture while those at lower levels, such as department heads and general managers, may depict a more negative picture. We found this to be the case, which could have an impact on how we could directly link acceleration to performance. We therefore introduced variables such as the stages of business growth to smooth out any variations in response.

Analysis showed that there was a strong positive correlation ($p < 0.01$) between our measure of acceleration (META) within the survey and the stage of the organization within its business cycle, irrespective of the respondents' role within the organization. In other words, if companies were accelerating they were more likely to be in the early-growth to mature phases while those that were derailing were more likely to be in the mature to decline phases.

Linking the stage in the business cycle with our objective measure CAGR (at seven years) we found a strong positive correlation ($p < 0.01$) between the two measures, indicating that those accelerating are more likely to have a higher revenue CAGR (at seven years).

3. Team Acceleration

The Team Accelerator Questionnaire (TAQ)

The TAQ is a 360-degree diagnostic tool that is used to assess teams' acceleration and to measure their progress over time (see Figure A.5). All aspects of this tool are grounded in evidence-based organizational research. The diagnostic is completed by members of the team, the team leader, the team commissioner, and, importantly, the team's stakeholders. More than 3,000 teams across industries and geographies have taken the TAQ, which allows us to provide our clients with benchmarks from comparable teams across the globe.

The TAQ is organized around four accelerators: Mobilize, Execute, Transform, and Agility (META). Within each accelerator, there are four drive factors (16 total):

- **Mobilize:** customer first, unique commission, shared purpose, and clear direction
- **Execute:** tight composition, explicit accountabilities, uncompromising standards, and focused grip
- **Transform:** stakeholder influence, distributed leadership, robust challenge, and disciplined decisions
- **Agility:** foresight, learning, adaptability, and resilience

FIGURE A.5 The TAQ model

Each drive factor has a corresponding drag factor. For example, "Shared purpose" is a drive factor for teams and its associated drag factor is "Competing agendas." Figure A.6 illustrates how a sample team might be assessed on two sets of factors. As the figure shows, three determinations form the basis of each drive factor; they are posed as robust questions in the diagnostic and the answers are rated on a scale from derailing to accelerating. Each drag factor is predicated on two conditions, which may or may not be present within the team.

FIGURE A.6 Sample team assessment: Focus on two sets of factors

Shared purpose vs **Competing agendas**		**Robust challenge** vs **Aggression**	
As a team, our strengths are:	**As a team, our constraints include:**	**As a team, our strengths are:**	**As a team, our constraints include:**
A clear team purpose		A climate of support and trust that enables us to speak candidly	
The way we focus on work that only this team can do	Finding it difficult to integrate different portfolios of each team member into a coherent purpose	Our readiness to robustly challenge each other to achieve the best outcome	Allowing competition to undermine team effectiveness
Mutual commitment to deliver on our priorities	Allowing too many priorities to pull it in competing directions	The way in which we rupture and repair quickly when there is conflict	A lack of diverse perspectives in the team

HOW THE TAQ WAS DEVELOPED   The TAQ was built by experts in team coaching, organizational health, and psychometric instrument design, and is based on many years of research. The tool has been used by teams in banking, engineering, telecommunications, health care, the public sector, academic and charitable institutions, and more. The large sample size (more than 3,000 teams have completed the assessment) has allowed for testing and retesting, so the TAQ has been measured and validated. The TAQ has been licensed and is now embedded in several organizations for leadership development.

RELIABILITY: INTERNAL CONSISTENCY   To explore the reliability of the TAQ drive factors, we calculated Cronbach's alpha to measure internal consistency. Coefficients ranged from 0.66 to 0.76, which sits around the acceptable threshold of 0.7.

CONVERGENT VALIDITY   Convergent validity refers to the degree to which two measures of constructs that theoretically should be related are, in fact, related. Moderate correlations were observed between team members' TAQ items and additional team effectiveness responses. TAQ scores from team members associated with higher evaluations of current effectiveness are:

- Shared purpose
- Coherent direction
- Unique commission
- Foresight
- Productive conflict

4. Individual-Leader Acceleration

The Leadership Accelerator Questionnaire (LAQ)

The LAQ is the tool that measures individual-leader acceleration. It is built around 11 drive factors following our META framework:

- **Mobilize:** put customers first, shape strategy, and inspire and influence
- **Execute:** build talent and teams, and drive for results
- **Transform:** lead innovation, disrupt and challenge
- **Agility:** foresight, learning, adaptability, and resilience

The LAQ can be used when assessing leaders and can provide information aggregated at the level of drive factor or its elements or at the level of individual behaviors (see Figure A.7).

FIGURE A.7 The LAQ model

HOW THE LAQ WAS DEVELOPED In 1999, Heidrick & Struggles developed a proprietary leadership capability framework known as LEEEDS. This model provided a library of 19 competencies, organized around five main categories (see Figure A.8).

This competency framework was applied more than 10,000 times between 2000 and 2015, mainly for the purpose of developing leaders, although it has also been used in selection and succession-planning situations.

In 2014, a team of Heidrick & Struggles consultants started work on refreshing the LEEEDS framework, recognizing the changing demands of leaders in a volatile, uncertain, complex, and ambiguous (VUCA) world. The main inputs into this work were:

- Experience and data collected with LEEEDS
- In-depth interviews with some 150 CEOs in partnership with the Saïd Business School at the University of Oxford, which resulted in *The CEO Report*, delivered at the 2015 World Economic Forum in Davos
- Internal and external research into accelerating leadership performance for individuals, teams, and organizations

FIGURE A.8 The LEEEDS competency framework

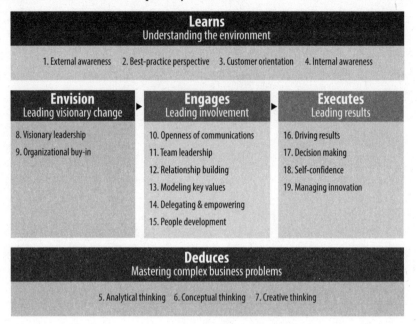

- Hands-on experience working with clients in accelerating their individual leaders
- Research conducted to design and deploy Leadership Signature®, a proprietary assessment tool

Leadership Signature

Heidrick & Struggles created its first online leadership psychometric assessment tool, Leadership Signature, to enhance the insight of its experienced consultants. The purpose of this tool is to provide an empirically grounded approach to heighten clients' and C-suite candidates' self-awareness, to better understand their leadership styles, and to further illuminate the types of environments in which they are most likely to succeed. The approach differentiates the tool from what currently exists in the market. The tool is underpinned by three constructs:

1. Thriving mind-set, based on the leader's level of purpose, learning orientation, and vitality

2. Leadership values, relative to culture fit, based on the leader's orientation around performance, ethics, collaboration, positive spirit, openness to change, and purpose
3. Growth potential, based on the leader's degree of social, self, and situational awareness

From the data collected and psychometric construction process, we discovered eight distinct leadership patterns of behavioral approaches. Individuals' responses on the assessment indicate their degree of access to each of the eight types, creating their individualized Leadership Signature.

Leadership Signature patterns are significant for several reasons. First, they help explain how an individual is likely to behave when in leadership positions. This can be useful in increasing self-awareness, in understanding contexts in which individuals are likely to be successful, and in coaching around strengths, potential downsides, or paradoxes inherent to each particular style. Second, they provide an explanation of an individual's degree of understanding of, and ability to flex into, the other types. Leaders who have greater access to different types are likely to be superior influencers and developers of people, as they have strong awareness and insight into how and why those around them behave in certain ways. Those with more limited access to the other types are likely less adept in flexing styles or in understanding behaviors in others.

THE CONSTRUCTS

Thriving Mind-Set Leaders are said to have a thriving mind-set if they possess a guiding sense of purpose where they maintain a clear vision for the future and take ownership over executing that vision. Leaders with this mind-set have a passionate and deep-seated commitment to learning and growth. They are curious, creative, and consistently attempt to better themselves. These leaders convey a sense of confidence and optimism, both to themselves and those around them. The thriving construct has substantial theoretical backing in the literature, and the authors believe it to be a critical component of successful leadership.

Leadership Values The leadership values are based on 37 years of research and experience compiled over the course of Senn Delaney's (a Heidrick & Struggles company) partnership with clients around enhancing organizational culture. The leadership values are:

1. **Performance orientation:** strong results focus, setting high expectations, focus on personal accountability
2. **Ethical:** integrity in actions, congruence in words and deeds

3. **Collaboration:** cross-functional teamwork, mutual respect, and support for peers and colleagues
4. **Positive spirit:** open and trusting, hopeful and optimistic
5. **Open to change:** encourage innovation, openness, exploration of new ideas
6. **Purpose:** focus on the organization's purpose and whom they serve (the customer or client)

Leaders who hold these values and display their associated behaviors are equipped to create the type of high-performance cultures desired by today's top organizations.

Growth Potential   This component involves a leader's potential and ability to grow and adapt and is grounded in various studies.[1] Our evaluation of potential includes the four drive factors underpinning agility—foresight, learning, adaptability, and resilience.

In this assessment, we ask:

1. What is the leader's intrinsic potential? This is informed by the leader's capability spikes and signature strengths. These are the things that come more naturally to him or her, and that he or she enjoys and is energized by (in other words, factors that play to the leader's strengths).
2. What is the key to this leader realizing his or her potential? This is answered by understanding both the capability spikes and the potential derailers that could inhibit this leader. Most commonly, a limiting mind-set is what underpins potential derailers.

DATA ANALYSIS   After reviewing the data on leaders, 73 items were entered into a factor analysis with Varimax rotation using SPSS, a statistics software package. The goal of the factor analysis was to understand empirically the diversity of the questions in the data set, to determine which items accounted for the greatest amount of variance, and to eliminate extraneous data. Twenty-nine factors were revealed, based on Kaiser's "eigenvalues greater than one" rule. After this initial analysis, the highest-loading item from each of the 29 factors was then entered into a second-order factor analysis, also with Varimax rotation. This second factor analysis revealed 11 distinct factors (again based on Kaiser's "eigenvalues greater than one" rule) that accounted for the vast majority of the variance. The purpose of running the additional factor analysis was to reduce the number of factors to home in on the most predictive items and, from a practical perspective, to create a more manageable data set.

The single item that accounted for the greatest amount of variance for each of the 11 factors was entered into a hierarchical agglomerate cluster analysis, which resulted in eight distinct groupings of respondents. The purpose of conducting the cluster analysis was to determine new variables that explained the relationship between the 11 items derived in the factor analysis. A K-Means cluster analysis was used, and clusters were manually forced from 1 to 11 cluster options. K-Means was chosen because it provided more control over the data (versus hierarchal clustering) and provided a more robust lens through which to make conceptual interpretations of the data. After examining the various options, the eight-cluster solution was deemed optimal, as it was the largest number of factors that returned significant results and because only 3 of the 1,006 participants did not fit the model while meeting the 25-iteration threshold. To confirm these findings, a similar cluster analysis was conducted with the top item from each of the original 29 factors, which also yielded eight distinct clusters.

Once the eight distinct groupings were formalized, discriminant analysis techniques were used to derive equations that classified individuals, based on their answers to the 11 items, into which of the eight types they were most similar to. In essence, this process was used to derive the equations that classify a respondent's most preferred leadership style. An additional set of equations was then created, again using discriminant analysis, to determine to what degree respondents have access to the remaining seven styles. The result is a rank-ordered system of "most-like" to "least-like" regarding degree of similarity of the eight leadership types.

The final survey is composed of 36 questions, the original 29 highest-ranking items from the initial factor analysis and an additional seven items to ensure that each of the three initial constructs was still accurately covered.

5. Board Acceleration

Heidrick & Struggles Board Analysis

Chapter 13 on the role of the board draws on evidence from two different sources: first, BoardEx corporate governance data, and second, recent global surveys on boards undertaken by Heidrick & Struggles.

a. Corporate Governance

Heidrick & Struggles has produced biennial reports on corporate governance, the most recent being in Europe and Asia Pacific in 2014. To identify any trends and their potential impact on the role of boards, data relating to these reports has been updated to take into account:

- Average number of directors per board
- Proportion of independent nonexecutives on the board
- Average number of board committees

- Average age of board directors
- Age profile of board directors
- Average age by role
- Average number of years on the board
- Proportion of women directors on the board
- Current role by gender
- Proportion of non-national directors on the board

Data was drawn from BoardEx, which uses company reports from (a) the top 400 publicly listed companies across 15 European countries (Austria, Belgium, Denmark, Finland, France, Germany, Italy, Netherlands, Norway, Poland, Portugal, Spain, Sweden, Switzerland, United Kingdom), (b) the top 170 publicly listed companies in Australia, China, Hong Kong, India, New Zealand, and Singapore, and (c) the top 500 companies publicly listed in the United States. In total, slightly fewer than 1,070 different companies were analyzed at the global level, allowing for dual and cross listings.

b. **Board Effectiveness Questionnaire**

The Heidrick & Struggles Board Effectiveness Questionnaire captured the views of board directors, CEOs/MDs, and chairs from across Europe, Asia Pacific, and North America. The aim was to assess how board members rated their own board with respect to (a) how important each of the following measures were for board effectiveness in general; and (b) how well the board performed in practice on each of the same measures:

- Achieving the right balance between executive and nonexecutive directors
- The empowered support of committees that exist for the board
- A formal board evaluation process
- A comprehensive review of top talent performance and engagement in succession planning
- A consistent number of board meetings held annually
- The right balance of skills, knowledge, and experience to constructively challenge senior management
- Clear criteria for the replacement of board members
- A clear vision that is shared by board members
- A clear strategy that is understood by each board member
- A leadership style by the chair that encourages excellent team dynamics
- The board's capacity to consider accepting appropriate risks
- Identifying board improvement opportunities
- The board's capacity to innovate and adapt

Scoring ranged from low (score of 1) to very high (score of 5). The analysis is based on 483 responses from Europe, Asia Pacific, and North America.

c. **High Performance Leadership Survey**

The Heidrick & Struggles High Performance Leadership Survey was developed following interviews with some 100 leaders in organizations in the private, public, and social sectors in 14 countries around the world. The survey focused on four core themes:

- Leadership qualities of the chair, the CEO/MD, the board, and the executive/management team
- Engagement at different levels, including (a) relationships between the chair and the CEO/MD, within the board as a whole, between the board and the executive/management team, and across the organization as a whole; and (b) the ability to handle awkward/sensitive issues on the board, on the executive/management team, and across the organization as a whole
- Diversity, and the degree to which the board has a global mindset, a diverse blend of knowledge/expertise, a diverse range of experiences/backgrounds, a diverse gender and nationality mix, and members who think differently
- Corporate strategy development, with respect to (a) the different degrees of input the chair, the CEO/MD, and the board as a whole have toward development; (b) the qualities of those involved in developing the strategy; and (c) the degree to which those determining the strategic direction of the organization use appropriate evidence, engage with other parts of the organization and external stakeholders, and understand the options and implications facing the organization

The analysis is based on 236 responses from across the globe and contributed toward the outcomes of the book *The Success Formula*.[2]

d. **Accelerating Performance Survey**

The Heidrick & Struggles Acceleration Performance Survey aimed to better understand how organizations can accelerate. The survey has been well-documented elsewhere in this book, where it provided supporting evidence not just on the role of boards but also for the book as a whole. In summary, the survey focuses on performance at the organization, team, and individual level.

To date, the analysis is based on 237 responses from across the globe.

We also gathered all governance-related information for the 23 superaccelerating companies. We then compared results from the superaccelerating companies with a set of nonaccelerating companies in the financial services sector. We used the Wilcoxon rank-sum test to assess whether there was a significant difference in mean ranks between the two groups. We found that:

- Boards of superaccelerators are significantly smaller than those of nonaccelerators, with a mean difference of approximately two members and significant at 0.0001.

- Boards of superaccelerators have significantly less outside-industry representation than those of nonaccelerators, with a mean difference of approximately 12.9 percent and significant at 0.0084.
- Boards of superaccelerators have significantly longer-tenured members than those of nonaccelerators, with a median difference of 2.34 years and significant at 0.0128.
- Boards of superaccelerators tend to have younger members (greater representation of directors below age 60) than those of nonaccelerators, with a mean difference of 6.3 percent and significant at 0.0039.
- Female and minority underrepresentation did not significantly differ between superaccelerators and nonaccelerators; it is an issue that affects all boards across performance categories.

To arrive at these findings, our methodology was to use the Wilcoxon rank-sum test on the number of board members for two samples: superaccelerators and nonaccelerators. The questions we posed to test each variable, and the corresponding statistical outcomes, are below:

Size. Are boards of superaccelerators smaller than those of nonaccelerators?

- Null hypothesis: there is no statistically significant difference between the two samples
- Alternate hypothesis: superaccelerator boards are significantly smaller than those of nonaccelerators
- Desired confidence interval: 95% (alpha = 0.05)

We found a p-value of 0.0001, which leads us to reject the null hypothesis, allowing us to conclude that the boards of superaccelerators are smaller than those of nonaccelerators in a statistically significant way, with a mean difference of approximately 2.28.

Industry. Do boards of superaccelerators have different levels of outside-industry representation than boards of nonaccelerators do?

- Null hypothesis: there is no statistically significant difference between the two samples
- Alternate hypothesis: superaccelerator boards have significantly less outside-industry representation than those of nonaccelerators
- Desired confidence interval: 95% (alpha = 0.05)

We found a p-value of 0.0084, which leads us to reject the null hypothesis, allowing us to conclude that the boards of superaccelerators have less outside-industry representation than those of nonaccelerators in a statistically significant way, with a mean difference of approximately 12.9 percent.

Tenure. Do boards of superaccelerators have longer-tenured members than boards of nonaccelerators do?

- Null hypothesis: there is no statistically significant difference between the two samples
- Alternate hypothesis: superaccelerator boards have significantly longer-tenured board members than those of nonaccelerators
- Desired confidence interval: 95% (alpha = 0.05)

We found a p-value of 0.0128, which leads us to reject the null hypothesis, allowing us to conclude that the boards of superaccelerators have longer-tenured members than those of nonaccelerators in a statistically significant way, with a median difference of 2.34 years.

Age. Do boards of superaccelerators have a greater percentage of members younger than 60 years old than boards of nonaccelerators do?

- Null hypothesis: there is no statistically significant difference between the two samples
- Alternate hypothesis: superaccelerator boards have significantly greater sub-60 board member representation than those of nonaccelerators
- Desired confidence interval: 95% (alpha = 0.05)

We found a p-value of 0.0039, which leads us to reject the null hypothesis, allowing us to conclude that the boards of superaccelerators have greater sub-60 representation than those of nonaccelerators in a statistically significant way, with a mean difference of 6.3 percent.

Diversity. Are boards of superaccelerators more diverse in terms of demographics?

Our analysis of the data did not substantiate this hypothesis. Female and minority underrepresentation is an issue that affects all boards across performance categories.

6. Superaccelerators Interviewed for This Book

Alphabet: Matt Brittin, president of EMEA business and operations, Google

BlackRock: Jeffrey Smith, global head of human resources

Cigna: David Cordani, president and CEO; John Murabito, executive vice president of human resources and services

Comcast: Allison Joyce, vice president of talent management; William Strahan, executive vice president of human resources, Comcast Cable

HDFC Bank: Paresh Sukthankar, deputy managing director

Intercontinental Exchange: Jeff Sprecher, founder and CEO

MasterCard: Ajay Banga, president and CEO

Starbucks: Scott Pitasky, executive vice president and chief partner resources officer

Taiwan Semiconductor Manufacturing Company (TSMC): Connie Ma, vice president of human resources

Tata Consultancy Services (TCS): Natarajan Chandrasekaran, CEO and managing director; Thyagi Thyagarajan, independent nonexecutive director

7. The 23 Superaccelerators

Outlined below is a brief description of the core business of each of the superaccelerators featured in this book, presented in order of their 2015 total revenue:

Apple designs, manufactures, and markets mobile communication and media devices, personal computers, and portable digital music players to consumers, small and mid-sized businesses, education institutions, and enterprise and government customers worldwide. The company also sells related software, services, accessories, networking solutions, and third-party digital content and applications. It offers: iPhone, a line of smartphones; iPad, a line of multipurpose tablets; and Mac, a line of desktop and portable personal computers. The company also provides a variety of other products that helps households connect with digital content in many platforms. Apple was founded in 1976 and is headquartered in Cupertino, California.

Ping An Insurance (Group) Company of China engages in life insurance, property and casualty insurance, trust, securities, banking, and other businesses in China. Its life insurance segment offers a range of products, including term, whole-life, endowment, annuity, investment-linked, universal life, and health care insurance products to individual and corporate customers. The company's property and casualty segment provides automobile, non-automobile, and accident and health insurance to individual and corporate customers. It also has a banking subsidiary, Ping An Bank. Ping An Insurance (Group) Company of China was founded in 1988 and is based in Shenzhen, China.

Alphabet, through its subsidiaries, provides online advertising services in the United States, the United Kingdom, and the rest of the world. The company offers performance and brand advertising services. It operates through Google and Other Bets segments. The Google segment includes principal Internet products, such as Search, Ads, Commerce, Maps, YouTube, Apps, Cloud, Android, Chrome, and Play, as well as technical infrastructure and newer efforts, such as Virtual Reality. This segment also sells hardware products comprising Chromecast, Chromebooks, and Nexus. Alphabet was founded in 1998 and is headquartered in Mountain View, California.

Comcast operates as a media and technology company worldwide. It operates through Cable Communications, Cable Networks, Broadcast Television, Filmed Entertainment, and Theme Parks segments. The company also owns the Philadelphia Flyers as well as the Wells Fargo Center arena in Philadelphia, Pennsylvania, and operates arena management-related businesses. Comcast was founded in 1963 and is headquartered in Philadelphia, Pennsylvania.

SoftBank Group operates in the information industry in Japan and internationally. Its mobile communications segment provides mobile communications and broadband services. The company's Sprint segment offers mobile and fixed-line communications services for individual consumers, businesses, government subscribers, and resellers and sells mobile devices and accessories. Its fixed-line telecommunications segment provides fixed-line telecommunications, data transmission/dedicated line, ICT, and other services to corporate customers and broadband services to individuals. SoftBank Group was founded in 1981 and is headquartered in Tokyo, Japan.

Cigna, a health-services organization, provides insurance and related products and services in the United States and internationally. It operates through three segments: Global Health Care, Global Supplemental Benefits, and Group Disability and Life. The company distributes its products and services through insurance brokers and insurance consultants or directly to employers, unions, and other groups or individuals and also through direct-response television and the Internet. Cigna was founded in 1792 and is headquartered in Bloomfield, Connecticut.

Gilead Sciences, a research-based biopharmaceutical company, discovers, develops, and commercializes medicines in areas of unmet medical needs in North America, South America, Europe, and Asia Pacific. The company markets its products through its commercial teams or in conjunction with third-party distributors and corporate partners. Gilead Sciences has collaboration agreements with Bristol-Myers Squibb Company, Janssen R&D Ireland, Japan Tobacco Inc., and Galapagos NV. The company was founded in 1987 and is headquartered in Foster City, California.

Taiwan Semiconductor Manufacturing Company engages in the computer-aided design, manufacture, packaging, testing, sale, and marketing of integrated circuits and other semiconductor devices. The company is also involved in researching, developing, designing, manufacturing, and selling renewable energy and energy-saving technologies and products. Taiwan Semiconductor Manufacturing Company was founded in 1987 and is headquartered in Hsinchu, Taiwan.

Danaher designs, manufactures, and markets professional, medical, industrial, and commercial products and services worldwide. The company's segments include Test & Measurement, Environmental, Life Sciences & Diagnostics, Dental, and Industrial Technologies. The company was formerly known as Diversified Mortgage Investors and changed its name to Danaher Corporation in 1984. The company was founded in 1969 and is headquartered in Washington, D.C.

Starbucks operates as a roaster, marketer, and retailer of specialty coffee worldwide. The company operates in four segments: Americas; Europe, Middle East, and Africa; China/Asia Pacific; and Channel Development. Its stores offer coffee and tea beverages, packaged roasted whole bean and ground coffees, single-serve and ready-to-drink coffee and tea products, juices, and bottled water. As of March 3, 2016, it operated approximately 22,000 cafes. Starbucks was founded in 1987 and is based in Seattle, Washington.

Tencent Holdings, an investment holding company, provides Internet and mobile value-added services (VAS) and online advertising services in mainland China, the United States, Europe, and internationally. The company operates through VAS, Online Advertising, and Others segments. The company's Internet platforms comprise Weixin/WeChat, QQmail, Foxmail, and QQ.com. In addition, the company provides trademark licensing, software development, software sales, information-system integration, and asset-management services. Tencent Holdings was founded in 1998 and is headquartered in Shenzhen, China.

Tata Consultancy Services (TCS) provides IT and IT-enabled services worldwide. The company offers assurance services, business intelligence and performance management, and business process services. It also provides consulting services comprising business change and business and technology optimization, eco-sustainability services, and engineering and industrial services. Additionally, the company offers software products, such as digital software and solutions, as well as ignio, TCS BaNCS, TCS MasterCraft, and TCS technology products. The company was founded in 1968 and is based in Mumbai, India. Tata Consultancy Services is a subsidiary of Tata Sons Limited.

Visa, a payments technology company, operates an open-loop payments network worldwide. The company facilitates commerce through the transfer of value and information among financial institutions, merchants, consumers, businesses, and government entities. It operates VisaNet—a processing network that enables authorization, clearing, and settlement of payment transactions—and offers fraud protection for account holders and assured payment for merchants. The company provides its services under the Visa, Visa Electron, Interlink, and Plus brands. Visa has a strategic alliance with Bottomline Technologies. The company was incorporated in 2007 and is headquartered in San Francisco, California.

Cognizant Technology Solutions provides IT, consulting, and business process services worldwide. The company operates through four segments: Financial Services, Healthcare, Manufacturing/Retail/Logistics, and Other. Its consulting and technology services include IT strategy consulting, program management consulting, operations improvement consulting, strategy consulting, and business consulting services and application design and development, systems integration, enterprise resource planning, and customer relationship management implementation services. The company markets and sells services through its professional staff, senior management, and direct sales personnel. Cognizant Technology Solutions was founded in 1994 and is headquartered in Teaneck, New Jersey.

BlackRock is a publicly owned investment manager. The firm primarily provides its services to institutional, intermediary, and individual investors. It also manages accounts for insurance companies, third-party mutual funds, endowments, foundations, charities, corporations, official institutions, banks, and corporate, public, union, and industry pension plans. The firm also provides global risk management and advisory services. It manages separate client-focused equity, fixed income, and balanced portfolios. BlackRock was founded in 1988 and is based in New York City.

Biogen discovers, develops, manufactures, and delivers therapies for the treatment of neurodegenerative diseases, hematologic conditions, and autoimmune disorders. The company has a strategic research collaboration with Ionis Pharmaceuticals. It offers products primarily through its own sales force, marketing groups, and third parties worldwide. Biogen was founded in 1978 and is headquartered in Cambridge, Massachusetts.

MasterCard, a technology company, provides transaction processing and other payment-related products and services in the United States and internationally. It facilitates the processing of payment transactions, including authorization, clearing, and settlement, and delivers related products and services. The company also offers value-added services, such as loyalty and reward programs, and information and consulting services. The company offers payment solutions and services under the MasterCard, Maestro, and Cirrus brands. MasterCard was founded in 1966 and is headquartered in Purchase, New York.

The Priceline Group provides online travel and restaurant reservation and related services. The company operates Booking.com, which provides online accommodation reservation services, and Priceline.com, which offers hotel, rental car, and airline ticket reservation services as well as vacation packages and cruises through its Name Your Own Price and Express Deals travel services. Priceline was founded in 1997 and is headquartered in Norwalk, Connecticut.

Shire, a biotech company, together with its subsidiaries, engages in the research, development, licensing, manufacture, marketing, distribution, and sale of medicines for patients with rare diseases and other select conditions. Shire plc markets its products through wholesalers and pharmacies. The company has collaboration and licensing activities with ArmaGen, Sangamo BioSciences, and Shionogi. Shire was founded in 1986 and is based in Dublin, Ireland.

HDFC Bank provides a range of banking and financial services to individuals and businesses in India, Bahrain, Hong Kong, and Dubai. The company operates in Treasury, Retail Banking, Wholesale Banking, and Other Banking Business segments. As of June 30, 2015, the company operated a network of 4,101 branches and 11,962 ATMs. HDFC was founded in 1994 and is based in Mumbai, India.

Cerner designs, develops, markets, installs, hosts, and supports health care information technology, health care devices, hardware, and content solutions for health care organizations and consumers in the United States and internationally. It serves integrated delivery networks, physician groups and networks, managed care organizations, hospitals, medical centers, reference laboratories, home health agencies, blood banks, imaging centers, pharmacies, pharmaceutical manufacturers, employers, governments, and public health organizations. Cerner was founded in 1979 and is headquartered in North Kansas City, Missouri.

Intercontinental Exchange operates regulated exchanges, clearinghouses, and listings venues for financial and commodity markets in the United States, the United Kingdom, Continental Europe, Asia, Israel, and Canada. It serves financial institutions, money managers, trading firms, commodity producers and consumers, institutional and individual investors, and other business entities. Intercontinental Exchange was founded in 2000 and is headquartered in Atlanta, Georgia.

Illumina provides sequencing and array-based solutions for genetic analysis. The company's sequencing by synthesis technology provides researchers with various applications and the ability to sequence mammalian genomes. The company markets and distributes its products directly to customers in North America, Europe, Latin America, and the Asia Pacific region as well as through life science distributors. Illumina was founded in 1998 and is headquartered in San Diego, California.

Notes

1. For more, see Rob Silzer and Allan H. Church, "The pearls and perils of identifying potential," *Industrial and Organizational Psychology*, November 16, 2009.
2. Andrew Kakabadse, *The Success Formula: How Smart Leaders Deliver Outstanding Value*, London: Bloomsbury, 2015.

Index